Lecture Notes in Computer Science   13065

More information about this subseries at http://www.springer.com/series/7408

Ezio Bartocci · Yliès Falcone ·
Martin Leucker (Eds.)

Formal Methods
in Outer Space

Essays Dedicated to Klaus Havelund
on the Occasion of His 65th Birthday

 Springer

Editors
Ezio Bartocci 🆔
TU Wien
Vienna, Austria

Yliès Falcone 🆔
Univ. Grenoble Alpes, Inria, CNRS,
Grenoble INP, LIG
Grenoble, France

Martin Leucker
University of Lübeck
Lübeck, Germany

ISSN 0302-9743   ISSN 1611-3349   (electronic)
Lecture Notes in Computer Science
ISBN 978-3-030-87347-9   ISBN 978-3-030-87348-6   (eBook)
https://doi.org/10.1007/978-3-030-87348-6

LNCS Sublibrary: SL2 – Programming and Software Engineering

This Springer imprint is published by the registered company Springer Nature Switzerland AG
The registered company address is: Gewerbestrasse 11, 6330 Cham, Switzerland

Klaus Havelund
(Picture by Gerard Holzmann)

Preface

We would have started this Preface as follows: *This Festschrift is dedicated to Klaus Havelund on the occasion of his 65th birthday that was celebrated on October 17, 2020.* However, due to the COVID-19 pandemic, basically all scientific events were cancelled, held digitally, or postponed in 2020. Klaus' Festschrift and its accompanying symposium, which is part of the ISoLA conference series, were postponed to 2021 and currently, August 2021, a physical symposium is planned, though a rising, fourth wave of the pandemic may require an adaption of the current plans. So we have adapted the beginning of our preface and are optimistic about holding the symposium:

This Festschrift is dedicated to Klaus Havelund on the occasion of his 66th birthday that was celebrated on October 17, 2021. This book contains the papers written by his closest friends and collaborators. These papers were presented during a one-day workshop organized in his honor that was held on October 24, 2021, at Rhodes, Greece, during the 9th International Symposium on Leveraging Applications of Formal Methods, Verification and Validation.

Klaus started his career during his university studies as a software programmer in various Danish companies. From 1984, he held several research positions at different institutes such as the Danish Datamatics Center, the École Polytechnique, LIP 6 Lab in Paris, the Computer Science Department at Aalborg University and NASA Ames. Since 2006 he has been working with NASA's Jet Propulsion Laboratory (JPL) where he was appointed Senior Research Scientist in 2009. JPL is a federally funded research and development center (FFRDC), managed by California Institute of Technology (Caltech), with the primary function to construct and operate planetary robotic spacecrafts.

Klaus has received numerous research awards attesting to the excellence of his work. He received the Turning Goals Into Reality Engineering Innovation Award for the Java PathFinder tool in 2003, a Contribution Award for a NASA tech article about innovation in 2006, an Outstanding Technology Development Award for Java PathFinder in 2009, the JPL Mariner Award for LogScope, the JPL Ranger Award for the development of a Java coding standard, the JPL Voyager Award in recognition of his research contributions, and the JPL Magellan Award for his excellence in research and contribution in the field of runtime verification of software systems.

Along with the JPL awards, he has received several best paper awards such as:

- 2020 SIGSOFT Impact Paper Award
- RV 2018 Test of Time Award
- ASE 2016 Most Influential Paper Award
- ASE 2014 Most Influential Paper Award

His research activities have generated more than 100 publications with more than 100 collaborators. His work has generated more than 12,000 citations. His publications have received several best paper and most influential awards.

Klaus has provided constant and generous service to the formal methods community and the Jet Propulsion Laboratory by organizing, participating, and chairing numerous committees.

The title of this volume is *Formal Methods in Outer Space*. It reflects Klaus's main research focus throughout his career: formal methods, often applied at NASA. The contributions, which went through a peer-review process, cover a wide spectrum of the topics related to Klaus's scientific research interests, including programming languages, static and dynamic analysis. The papers cover topics on *programming*, ranging over domain analysis, abstract interpretation, foundations of programming language design and analysis, characterizations of the safety- and liveness properties, on *runtime verification* like hardware-assisted data race detection, confidence monitoring, and *automata learning* like runtime verification and automata learning and reverse engineering through automata learning, as well as runtime verification and control.

Dear Klaus, on behalf of all your friends and colleagues, we thank you for everything and wish you all the best.

August 2021

Ezio Bartocci
Yliès Falcone
Martin Leucker

Organization

Program Committee Chairs

Bartocci, Ezio	TU Wien, Austria
Falcone, Yliès	Univ. Grenoble Alpes, France
Leucker, Martin	University of Lübeck, Germany

Reviewers

Bollig, Benedikt	CNRS and ENS Paris-Saclay, France
Colombo, Christian	University of Malta, Malta
Holzmann, Gerard	Nimble Research, USA
Kallwies, Hannes	University of Lübeck, Germany
Ničković, Dejan	Austrian Institute of Technology, Austria
Pace, Gordon	University of Malta, Malta
Schmitz, Malte	University of Lübeck, Germany
Sokolsky, Oleg	University of Pennsylvania, USA
Soueidi, Chukri	Inria Grenoble, France
Stolz, Volker	Høgskulen på Vestlandet, Norway
Thoma, Daniel	University of Lübeck, Germany

Contents

Foundations

The $\mathbb{K}$ Vision for the Future of Programming Language Design
and Analysis. 3
   Xiaohong Chen and Grigore Roşu

Refining the Safety-Liveness Classification of Temporal Properties
According to Realizability 10
   Manfred Broy

Static Analysis

Domain Analysis and Description – Sorts, Types, Intents. 35
   Dines Bjørner

Dynamic interval analysis by abstract interpretation. 61
   Patrick Cousot

Runtime Verification

Runtime Verification: Passing on the Baton 89
   Christian Colombo, Gordon J. Pace, and Gerardo Schneider

Hardware-Assisted Online Data Race Detection 108
   *Faustin Ahishakiye, José Ignacio Requeno Jarabo, Violet Ka I Pun,
   and Volker Stolz*

Comparing Two Methods for Checking Runtime Properties 127
   Gerard J. Holzmann

Dynamic Assurance

Confidence Monitoring and Composition for Dynamic Assurance
of Learning-Enabled Autonomous Systems: Position Paper. 137
   Ivan Ruchkin, Matthew Cleaveland, Oleg Sokolsky, and Insup Lee

Collision-Free 3D Flocking Using the Distributed Simplex Architecture. 147
   Usama Mehmood, Scott D. Stoller, Radu Grosu, and Scott A. Smolka

Automata Learning

A Context-Free Symbiosis of Runtime Verification
and Automata Learning   159
   Markus Frohme and Bernhard Steffen

Reverse Engineering Through Automata Learning   182
   Doron Peled

Author Index   193

Foundations

The $\mathbb{K}$ Vision for the Future of Programming Language Design and Analysis

Xiaohong Chen[1,2]([✉]) [iD] and Grigore Roşu[1,2]([✉]) [iD]

[1] University of Illinois at Urbana-Champaign, Champaign, USA
{xc3,grosu}@illinois.edu
[2] Runtime Verification Inc., Urbana, USA

Abstract. Formal programming language semantics should be a unique opportunity to give birth to a better language, not a cumbersome post-mortem activity. Moreover, language implementations and analysis tools should be automatically generated from the formal semantics in a correct-by-construction manner, at no additional cost. In this paper, we discuss how we are pursuing this vision of programming language design and analysis within the context of the $\mathbb{K}$ framework (http://kframework. org), where it is easy and fun to design and deploy new programming languages; where language designers can focus on the desired features and not worry about their implementation; and where the correctness of all auto-generated language implementations and tools is guaranteed on a case-by-case basis, and every individual task, be it parsing, execution, verification, or anything else, is endorsed by its own proof object that can be independently checked by third-party proof checkers, making no compromise to safety or correctness.

Keywords: $\mathbb{K}$ framework · Programming language design · Language frameworks

1 Background

A formal semantics of a programming language is a precise, rigorous, and non-ambiguous mathematical definition of the behaviors of all programs of that language. Consider syntax first. A formal syntax of a language is a precise, rigorous, and non-ambiguous mathematical definition of which sequences of characters construct a well-formed program of that language. Scientists and engineers have found and converged on ways to write formal syntax definitions of programming languages, where regular expressions are often used to define the lexical structures and Backus-Naur form (BNF) grammars define the grammatical structures. Additionally, they developed automatic tools, like Yacc [11], that take the syntax definition and generate syntax tools such as lexers and parsers, which are specific to that language. Undoubtedly, these automatic tools greatly reduce the amount of work in designing and developing new programming languages.

© Springer Nature Switzerland AG 2021
E. Bartocci et al. (Eds.): Havelund Festschrift, LNCS 13065, pp. 3–9, 2021.
https://doi.org/10.1007/978-3-030-87348-6_1

But why stop at syntax? Why not do the same for language *semantics*, too? This is a question that the second author and Klaus Havelund have reflected upon numerous times during their meetings and walks as colleagues at NASA Ames during the years 2000 and 2002, to a point where the second author found it so fascinating as a question that answering it has became his main scientific goal. The second author is thus grateful to Klaus Havelund not only for introducing him to and a life-time collaboration on the topic we call today "runtime verification", but also for shaping his belief that formal semantics can and should be accessible and practical. But this was not going to be easy. Many great logicians and computer scientists have been conducting research for decades on formal semantics of programming languages, though. Since the 1960s, various semantics notions and styles have been proposed, including Floyd-Hoare axiomatic semantics [6,10], Scott-Strachey denotational semantics [17], and various types of operational semantics [1,12,13,15].

Unfortunately, it turned out that semantics is much harder than syntax. After nearly 50 years of research, semantics-based tools are still far from syntax-based tools in terms of scalability, usability, robustness, popularity, and reusability across different languages. Worse, practitioners tend to think that formal semantics of real programming languages are hard to define, difficult to understand, and ultimately useless. In practice, many language designers simply forgo defining a formal semantics for their language altogether, and just manually implement adhoc interpreters, compilers, or whatever tools are desired or needed, with little or no correctness guarantees. As a result, programs in such languages may end up manifesting unexpected behaviors after they are deployed, sometimes with catastrophic consequences.

2   The Vision of an Ideal Language Framework

We can change the status quo and make programming language design faster, easier, fun, economical, and mathematically rigorous, by using an *ideal language framework* that incentivizes programming language designers to design and implement their languages by defining a formal semantics and nothing else. All the above-mentioned language tools for their languages will be automatically generated as a bonus, as illustrated in Fig. 1. For existing languages, we are also better off defining a post-mortem formal semantics that yields the language tools following a principled, correct-by-construction way. Our main message is the following.

> It is *hard* to define a complete formal semantics of any real-world programming language, but if the objective is to tolerate no imprecision or ambiguity in the language, there is no way around it. But we can do it *once and for all*. Nothing else should be needed besides the canonical formal semantics, from which all implementations, tools, and documentations are auto-generated by the framework.

Based on our experience and thinking, an ideal language framework—*the* framework—is distinguished by the following characteristics.

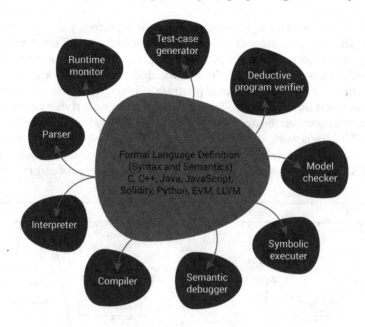

Fig. 1. 𝕂 vision: an ideal language framework

The framework should have an intuitive and user-friendly front-end interface (i.e., a meta-language) to define the formal language semantics. Language designers can use the framework as a natural means to create and experiment with their languages. Since the basic language tools like the parser and the interpreter are auto-generated, the semantics can be executed and easily tested while it is designed, simply by running lots of test programs using the semantics and check the results.

The framework should make language semantic definitions modular and extensible. Language features are loosely coupled, and language designers can easily add new features without revisiting existing definitions. This is because the modern programming languages in emerging areas such as blockchains and smart contracts are constantly evolving, with a rapid development cycle where a new release is deployed on a weekly basis.

The framework should have a solid logical foundation. The semantic definition should have a clear mathematical meaning so it can serve a basis for formal reasoning about programs. The underlying *core logic* of the framework should be highly expressive so arbitrarily complex language features can be formalized in reasonably amount of effort. Auto-generated language tools are (1) correct-by-construction, so there is no "modeling gap" between the formal semantics and the actual tools, and (2) efficient, so there is no need to waste time in handcrafting language-specific tools.

Finally, the framework should have a minimal *trust base* that is fully comprehensible and accessible to all its users. The complexity of the framework implies that it is practically impossible to give it a perfect, bug-free implementation, which can have tens of thousands of lines of code. Therefore, instead of aiming at the correctness of the entire framework implementation, we generate *proof objects* for every individual task that the framework does, such as parsing a piece of code, executing a program snippet, verifying a formal property. These proof objects encode formal proofs of the underlying core logic and become correctness certificates that can be proof-checked by independent proof checkers. The framework users need not trust any particular implementations of the framework. Instead, correctness is established on a case-by-case basis for each individual task, each endorsed by its corresponding proof object.

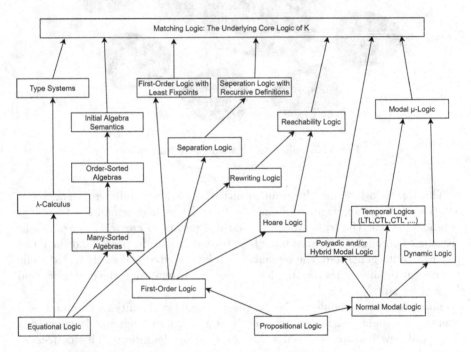

Fig. 2. The logical foundation of $\mathbb{K}$ is matching logic; it captures various logical systems and/or semantic approaches as its theories.

3   The $\mathbb{K}$ Language Framework

$\mathbb{K}$ (http://kframework.org) is a 20-year continuous effort in pushing towards the ideal vision as illustrated in Fig. 1. We have used $\mathbb{K}$ to define the complete, executable semantics of many real-world languages and automatically generate implementations and analysis tools for those languages, including C [8], Java [2], JavaScript [14], Python [7], Ethereum virtual machine bytecode [9], and x86-64 [5]. The research study and practical applications of $\mathbb{K}$ prove that the ideal scenario is within our reach to achieve in the short term.

K provides an intuitive and user-friendly meta-language to define the formal semantics of programming languages, based on configurations, computations, and rewrite rules. For example, the following K code[1] defines the formal semantics of variable lookup in a simple imperative language that has a C-like syntax:

```
rule <k> X : Id => V ... </k>
     <env >... X |-> L ...</env>
     <store >... L |-> V ...</store>
```

where `<k> ... </k>` is a configuration cell that holds the current computation. `<env> ... </env>` holds a mapping from variables to locations and `<store> ... </store>` holds a mapping from locations to values, respectively. The complete configuration can include many other user-defined, possibly nested cells that include all the information needed to execute programs, but only those which are relevant need to be mentioned in the semantic rule. Intuitively, the rule states that if the program variable `X` is mapped to location `L`, and `L` is mapped to value `V`, then rewrite `X` to `V` in the current computation, and do not change the rest of the computation, environment, or store. K uses the three dots "..." to denote the computation frames.

K definitions are highly modular and extensible. Not only that language semantics can be organized into different K modules, semantic definitions themselves are extension-friendly. For example, the above variable lookup rule only mentions the configuration cells that are relevant to variable lookup, and does not require to write the irrelevant computation frames. Therefore, we can extend or modify the language however we like and do not need to revisit and update the variable lookup rule, as long as we do not change how environments and stores are represented in the semantics. Language features that are loosely-coupled have their semantic definitions also loosely-coupled in K, giving users (nearly) the maximum modularity and extensibility.

K has a solid logical foundation called *matching logic* [3, 4, 16], whose formulas are called patterns and the key concept is that of pattern matching, meaning that the semantics of a pattern is the set of elements that match it. Matching logic is highly expressive and is able to define, as logical theories, all the common logical formalisms that semanticists use to formalize languages; see Fig. 2 for some of them. Every K language definition yields a logical theory of matching logic, and all language tools auto-generated by K are best-effort implementations of heuristics of proof search within the matching logic theories.

Matching logic follows a minimalism design, requiring only the simplest building blocks, from which more complex and heavier concepts are defined using axioms, notations, and theories. One major advantage of matching logic is that it has a small Hilbert-style proof system with only a few proof rules, and checking Hilbert-style proofs, i.e., sequences of patterns $\varphi_1, \ldots, \varphi_n$, is very (!) simple. One only needs to check that every φ_i is either an axiom of the proof system,

---

[1] The code is extracted from the complete K definition of an academic language named IMP^{++}; see https://github.com/kframework/k/blob/master/k-distribution/tutorial/1_k/4_imp++/lesson_8/imp.md.

or is obtained from a proof rule. A proof object simply encodes a Hilbert-style proof $\varphi_1, \ldots, \varphi_n$, decorated with proof annotations that state how each φ_i is proved, so it contains all necessary details to be easily checked by third-party checkers.

4 Conclusion

We are witnessing a bright future, where designing and implementing programming languages can be easy, fun, well-principled, mathematically rigorous, and accessible to non-expert users. This future is made possible by holding the vision of an ideal language framework, where programming languages must have formal semantics, and all language implementations, tools, documentations, etc. are automatically generated from the formal semantics by the framework in a correct-by-construction manner, at no additional costs. We have been pursuing this ideal vision with the $\mathbb{K}$ framework and we believe with strong evidence that the ideal vision is feasible within our reach in the near future. We warmly thank our visionary friend Klaus Havelund for various discussions on this topic and for countless encouragements along the way.

References

1. Berry, G., Boudol, G.: The chemical abstract machine. Theor. Comput. Sci. **96**(1), 217–248 (1992). https://doi.org/10.1016/0304-3975(92)90185-I
2. Bogdanas, D., Roşu, G.: K-Java: a complete semantics of Java. In: Proceedings of the 42nd Annual ACM SIGPLAN-SIGACT Symposium on Principles of Programming Languages, POPL 2015, pp. 445–456. ACM, New York (2015). https://doi.org/10.1145/2676726.2676982
3. Chen, X., Roşu, G.: Matching μ-logic. In: Proceedings of the 34th Annual ACM/IEEE Symposium on Logic in Computer Science (LICS 2019), Vancouver, BC, Canada, pp. 1–13. IEEE (2019)
4. Chen, X., Roşu, G.: A general approach to define binders using matching logic. Technical report, University of Illinois at Urbana-Champaign (2020). http://hdl.handle.net/2142/106608
5. Dasgupta, S., Park, D., Kasampalis, T., Adve, V.S., Roşu, G.: A complete formal semantics of x86-64 user-level instruction set architecture. In: Proceedings of the 40th ACM SIGPLAN Conference on Programming Language Design and Implementation (PLDI 2019), pp. 1133–1148. ACM, June 2019. https://doi.org/10.1145/3314221.3314601
6. Floyd, R.W.: Assigning meaning to programs. In: Symposium on Applied Mathematics, vol. 19, pp. 19–32 (1967)
7. Guth, D.: A formal semantics of Python 3.3. Master's thesis, University of Illinois at Urbana-Champaign, August 2013. http://hdl.handle.net/2142/45275
8. Hathhorn, C., Ellison, C., Roşu, G.: Defining the undefinedness of C. In: Proceedings of the 36th ACM SIGPLAN Conference on Programming Language Design and Implementation, PLDI 2015, pp. 336–345. ACM, New York (2015). https://doi.org/10.1145/2737924.2737979

9. Hildenbrandt, E., et al.: KEVM: a complete semantics of the Ethereum virtual machine. In: Proceedings of the 31st IEEE Computer Security Foundations Symposium (CSF 2018). IEEE (2018). http://jellopaper.org
10. Hoare, C.A.R.: An axiomatic basis for computer programming. Commun. ACM **12**(10), 576–580 (1969)
11. Johnson, S.C.: Yacc: Yet another compiler-compiler (1975). http://dinosaur. compilertools.net/yacc/
12. Kahn, G.: Natural semantics. In: Brandenburg, F.J., Vidal-Naquet, G., Wirsing, M. (eds.) STACS 1987. LNCS, vol. 247, pp. 22–39. Springer, Heidelberg (1987). https://doi.org/10.1007/BFb0039592
13. Mosses, P.D.: Modular structural operational semantics. J. Log. Algebraic Program. **60–61**, 195–228 (2004)
14. Park, D., Stefănescu, A., Roşu, G.: KJS: a complete formal semantics of JavaScript. In: Proceedings of the 36th ACM SIGPLAN Conference on Programming Language Design and Implementation, PLDI 2015, pp. 346–356. ACM, New York (2015). https://doi.org/10.1145/2737924.2737991
15. Plotkin, G.: A structural approach to operational semantics. J. Log. Algebraic Program. **60–61**, 17–139 (2004)
16. Roşu, G.: Matching logic. Log. Methods Comput. Sci. **13**(4), 1–61 (2017)
17. Scott, D.S.: Domains for denotational semantics. In: Nielsen, M., Schmidt, E.M. (eds.) ICALP 1982. LNCS, vol. 140, pp. 577–610. Springer, Heidelberg (1982). https://doi.org/10.1007/BFb0012801

Refining the Safety-Liveness Classification of Temporal Properties According to Realizability

Manfred Broy[(✉)]

Institut für Informatik, Technische Universität München, 80290 München, Germany
broy@in.tum.de

Dedicated to Klaus Havelund on the Occasion of his 65th Birthday

As Time Goes By
Casablanca - Original Song by Sam (Dooley Wilson)

Abstract. In the specification approach FOCUS (see [2]), systems are specified by interface predicates which relate input histories to output histories. In such interface predicates, required safety and liveness properties of systems are formulated for the output histories in terms of their dependencies on the properties of input histories. In the following, we show how safety and liveness properties in systems specifications relate to questions of refinement, causality, and realizability. In particular, we study the effect of logical operations onto safety and liveness properties and how this relates to specification refinement. In addition, we analyze which safety and liveness properties used in implicative formulas can be realized by Moore machines. The requirements about the realizability by Moore machines are reflected in respective refinements simplifying or strengthening the original specifications.

Keywords: Safety · Liveness · Causality · Realizability · Refinement

1 Introduction

In their paper, Peled and Havelund publish results on the refinement of the safety-liveness classification of temporal properties according to monitorability [12]. In the following, we take up their approach for a classification of properties in interface specifications and their relationship to realizability (see [6]). Realizability for a specification leads to a refined – a logically stronger – specification by taking into account questions of implementability of Moore machines (see [11] and also [10] and [8]).

© Springer Nature Switzerland AG 2021
E. Bartocci et al. (Eds.): Havelund Festschrift, LNCS 13065, pp. 10–31, 2021.
https://doi.org/10.1007/978-3-030-87348-6_2

1.1 Relating Realizability to Time-Sensitive Requirements Specifications

As shown in [2] and [4], systems can be specified by interface predicates, for which a relatively complete and sound specification and verification calculus can be given (see [8]). In this calculus, given systems specifications are refined by adding properties of causality and realizability that capture the properties of implementations by Moore machines (see [11] and also [5, 8] and [10]). In the following, we show, how such system properties can be classified into safety and liveness as well as bounded and unbounded properties. In particular, we talk about the manipulation by logical connectors such as negation, disjunction, and conjunction of bounded and unbounded safety and liveness properties.

On this basis, specifying predicates can be classified according to these properties. Moreover, it can be discussed to which extent these properties may come into conflict with causality and realizability. We show what happens if we refine predicates according to strong causality and realizability.

1.2 Content of the Paper

In the following, we first introduce special forms of temporal predicates which we call "bounded" and "unbounded" and then the well-known definitions of safety and liveness (see [1, 9] and [12]). We analyze how logical operations on safety and liveness, on bounded and unbounded predicates lead to properties which can be characterized again as safety and liveness properties, as bounded and unbounded properties.

On this basis, we study specific forms of specifications which have the form of implications with predicates on input histories that serve as premises, called *assumptions*, and conclusions being predicates on the output histories, called *commitments*. We discuss the different possibilities of assumptions being safety and liveness, bounded and unbounded properties, and the same for the commitments and show that certain forms of specifications can be simplified and properties can be strengthened under the assumption of causality and realizability. The main result is the demonstration how properties implied by the requirement of realizability of behaviors on Moore machines induce further properties on the specification that are made explicit considering safety and liveness as well as boundedness and unboundedness of the specifying predicates.

In contrast to [12], we do not use temporal logic with its restricted expressiveness, but general formulas of higher-order predicate logic. Temporal logic formulas form a subset thereof.

2 The System Model

In this chapter, we introduce a model of concurrent, distributed interactive systems. We work with simple discrete global time (see [3]).

2.1 Streams, Time, and Behaviors

We consider *timed streams* over a message set M defined as follows ($\mathbb{N}$ denotes the natural numbers including 0, $\mathbb{N}_+ = \mathbb{N}\backslash\{0\}$; M^* denotes the set of finite sequences over the set M). The set of infinite streams over a set of messages M is denoted by M^ω. We define

$$M^\omega = (\mathbb{N}_+ \to M)$$

A stream $x \in (M^*)^\omega$ is called *timed*, since we understand $\mathbb{N}_+$ to represent a discrete time in terms of an infinite sequence of time intervals (see [3]). Each time interval is denoted by a number $t \in \mathbb{N}_+$. Then $x(t)$ with $t \in \mathbb{N}_+$ denotes the sequence of messages communicated via the timed stream x in time interval t.

We introduce the set of finite timed streams defined as follows:

$$(M^*)^* = \cup_{n \in \mathbb{N}} ([1{:}n] \to M^*),$$

where for $n \in \mathbb{N}: [1{:}n] = \{i \in \mathbb{N}_+ : i \leq n\}$. For a timed stream x over a set M and a subset $D \subseteq M$ we denote by

$$D\#x$$

the sum of the number of copies of elements from set D in x; we also write a#x for $\{a\}\#x$ and #x for M#x.

2.2 Syntactic Interfaces and Interface Behavior

Often, we consider interfaces with not just one stream as input and one as output but a finite family of streams. To handle this in a convenient notational way we introduce finite sets X and Y of channels that serve as names for timed streams. We assume that every channel has an associated data type which describes the type of messages sent over this channel. We write

$$X = \{x_1 : S_1, \ldots, x_m : S_m\}$$
$$Y = \{y_1 : T_1, \ldots, y_n : T_n\}$$

where $S_k (1 \leq k \leq m)$ and $T_k (1 \leq k \leq n)$ are data types. By $\vec{X}$ we denote channel histories by families of timed streams.

$$\vec{X} = (X \to (M^*)^\omega)$$
$$\vec{X}_{fin} = (X \to (M^*)^*)$$

Thus, every timed history $x \in \vec{X}$ denotes an evaluation for the channels in X by streams. We call the elements of $\vec{X}$ (channel) histories or families of streams. If $x \in \vec{X}$ then x(c) denotes a timed stream for every channel $c \in X$. We assume that each stream x(c) carries only elements of the data type associated with channel c.

For $z \in \vec{X}_{fin}$ we denote by $|z| \in \mathbb{N}$ the length of finite history z. For $z \in \vec{X}_{fin}, x \in \vec{X}$ by $z^\frown x$ we denote the concatenation of z with x.

We use the following notation both for timed streams $s \in (M^*)^\omega$ and for timed channel histories $x \in \vec{X}$; let $t \in \mathbb{N}$:

$$s \downarrow t \in (M^*)^* \qquad \text{finite timed stream until (and including) time } t$$
$$x \downarrow t \in \vec{X}_{fin} \qquad \text{finite timed channel history till (and including) time } t$$
$$x \uparrow t \in \vec{X}_{fin} \qquad \text{timed channel history after (and excluding) time } t$$

We get:

$$(x \downarrow t)^\wedge(x \uparrow t) = x$$
$$(x \downarrow t)(i) = x(i) \Leftarrow 1 \leq i \leq t$$
$$x(c) \downarrow t = (x \downarrow t)(c)$$

We consider the following types of interface behaviors

$$f: (M^*)^\omega \to (M^*)^\omega \qquad \text{functions on timed streams}$$
$$f: \vec{X} \to \vec{Y} \qquad \text{functions on channel histories over timed streams}$$
$$F: (M^*)^\omega \to \wp((M^*)^\omega) \qquad \text{set-valued functions representing relations on timed streams}$$
$$F: \vec{X} \to \wp(\vec{Y}) \qquad \text{set-valued functions representing relations on histories of timed streams}$$

The syntactic interface of relations on channel histories over timed streams is denoted by $(X \blacktriangleright Y)$ called *syntactic interface*. For simplicity, we assume that X and Y are disjoint.

Notation: Extension of predicates on infinite histories to predicates on finite histories:

Throughout the paper, we use the following notation: Given a predicate

$$p: \vec{X} \to \mathbb{B}$$

on infinite histories, we extend the predicate p to predicates on

$$p^\exists, p^\forall: \vec{X}_{fin} \to \mathbb{B}$$

on finite histories $z \in \vec{X}_{fin}$ by the following definition:

$$p^\exists(z) \equiv \exists x \in \vec{X} : z = x' \downarrow |z| \wedge p(x)$$
$$p^\forall(z) \equiv \forall x \in \vec{X} : z = x' \downarrow |z| \Rightarrow p(x)$$

In the following, example predicates p are mostly of the type $p: (\mathbb{N}^*)^\omega \to \mathbb{B}$ to keep them simple and readable. The general definitions are formulated for predicates of the type $p: \vec{X} \to \mathbb{B}$, however.

3 Temporal System Properties

In this section, we give definitions of bounded and unbounded properties as well as liveness and safety properties and how they behave in system predicates.

3.1 Bounded and Unbounded System Properties

A property

$$p: \vec{X} \to \mathbb{B}$$

on histories of timed streams is called *bounded* if

$$\forall x \in \vec{X}: \left(p(x) \Rightarrow \left(\exists t \in \mathbb{N}: p^{\vee}(x \downarrow t)\right)\right)$$

and *unbounded* if

$$\forall x \in \vec{X}: \left(p(x) \Rightarrow \left(\forall t \in \mathbb{N}: (\neg p)^{\exists}(x \downarrow t)\right)\right)$$

A property p is called *uniformly bounded*, if

$$\exists t \in \mathbb{N}: \forall x \in \vec{X}: \left(p(x) \Rightarrow p^{\vee}(x \downarrow t)\right)$$

Note that uniformly bounded means that the choice of the $t \in \mathbb{N}$ such that $p^{\vee}(x \downarrow t)$ can be the same for all x while bounded only requires that there exists an individual t for each x.

Every property is either bounded or unbounded or a mixture of both. In the latter case, there is a subset of $\vec{X}$ for which p is bounded and the complementary subset for which p is unbounded.

In [12], what we call a bounded property is called guarantee and what we call an unbounded property is called morbidity.

3.2 Safety

A specifying predicate

$$e: \vec{X} \to \mathbb{B}$$

is a *safety property* (see [1, 9]) if

$$\forall x \in \vec{X}: \left(e(x) \Leftarrow \forall t \in \mathbb{N}: e^{\exists}(x \downarrow t)\right)$$

Consider a specifying predicate

$$p: \vec{X} \to \mathbb{B}$$

Its safety part p^S for p is defined by the equation

$$p^S(x) = \left(\forall t \in \mathbb{N}: p^{\exists}(x \downarrow t)\right)$$

The proof that p^S is a safety property is straightforward.

3.3 Liveness

A specifying predicate

$$v: \vec{X} \to \mathbb{B}$$

is called a *liveness property* (see [1, 9]) if

$$\forall x \in \vec{X}, t \in \mathbb{N}: v^{\exists}(x \downarrow t)$$

Consider a predicate

$$p: \vec{X} \to \mathbb{B}$$

Its liveness part p^L for its output histories is not unique, in general. There are several liveness properties v, in general, such that

$$p = \left(p^S \wedge v \right)$$

This reflects the well-known fact that every property can be represented as a conjunction of a safety with a liveness property.

Note that, in general, by the formula

$$p = \left(p^S \wedge p^L \right)$$

the safety part p^S is uniquely determined, whereas the liveness part p^L is not. For instance, if p^S = false, then p^S = false. Then, in fact, we may choose any liveness property to fulfill the formula. We define the canonical liveness part p^L by the weakest liveness property that fulfills the formula. If p^S = false then p^L = true. Generally, let ALV to be the set of all liveness properties; we define the set of all liveness properties that fulfil the equation above for a predicate p by LV(p)

$$LV(p) = \left\{ v \in ALV : p = p^S \wedge v \right\}$$

and based on ALV

$$p^L(x) = \exists v \in LV(p): v(x)$$

For an unbounded liveness property v we get

$$\forall x \in \vec{X}, t \in \mathbb{N}: v^{\exists}(x \downarrow t) \wedge (\neg V)^{\exists}(x \downarrow t)$$

This formula already shows that the negation of unbounded liveness properties yields unbounded liveness properties and vice versa.

3.4 Refining Safety and Liveness

Given a specifying predicate

$$p: \vec{X} \to \mathbb{B}$$

we may add a safety property

$$e: \vec{X} \to \mathbb{B}$$

to p and get the property q:

$$q = (p \wedge e)$$

Predicate q is a *refinement* of p, since $q \Rightarrow p$.

$$q^S = \left(p^S \wedge e\right)$$

For q^L we get from

$$\begin{aligned}
&v \in LV(p) \\
&\Rightarrow p = p^S \wedge v \\
&\Rightarrow p \wedge e = p^S \wedge v \wedge e \\
&\Rightarrow q = q^S \wedge v \\
&\Rightarrow v \in LV(q)
\end{aligned}$$

the implication

$$\begin{aligned}
&p^L(x) \\
&= \exists v \in LV(p): v(x) \\
&\Rightarrow \exists v \in LV(q): v(x) \\
&= q^L(x)
\end{aligned}$$

Choose e = false, then true $\in LV(q)$. This illustrates that a refinement by the conjunction of a safety property to a predicate also changes the associated weakest liveness property, in general.

However, the "old" liveness property p^L also fulfils the equation $q = q^S \wedge p^L$. This shows that strengthening ("refining") using a safety property results at most in weakening the weakest liveness property.

Given a specifying predicate

$$p: \vec{X} \to \mathbb{B}$$

we may add a liveness property

$$v: \vec{X} \to \mathbb{B}$$

to p and get

$$q = (p \wedge v)$$

Predicate q is a *refinement* of p, since q $\Rightarrow$ p. This is also true for the safety part of p and q, since we q^S $\Rightarrow$ p^S. In fact, in general, q^S is stronger than p^S.

This is shown by a simple example. Consider a predicate p: $(\mathbb{N}^*)^\omega \to \mathbb{B}$ where

$$p(x) = (\#x < \infty)$$

and

$$v(x) = (\#x = \infty)$$

Both p and v are liveness properties. Thus p^S = true. We deduce

$$
\begin{aligned}
& q^S(x) \\
&= (p(x) \wedge v(x))^S \\
&= (\#x < \infty \wedge \#x = \infty)^S \\
&= \text{false}^S \\
&= \text{false}
\end{aligned}
$$

Actually, in this case $(p(x) \wedge v(x))$ = false, and thus the weakest liveness part of $(p(x) \wedge v(x))$ is true. This illustrates that a refinement by the conjunction of a liveness property to a predicate may lead to a predicate with a safety part stronger or at least equally strong as the original safety part. Note, moreover, that for the resulting specification q = $(p \wedge v)$ the weakest liveness part may be much weaker than p^L $\wedge$ v. Refining the liveness part of a temporal property may weaken the weakest liveness part and strengthen the safety part. The example also demonstrates that the conjunction of liveness properties is not guaranteed to result in liveness properties.

4 Logical Operations on Safety and Liveness Properties

In this section, we study the effect of logical operations on unbounded safety and liveness properties as they may occur when putting together specifications.

4.1 Negation

For a bounded specifying predicate

$$p: \overrightarrow{X} \to \mathbb{B}$$

its negation is a safety property.

This is seen as follows: boundedness gives

$$\forall x \in \overrightarrow{X}: p(x) \Rightarrow \exists t \in \mathbb{N}: p^\forall(x \downarrow t)$$

Applying contraposition to boundedness yields

$$\forall x \in \overrightarrow{X}: \neg p(x) \Leftarrow \forall t \in \mathbb{N}: (\neg p)^\exists(x \downarrow t)$$

which shows that ¬p is a safety property.

If we negate a safety property

$$e: \overrightarrow{X} \to \mathbb{B}$$

we get from the definition of safety

$$e(x) \Leftarrow \left(\forall t \in \mathbb{N} : e^{\exists}(x \downarrow t) \right)$$

by contraposition

$$\neg e(x) \Rightarrow \left(\exists t \in \mathbb{N} : (\neg e)^{\vee}(x \downarrow t) \right)$$

This shows that property ¬e is bounded.

As a corollary, we get: If e is a safety property and bounded, then ¬e is a safety property and bounded.

If e is a safety property and unbounded, then ¬e is a liveness property and bounded. This is seen as follows. If the safety property e is unbounded, then

$$\forall x \in \overrightarrow{X} : e(x) \Rightarrow \forall t \in \mathbb{N} : (\neg e)^{\exists}(x \downarrow t) \Big)$$

Trivially, moreover

$$\forall x \in \overrightarrow{X} : \neg e(x) \Rightarrow \forall t \in \mathbb{N} : (\neg e)^{\exists}(x \downarrow t) \Big)$$

We get

$$\forall x \in \overrightarrow{X}, t \in \mathbb{N} : (\neg e)^{\exists}(x \downarrow t) \Big)$$

which shows that ¬e is a liveness property. As we have shown, the negation of a safety property is bounded. Hence, for every unbounded safety property e its negation ¬e is a bounded liveness property.

As shown, the negation ¬v of a bounded liveness property v is a safety property since the negation of bounded properties yields a safety property.

By the liveness of a specifying predicate v we get

$$\forall x \in \overrightarrow{X}, t \in \mathbb{N} : v^{\exists}(x \downarrow t)$$

which gives

$$\forall x \in \overrightarrow{X} : \neg v(x) \Rightarrow \forall t \in \mathbb{N} : v^{\exists}(x \downarrow t)$$

which shows that every negation ¬v of a liveness property is unbounded. Thus, the negation of a bounded liveness property yields an unbounded safety property.

If we negate an unbounded liveness property

$$v: \overrightarrow{X} \to \mathbb{B}$$

we get by the definition of unboundedness

$$\forall x \in \vec{X} : v(x) \Rightarrow \forall t \in \mathbb{N} : (\neg v)^{\exists}(x \downarrow t)$$

Trivially, moreover

$$\forall x \in \vec{X} : \neg v(x) \Rightarrow \forall t \in \mathbb{N} : (\neg v)^{\exists}(x \downarrow t)$$

which proves

$$\forall x \in \vec{X} : \forall t \in \mathbb{N} : (\neg v)^{\exists}(x \downarrow t)$$

This shows that $\neg v$ is an unbounded liveness property if v is an unbounded liveness property.

4.2 Conjunction

The conjunction of safety properties yields safety properties. This is shown as follows.
Let p and q be safety properties. We have to show

$$(p(x) \wedge q(x)) \Leftarrow \forall t \in \mathbb{N} : (p \wedge q)^{\exists}(x \downarrow t)$$

If

$$\forall t \in \mathbb{N} : (p \wedge q)^{\exists}(x \downarrow t)$$

yields true then both

$$\forall t \in \mathbb{N} : p^{\exists}(x \downarrow t)$$
$$\forall t \in \mathbb{N} : q^{\exists}(x \downarrow t)$$

hold which implies $p(x)$ and $q(x)$ since they are safety properties and thus $p \wedge q$ is a safety property.

The conjunction of liveness properties does not necessarily yield liveness properties. Take the example $(\#x < \infty \wedge \#x = \infty)$ from above; both $\#x < \infty$ and $\#x = \infty$ are liveness properties but their conjunction yields false which is not a liveness property.

If we combine a safety property e with a property q by conjunction, we do not get a safety property, in general, since

$$(q(x) \wedge e(x)) \Leftarrow \forall t \in \mathbb{N} : (q \wedge e)^{\exists}(x \downarrow t)$$

does not follow from

$$e(x) \Leftarrow \forall t \in \mathbb{N} : e^{\exists}(x \downarrow t)$$

For instance, if q is a liveness property, then $\forall t \in \mathbb{N} : \exists x' : x \downarrow t = x' \downarrow t \wedge q(x')$ does hold but nevertheless $q(x)$ may not hold.

The same is obviously true, if we combine a liveness property v with a property q by conjunction. Take again the counterexample ($\#x < \infty \wedge \#x = \infty$) from above.

If we combine a bounded liveness property v' with an unbounded liveness property v by conjunction we get an unbounded property:

$$\forall x \in \vec{X}: \big(v(x) \wedge v'(x)\big) \Rightarrow \forall t \in \mathbb{N}: \big(\neg(v \wedge v')\big)^{\exists}(x \downarrow t)$$

which follows from

$$\forall x \in \vec{X}: v'(x) \Rightarrow \forall t \in \mathbb{N}: \big(\neg v'\big)^{\exists}(x \downarrow t)$$

A conjunction of nontrivial liveness and safety properties yields a mixture of safety and liveness, in general.

If we add a liveness property v to property p, as demonstrated in Sect. 3.4 its safety part of p may be affected. In any case, adding a liveness property v to a predicate p by conjunction leads to a predicate $p \wedge v$ the safety property of which is a refinement of the safety property p^S since

$$(p \wedge v)^S(x) = \forall t \in \mathbb{N}: (v \wedge p)^{\exists}(x \downarrow t)$$

which is stronger than

$$\forall x \in \vec{X}, t \in \mathbb{N}: p^{\exists}(x \downarrow t)$$

Adding a safety property e to a predicate p leaves its associated (weakest) liveness property unchanged or makes it weaker.

As demonstrated in Sect. 3.4, in general, there are several distinct liveness properties v and v' that satisfy the equation

$$p = \big(p^S \wedge v\big)$$

and

$$p = \big(p^S \wedge v'\big)$$

The liveness property p^L is the weakest one. We get by simple propositional logic

$$p = \big(p^S \wedge p^L\big)$$

Both liveness properties v and v' imply the liveness property p^L.

4.3 Disjunction

The disjunction of safety properties yields safety properties. Let p and q be safety properties. We prove

$$\forall x \in \vec{X}: \big((p(x) \vee q(x)) \Leftarrow \forall t \in \mathbb{N}: (p \vee q)^{\exists}(x \downarrow t)\big)$$

If

$$\forall t \in \mathbb{N}: (p \vee q)^{\exists}(x \downarrow t)$$

then if both $\forall t \in \mathbb{N}: p^{\exists}(x \downarrow t)$ and $\forall t \in \mathbb{N}: p^{\exists}(x \downarrow t)$ hold then $p(x) \vee q(x)$ holds.
  Assume without loss of generality that

$$\forall t \in \mathbb{N}: p^{\exists}(x \downarrow t)$$

does not hold. Then there exists some $t' \in \mathbb{N}$ such that

$$\forall t \in \mathbb{N}: t' \leq t \Rightarrow \neg p^{\exists}(x \downarrow t)$$

Hence from $\forall t \in \mathbb{N}: (p \vee q)^{\exists}(x \downarrow t)$ we conclude

$$\forall t \in \mathbb{N}: q^{\exists}(x \downarrow t)$$

and thus $p(x) \vee q(x)$, which concludes the proof.
  If we combine a nontrivial bounded liveness property v with an unbounded liveness property v by disjunction, in general, we get a liveness property that is bounded for some x and unbounded for others.
  If we combine a liveness property v with a property q by disjunction, we always get a liveness property, since

$$\forall x \in \vec{X}, t \in \mathbb{N}: (q \vee v)^{\exists}(x \downarrow t)$$

follows from

$$\forall x \in \vec{X}, t \in \mathbb{N}: v^{\exists}(x \downarrow t)$$

which holds, since v is a liveness property. This shows also, that the disjunction of liveness properties yields liveness properties.
  If we combine a predicate p with a bounded predicate q by disjunction, we do not get a bounded property, in general, since from

$$\forall x \in \vec{X}: q(x) \Rightarrow \exists t \in \mathbb{N}: q^{\vee}(x \downarrow t)$$

we cannot deduce

$$\forall x \in \vec{X}: (p(x) \vee q(x)) \Rightarrow \exists t \in \mathbb{N}: (p \vee q)^{\vee}(x \downarrow t)$$

since if $p(x) \wedge \neg q(x)$ holds and p is unbounded, then there does not exist, in general, an x such that for all x with $x \downarrow t = x' \downarrow t$ the property p holds. Take as a simple example $q = \text{false}$; then q is bounded. Take an arbitrary property p that is unbounded. Then $(p \vee q) = p$ is unbounded.

4.4 Approximating Liveness

Given a specifying predicate

$$v: \vec{X} \to \mathbb{B}$$

which is a liveness property, v is called *approximatively bounded* if there exists a set of bounded liveness properties

$$v_k: \vec{X} \to \mathbb{B}$$

such that

$$\forall k \in \mathbb{N}: v_{k+1} \Rightarrow v_k$$

and

$$\forall x \in \vec{X}: (\forall k \in \mathbb{N}: v_k(x)) \Rightarrow v(x)$$

We make use of approximately bounded liveness properties in Sect. 7.

5 Specification by Interface Assertions and Interface Predicates

We work with *specifying predicates* which are predicates over syntactic interfaces. A specifying predicate q for the syntactic interface $(X \blacktriangleright Y)$ is a predicate

$$p: \vec{X} \times \vec{Y} \to \mathbb{B}$$

To express this, we write

$$p:(X \blacktriangleright Y)$$

Given p, with $x \in \vec{X}, y \in \vec{Y}$ we form propositions p(x, y). We write

$$(X \blacktriangleright Y): p(x, y)$$

for the specification of a system with syntactic interface $(X \blacktriangleright Y)$ that fulfills p(x, y).

To keep our examples simple, we work with the syntactic interface

$$(\{x : Nat\} \blacktriangleright \{y : Nat\})$$

In this case, for $(\{x : Nat\} \blacktriangleright \{y : Nat\})$ we also write p(x, y) where x and y are timed streams of natural numbers.

6 Strong Causality and Realizability of Specifications

We work with logical formulas formed by *interface predicates* over syntactic interfaces. An interface predicate defines an interactive behavior.

A function

$$f: \vec{X} \to \vec{Y}$$

is called *strongly causal* if for all $t \in \mathbb{N}$ and $x \in \vec{X}$

$$x \downarrow t = x' \downarrow t \Rightarrow f(x) \downarrow t+1 = f(x') \downarrow t+1$$

In other words, the output $f(x) \downarrow t+1$ – the output till time $t+1$ – depends only on the input $x \downarrow t$, the input until time t. Similarly, a specifying predicate p: $(X \triangleright Y)$ is called *strongly causal* if for all $t \in \mathbb{N}$ and $x \in \vec{X}$

$$x \downarrow t = x' \downarrow t \wedge p(x, y) \Rightarrow \exists y \in \vec{Y}: y \downarrow t+1 = y' \downarrow t+1 \wedge p(x', y')$$

A specifying predicate p: $(X \triangleright Y)$ is called *realizable* if there exists a strongly causal function

$$f: \vec{X} \to \vec{Y}$$

such that $p(x, f(x))$ for all input histories x. Then f is called *realization* of p.

A specifying predicate p: $(X \triangleright Y)$ is called *realizable* if there exists a realization for it. It is called *fully realizable* if for every input history x and every output history y for which $p(x, y)$ holds there exist a causal realization f of p with $y = f(x)$. Note that full realizability implies strong causality. Every fully realizable predicate is strongly causal. Note, moreover, that, as a paradox, the specification false is fully realizable but not realizable.

As shown in [8], behaviors of Moore machines are fully realizable. Therefore, every specification p of a behavior of a system that supposed to be implemented by a Moore machine is refined – strengthened – to the weakest fully realizable refinement of p which is the result of implementing p on a Moore machine. A refined specification includes both the original specification p – is a refinement of p – and the property of full realizability as induced by Moore machines (see also [5]). Why considering Moore machines? Mealy machines are perfect operational models for interactive systems and Moore machines are a subclass for which parallel composition is well defined (for details, see [5]).

7 Effects of Safety and Liveness onto Realizability

We specify systems by predicates on input and output histories. If a system specification p: $(X \triangleright Y)$ is implemented by Moore machines this implies that a stronger specification $p^{\circledR}$: $(X \triangleright Y)$ which holds for all the Moore machines that implement p. $p^{\circledR}$ is a refinement of p where $p^{\circledR}(x, y)$ holds if and only if there exists a realization f of p (which means f is strongly causal and $p(x, f(x))$ holds for all x) where $p^{\circledR}(x, f(x))$, formally (see [5]).

$$p^{\circledR}(x, y) = \exists f: \vec{X} \to \vec{Y}: \text{strongly\_causal}(f) \wedge (\forall x \in \vec{X}: p(x, f(x)))$$

where strongly_causal(f) = $\forall t \in \mathbb{N}, x, x' \in \vec{X} : x \downarrow t = x' \downarrow t \Rightarrow f(x) \downarrow t+1 = f(x') \downarrow t+1$.

$p^{\circledR}$ is called the *fully realizable specification* induced by p.

We study a more specific structured form of specifications being implications between premises ae – called assumptions – and conclusions ct – called commitments

$$p(x, y) = (ae(x) \Rightarrow ct(y))$$

Assumption ae(x) talks about the input histories $x \in \vec{X}$ and commitment ct(y) speaks about the output history y. We study the refinement of p to the weakest fully realizable specification $p^{\circledR}$.

Note that $p(x, y) = (\neg ae(x) \vee ct(y))$. Therefore, according to our analysis p(x, y) is a safety property iff both $\neg ae$ and ct are safety properties. The predicate $\neg ae$ is a safety property iff ae is bounded. For a comprehensive treatment of assumptions and commitments in specifications, see [7].

Since in realizations – due to their strong causality – the output $y \downarrow t+1$ is determined exclusively by the input $x \downarrow t$, we refine the proposition p(x, y) to the following weakest refinement of p that is a fully realizable specification:

$\exists f : \vec{X} \rightarrow \vec{Y} : \text{strongly\_ causal}(f) \wedge \forall x \in \vec{X} :$

$$\left(\forall t \in \mathbb{N} : ae^{\exists}(x \downarrow t) \Rightarrow ct^{\exists}(f(x) \downarrow t+1) \right) \wedge (ae(x) \Rightarrow ct(f(x)))$$

The formula

$$ae^{\exists}(x \downarrow t) \Rightarrow ct^{\exists}(f(x) \downarrow t+1)$$

is obtained from

$$(ae(x) \Rightarrow ct(f(x)))$$

by the strong causality of f, since

$$ae^{\exists}(x \downarrow t)$$

stands for

$$\exists x' \in \vec{X} : x \downarrow t = x' \downarrow t \wedge ae(x')$$

Using $ae(x') \Rightarrow ct(f(x'))$ we derive from

$$ct^{\exists}(f(x') \downarrow t+1)$$

by $x \downarrow t = x' \downarrow t \Rightarrow f(x) \downarrow t+1 = f(x') \downarrow t+1$

$$ct^{\exists}(f(x) \downarrow t+1)$$

which gives

$$ae^{\exists}(x \downarrow t) \Rightarrow ct^{\exists}(f(x) \downarrow t+1)$$

Thus, the fully realizable specification for the specification p implies

$$\left(\forall t \in \mathbb{N}: ae^{\exists}(x \downarrow t) \Rightarrow ct^{\exists}(y \downarrow t+1)\right) \wedge (ae(x) \Rightarrow ct(y))$$

In the following, we consider the different cases of ae and ct being safety or liveness properties and how this allows us to simplify or strengthen the fully realizable specification.

ae is a safety property:

ct is a safety property: then the fully realizable specification simplifies to

$$\forall t \in \mathbb{N}: ae^{\exists}(x \downarrow t) \Rightarrow ct^{\exists}(y \downarrow t+1)$$

Note that this formula implies

$$ae(x) \Rightarrow ct(y)$$

since by the safety of ae and ct we have

$$ae(x)$$
$$= \forall t \in \mathbb{N}: \exists x' \in \overrightarrow{X}: x \downarrow t = x' \downarrow t \wedge ae(x')$$
$$= \forall t \in \mathbb{N}: ae^{\exists}(x \downarrow t)$$

as well as

$$ct(y)$$
$$= \forall t \in \mathbb{N}: \exists y' \in \overrightarrow{Y}: y \downarrow t+1 = y' \downarrow t+1 \wedge ct(y')$$
$$= \forall t \in \mathbb{N}: ct^{\exists}(y \downarrow t+1)$$

and therefore from

$$\forall t \in \mathbb{N}: ae^{\exists}(x \downarrow t) \Rightarrow ct^{\exists}(y \downarrow t+1)$$

the proposition

$$ae(x) \Rightarrow ct(y)$$

follows

ct is a liveness property: then the fully realizable specification simplifies to

$$ae(x) \Rightarrow ct(y)$$

since $\forall t \in \mathbb{N}: ae(x \downarrow t) \Rightarrow ct(y \downarrow t+1)$ trivially holds due to the fact that ct is a liveness property and hence, $ct(y \downarrow t+1) = \text{true}$ for all t.

ae is a liveness property:

ct is a safety property: then the fully realizable specification simplifies to

$$ct(y)$$

since $ae^{\exists}(x \downarrow t) \Rightarrow ct^{\exists}(y \downarrow t+1)$ simplifies to $ct^{\exists}(y \downarrow t+1)$, since ae is a liveness property and thus $ae^{\exists}(x \downarrow t) = \text{true}$; hence, $\forall t \in \mathbb{N}: ct^{\exists}(y \downarrow t+1)$ is equivalent to the property ct(y), since ct is a safety property.

ct is a liveness property: then the fully realizable specification simplifies, in general, to

$$ae(x) \Rightarrow ct(y)$$

since $ae^{\exists}(x \downarrow t) = ct^{\exists}(y \downarrow t+1) = \text{true}$ for all $t \in \mathbb{N}$. A simply strategy to guarantee this formula is to guarantee ct(y), anyway.

However, depending on specific properties of ae and ct we can simplify and strengthen this further. In fact, the question is, if there is a strategy to compute the output y from the input x stepwise, such that ct(y) holds if ae(x) holds but at least in some cases, where ¬ae(x), we may end up with output histoies y with ¬ct(y). Otherwise, if such a strategy does not exist, the output y has to fulfill ct(y) independently of the question whether ae(x) holds or does not. In the most extreme case, there is no strategy at all such that $(ae(x) \Rightarrow ct(y))$ holds. Then the specification is not realizable and is refined to false. We illustrate this by examples.

Consider the following three examples of specifications by implications between assumptions and commitments – both being liveness properties

$$\#x > k \Rightarrow \#y = \infty$$
$$\#x = \infty \Rightarrow \#y = \infty$$
$$\#x < \infty \Rightarrow \#y = \infty$$

First, we treat the case, where ae is bounded. Then ¬ae is a safety predicate and thus

$$\left(\forall t \in \mathbb{N}: \neg ae^{\exists}(x \downarrow t)\right) \Rightarrow \neg ae(x)$$

In other words, as long as $\neg ae^{\vee}(x \downarrow t)$ holds it is not excluded that ¬ae(x) holds and therefore ct(y) would not be required. Therefore, only if for some t the proposition $ae^{\vee}(x \downarrow t)$ holds, ¬ae(x) surely does not hold; thus ct(y) has to be fulfilled. Therefore it is sufficient to choose a strategy that starts to ensure ct(y) only if for some t the proposition $ae^{\vee}(x \downarrow t)$ holds.

Thus, there are cases where both ¬ct(f(x)) and ¬ae(x) hold and during the interaction it can observed that ae(x) does not hold. Fully realizability does not imply the stronger specification ct(f(x)) since due to the boundedness of ae there is for all x with ae(x) a time t such that $ae^{\vee}(x \downarrow t)$ holds. As soon as a time t is reached such that $ae^{\vee}(x \downarrow t)$ holds and thus all continuations of input after time t are guaranteed to fulfill ae(t) the function f produces some output f(x) with ct(f(x)). If such a time t is never reached then ae(x) is false and there is no need to guarantee ct(f(x)).

We look at the first example:

$$ae(x) = (\#x > k)$$
$$ct(y) = (\#y = \infty)$$

In this case, there are realizations f with $ae(x) \Rightarrow ct(f(x))$ as well as with $\neg ae(x)$ and $\neg ct(f(x))$. Choose the following realization (for all $t \in \mathbb{N}$):

$$\#x \leq k \Rightarrow f(x) = \varepsilon$$
$$\#(x \downarrow t) > k \Rightarrow f(x) = (\varepsilon \downarrow t + 1)^\wedge y \quad \text{with} \, \#y = \infty \, \text{and} \, t = \min\{t' \in \mathbb{N}: \#(x \downarrow t') > k\}$$

Let here ε be the empty timed stream, $\#\varepsilon = 0$. Then in the case $\#x = 0$ we get $y = f(x) = \varepsilon$ and thus $\neg ae(x)$ and $\neg ct(y)$.

The formulas show that in case of ae being a bounded liveness property there are realizations f for which $\neg ct(f(x))$ and $\neg ae(x)$ hold; thus, the fully realizable specification is $ae(x) \Rightarrow ct(y)$ need not to be simplified to $ct(f(x))$. In our example, choose $x = \varepsilon$; then $f(x) = \varepsilon$ and $\neg ae(x)$ as well as $\neg ct(f(x))$ hold.

Next, assume that ae is approximatively bounded. Then there exists a family of properties for $k \in \mathbb{N}$

$$v_k: \overrightarrow{X} \rightarrow \mathbb{B}$$

such that $\forall x \in \overrightarrow{X}$:

$$(\forall k \in \mathbb{N}: v_k(x)) \Leftrightarrow ae(x)$$
$$\forall k \in \mathbb{N}: v_{k+1}(x) \Rightarrow v_k(x)$$

Now assume a family of properties

$$w_k: \overrightarrow{Y} \rightarrow \mathbb{B}$$

such that $\forall x, \in \overrightarrow{X}, y \in \overrightarrow{Y}$:

$$(\forall k \in \mathbb{N}: w_k(y)) \Rightarrow ct(y)$$
$$\forall k \in \mathbb{N}: w_{k+1}(y) \Rightarrow w_k(y)$$

We get from this formula for the fully realizable specification: if

$$\forall k \in \mathbb{N}: v_k(x) \Rightarrow w_k(y)$$

then

$$ae(x) \Rightarrow ct(y)$$

holds. If for some k the proposition $v_k(x)$ does not hold then $ae(x)$ is false and there is no need that $ct(y)$ is true.

Let us look at our second example.

$$ae(x) = (x = \infty)$$
$$ct(y) = (y = \infty)$$

Hence, we consider the specification

$$\#x = \infty \Rightarrow \#y = \infty$$

We choose

$$v_k(x) = \#x > k$$

and

$$w_k(y) = \#y > k$$

We get

$$(\forall k: w_k(y)) \Rightarrow \#y = \infty$$
$$(\forall k \in \mathbb{N}: v_k(x)) \Leftrightarrow \#x = \infty$$

and further

$$\forall k \in \mathbb{N}: (\#x > k \Rightarrow \#y > k)$$

which is a proposition stronger than

$$\#x = \infty \Rightarrow \#y = \infty$$

but weaker than

$$\#y = \infty$$

In particular, there are realizations f with the property that $\#f(x) = \infty$ is only true if $\#x = \infty$.

Actually, the assertion $(\#x = \infty \Rightarrow y = \infty)$ is fully realizable. This is shown as follows. For every pair of streams (x', y') that fulfil the assertion there is a realization f such that $y' = f(x')$ and $(\#x = \infty \Rightarrow f(x) = \infty)$. Take an arbitrary strongly causal function f' the fulfils the assertion $(\#x = \infty \Rightarrow f'(x) = \infty)$. Define f as follows

$$f(x) = (y' \downarrow t + 1)^\wedge(f'(x) \uparrow t + 1) \text{ if } x' \neq x \text{ where } t = \max\{t': x' \downarrow t = x \downarrow t\}$$
$$f(x') = y'$$

Function f is strongly causal since f' is strongly causal (proof left to the reader).

Finally, we consider our third example

$$ae(x) = (\#x < \infty)$$
$$ct(y) = (\#y = \infty)$$

For every given realization f we construct some input history $x \in \vec{X}$ with

$$\#x = \infty \text{ and } f(x) = \infty$$

We define $x_k \in \vec{X}$ and $t_k \in \mathbb{N}$ inductively such that

$$\#(x_k \downarrow t_k) \geq k \text{ and } \#x_k < \infty$$

as follows: Let x_0 and t_0 be defined by $\#x_0 = 0$, $t_0 = 0$.

Given x_k and t_k with $\#x_k < \infty$ by the specification, $\#fx_k = \infty$ holds. Hence, there exists some $t \in \mathbb{N}$ with

$$t_k < t \text{ and } f(x_k) \downarrow t \geq k + 1$$

Define $t_{k+1} = t + 1$ and $x_{k+1} = (x_k \downarrow t)^\wedge \langle\langle 1 \rangle\rangle^\wedge \varepsilon$; here $x^\wedge z$ denotes the concatenation of two sequences or streams and $\langle e \rangle$ denotes the one element sequence with element e; thus, $\langle\langle 1 \rangle\rangle$ is the one element sequence with element $\langle 1 \rangle$ which is the one element sequence with element 1. We get

$$\#(x_{k+1} \downarrow t_{k+1}) \geq k + 1 \text{ and } \#x_{k+1} < \infty$$

We get for x with $x \downarrow t_k = x_k \downarrow t_k$ for all k the equation $f(x) = \infty$, since by causality $\#(f(x) \downarrow t_k) = \#(f(x_k) \downarrow t_k) \geq k$ for all k, although $\#x = \infty$. As a result, we get that for all realizations f of the specification

$$\#x < \infty \Rightarrow \#y = \infty$$

which requires for all realizations f that

$$\#x < \infty \Rightarrow \#f(x) = \infty$$

Then there exists some x such that $\#x = \infty$ and $f(x) = \infty$. If we control the input x, we can force each realization to observe $ct(f(x))$ although x is chosen in a way such that $ae(x)$ does not hold.

Moreover, the specification

$$(\#x = \infty \Rightarrow \#f(x) < \infty) \wedge (\#x < \infty \Rightarrow \#f(x) = \infty)$$

leads under the assumption of full realizability to the non-realizable specification false as demonstrated in the following section.

8   Liveness Leading to Unrealizability

We show how logically consistent specifications may lead by a refinement of full realizability to fully realizable specifications that are unrealizable since they are equivalent to false. As we show, there are conditional formulas for which there do not exist realizations although they are logically not contradictory. Consider the example

$$p(x, y) = (\#x = \infty \Rightarrow \#y < \infty) \wedge (\#x < \infty \Rightarrow \#y = \infty)$$

Assume a realization f exists such that

$$(\#x = \infty \Rightarrow \#f(x) < \infty) \wedge (\#x < \infty \Rightarrow \#f(x) = \infty)$$

We construct some input x with $\#x = \infty$ and $\#f(x) = \infty$, which is in contradiction to the specification.

Assume there exists a strongly causal function f that realizes the specification. We inductively define input histories x_n and time points $t_n \in \mathbb{N}$. Choose x_0 as the empty history, formally $\#x_0 = 0$, and $t_0 \in \mathbb{N}$ as follows: select for t_0 smallest number such that

$$\#(f(x_0) \downarrow t_0) > 0 \text{ and } \#x_0 \downarrow t_0 = 0$$

Such a number exists since according to the specification $\#f(x_0) = \infty$. We continue as follows: assume that the induction hypothesis

$$\#(f(x_n) \downarrow t_n) > n \text{ and } \#(x_n \downarrow t_n) = n$$

Choose x_{n+1} such that

$$x_n \downarrow t_n = x_{n+1} \downarrow t_n \text{ and } \#x_{n+1} = n + 1$$

and choose t_{n+1} as follows: select for the $t_{n+1} \in \mathbb{N}$ smallest number such that

$$\#(f(x_{n+1}) \downarrow t_{n+1}) > n + 1 \text{ and } \#(x_{n+1} \downarrow t_{n+1}) = n + 1$$

Such a number exists since $\#f(x_{n+1}) = \infty$. We define $x \in \overrightarrow{X}$ as follows

$$\forall n \in \mathbb{N}: x \downarrow t_n = x_n \downarrow t_n$$

We get $\#x = \infty$ since $x \downarrow t_n = \#x_n \downarrow t_n = n$ and $\#f(x) = \infty$ since $f(x) \downarrow t_n = f(x_n) \downarrow t_n > n$; we get a contradiction. The fully realizable specification for p is false since as shown realizations do not exist.

This an example that certain liveness properties may lead to false under the assumption of realizability. Liveness may be in conflict with realizability.

9 Related Work and Conclusion

Peled and Havelund (see [12]) studied monitorability of system properties according to a classification of safety and liveness properties. As we have shown, this issue is also of interest for specifications and their realizability. The key is that for a realizable specification there is a strategy such that the output is produced by a realizable function that generates step by step in each time interval output from the input received so far. Understanding that more in a game-theoretic way, we require a strategy that allows the system to win the interaction game, where the interaction game is defined by the interaction between the context that generates the input to the system and the replies generated by the system. In such a game, the system wins, if it manages to produce an output history for the input provided by the context which is correct with respect to the specification, and the context wins, if such an output, which is correct with respect to the specification, cannot be or is not produced. Strong causality makes sure that the system never does a step ("produces some output") such that the context may later generate some input for which no correct output is specified. A specification is realizable, if there exists a strategy for the system which allows the system to always win the game.

As we have shown, the existence of such a strategy is closely related to safety and liveness properties as they occur in specifications. This leads to an interesting observation: In interactive systems, we do not only speak about computability as an important notation, but also about the existence of a strategy or – in other terms – the existence of realizations. Accordingly, a specification is only implementable, if a realization exists, which gives for interactive systems additional criteria that have to hold to make interface specifications realizable.

References

1. Alpern, B., Schneider, F.B.: Recognizing safety and liveness. Distrib. Comput. **2**(3), 117–126 (1987)
2. Broy, M., Stølen, K.: Specification and Development of Interactive Systems: Focus on Streams, Interfaces, and Refinement. Springer, New York (2001). https://doi.org/10.1007/978-1-4613-0091-5
3. Broy, M.: Relating time and causality in interactive distributed systems. In: Broy, M., Sitou, W., Hoare, T. (eds.) Engineering Methods and Tools for Software Safety and Security, NATO Science for Peace and Security Systems, D: Information and Communication Security, vol. 22, pp. 75–130. IOS Press (2009)
4. Broy, M.: A logical basis for component-oriented software and systems engineering. Comput. J. **53**(10), 1758–1782 (2010)
5. Broy, M.: Verifying of interface assertions for infinite state Mealy machines. J. Comput. Syst. Sci. **80**(7), 1298–1322 (2014)
6. Broy, M.: Computability and realizability for interactive computations. Inf. Comput. **241**, 277–301 (2015)
7. Broy, M.: Theory and methodology of assumption/commitment based system interface specification and architectural contracts. Formal Methods Syst. Design **52**(1), 33–87 (2018)
8. Broy, M.: Specification and Verification of Concurrent System by Causality and Realizability (to appear)
9. Lamport, L.: Proving the correctness of multiprocess programs. IEEE Trans. Software Eng. **3**(2), 125–143 (1977)
10. Mealy, G.H.: A method for synthesizing sequential circuits. Bell Syst. Tech. J. 34, 1045–1079 (1955)
11. Moore, E.F.: Gedanken-experiments on Sequential Machines. Automata Stud. Ann. Math. Stud. (34), 129–153 (1956). Princeton University Press, Princeton
12. Peled,D., Havelund, K.: Refining the safety-liveness classification of temporal properties according to monitorability. In: Models, Mindsets, Meta, pp. 218–234 (2018)

Static Analysis

Domain Analysis and Description – Sorts, Types, Intents

Dines Bjørner[✉]

Technical University of Denmark, Fredsvej 11, DK-2800 Kgs. Lyngby,
2840 Holte, Denmark
http://www.imm.dtu.dk/dibj

Abstract. In earlier publications on **domain analysis & description**
[3–6,8,10,12] we introduced the notion of discrete endurants, both natural and artefactual, being parts and characterised classes of these as
sorts. Parts were then analysed with respect to internal qualities such
as unique identifiers, mereologies and attributes and these were characterised in terms of **types**. In [9,12] we show how Kai Sørlander's philosophy [26–28] justifies our ontology of entities not on empirical grounds,
but on philosophical grounds – and we brought forward the notion of
intentional pull mentioned only briefly in [10]. In [7] we further analysed certain attribute types in terms of the *SI: The International System of Units*[1] . In this paper we shall examine some aspects of sorts,
types and intents not covered in [3–10]. (https://en.wikipedia.org/wiki/
International_System_of_Units)

1 Motivation

1.1 Rôle of Domains

Before **software** can be **designed**
we must **understand**, that is, we must **analyse** and **prescribe** its **requirements**.
Before **requirements** can be **analysed** and **prescribed**
we must **understand**, that is, we must **analyse** and **describe** its **domain**.

1.2 What Are Domains?

By a **domain** we shall understand a **rationally describable** segment of a **human
assisted** reality, i.e., of a world, its **physical parts: natural** ["God-given"] and
artefactual ["man-made"], and **living species: plants** and **animals** including,
notably, **humans**. These entities are **endurants** ("still"), as well as **perdurants**
("alive"). Emphasis is placed on **"human-assistedness"**, that is, there is *at least
one (man-made)* **artifact** and, therefore, that **humans** are a primary cause for
change of endurant **states** as well as perdurant **behaviours**.

Submission for the Klaus Havelund Festschrift, 24 October 2021 ISoLA Conference
2021, Rhodes, Greece.

© Springer Nature Switzerland AG 2021
E. Bartocci et al. (Eds.): Havelund Festschrift, LNCS 13065, pp. 35–60, 2021.
https://doi.org/10.1007/978-3-030-87348-6_3

1.3   Why This Paper ?

A proper domain description consists, therefore, of (i) a description of the manifest phenomena, those we can see and touch, that is, of the **external qualities** of **endurants**; (ii) a description of the **internal qualities** of **endurants**, that is, of the general properties of domain endurants that are not necessarily visible, but can be measured by various means (**internal qualities** can be analysed into **unique identifiers, mereology** and **attributes**); and (iii) a description of the perdurants: events, actions and behaviours over endurants. We shall, in this contribution, focus on endurants.

The specific issues are those of the **sorts** of endurants and **types** and **intents** of unique identifiers, mereologies and attributes.

We distinguish between **sorts** and **types** as follows: **types** are meant as concrete types (for example in the form of atomic types (**integers, reals, characters** or **Boolean**s) or composite types (for example sets, Cartesians, lists, maps, or compositions of concrete types), while **sorts** are abstract types, i.e., types for which no representation is specified.

For software designs and for requirements sorts and types are necessarily **computable.** For domains sorts and types are often not computable. As we shall describe phenomena that obey **Newton's Laws** we shall find that continuous functions are de rigeur. From that derives facts that we shall likewise touch upon.

1.4   Ontologies

By the **main ontology** of domain descriptions we shall understand the general way on which a domain can be composed from solid and fluid endurants. By the **ontology** of a domain we shall understand the specific way in which a domain can be composed from solid an We shall focus here on solid endurants which we shall refer to as **parts**. Parts are either atomic or composite – typically sets or Cartesians.

1.4.1   Entities, Endurants and Perdurants
We identify "upper-most" domain phenomena.

1.4.2   Entity
By an **entity** we shall understand a **phenomenon**, i.e., something that can be *observed*: touched by humans, *or* that can be *conceived* as an *abstraction* of an entity; alternatively, a phenomenon is an entity, *if it exists, it is* **"being"**, *it is that which makes a "thing" what it is: essence, essential nature* [24, Vol. I, pg. 665] ■ **Examples:** A train, a train ride, an aircraft, a flight ■

1.4.3   Endurant
By an **endurant** we shall understand an entity that can be observed, or conceived and described, as a "complete thing" at no matter which given snapshot of time; alternatively an entity is endurant if it is capable of *enduring*, that is *persist*, *"hold out"* [24, Vol. I, pg. 656]. Were we to "freeze" time we would still be able to observe the entire endurant ■ **Examples:** A road, an automobile, a human driver ■

1.4.4   Perdurant

By a **perdurant** we shall understand an entity for which only a fragment exists if we look at or touch them at any given snapshot in time. Were we to freeze time we would only see or touch a fragment of the perdurant, alternatively an entity is perdurant if it endures continuously, over time, persists, lasting [24, Vol. II, pg. 1552] ■   **Examples:** A train ride, an aircraft flight ■

1.4.5   Discrete [Solid] and Continuous [Fluid] Endurants

We proceed in our analysis of manifest domain phenomena.

1.4.5.1   **Discrete [Solid] Endurant**. By a **discrete endurant** we shall understand an endurant which is separate, individual or distinct in form or concept ■   **Examples:** A pipeline and its individual units: pipes, valves, pumps, forks, etc. ■

1.4.5.2   **Continuous [Fluid] Endurants**. By a **continuous endurant** (a **fluid**) we shall understand an endurant which is prolonged, without interruption, in an unbroken series or pattern ■   **Examples:** Water, oil, gas, compressed air, etc. A container, which we consider a discrete endurant, may contain a non-solid, like a gas pipeline unit may contain gas ■

1.4.6   A Domain Description Ontology

Figure 1 graphs an essence of the domain ontology of entities, endurants, perdurants, etc. Sections 1.4.1-1.4.5 covered some aspects of the first three layers, from the top, of that domain ontology. Following [10, 12] (and also justified,

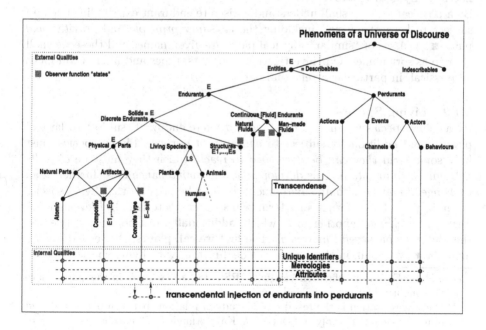

Fig. 1. A domain ontology

on grounds of philosophy by [9]), we shall claim that the manifest world, i.e., the *physical* and *living endurants*, can be analysed with respect to their observable, i.e., viewable and touchable, i.e., **external qualities**, respectively their measurable, i.e., **internal qualities**. The external qualities are summarised in **sorts**. Values of sorts, i.e., *physical* and *living endurants* [we shall omit treatment of *structures* in this paper], can be summarised in three (*internal quality*) categories: *unique identifiers*, *mereologies*, and *attributes*. These *internal qualities* are summarised by **types**[1].

• • •

We shall, in this paper, also make a pragmatic distinction between sorts and types. Sorts will be used to characterise observable endurants. Types will be used to characterise sorts! Intents are then [something] associated with man-made endurants.

2   Sorts

By a **sort** we shall generally mean a named set of endurants which we shall later further characterise.

2.1   Physical Parts, Living Species and Structures

With discrete endurants we associate sorts.

2.1.1   Physical Parts

By a *physical part* we shall understand a discrete endurant existing in time and subject to laws of physics, including the *causality principle* and *gravitational pull*[2] ∎ Classes of "similar" physical parts are given names and these we shall refer to as sort names. Our investigation into sorts, types and intents will focus on physical, in particular artefactual parts.

2.1.2   Living Species

By a *living species* we shall understand a discrete endurant, subject to laws of physics, and additionally subject to *causality of purpose*. Living species must have some *form they can be developed to reach*; which they must be *causally determined to maintain*. This *development and maintenance* must further in an *exchange of matter with an environment*. It must be possible that living species occur in one of two forms: one form which is characterised by *development, form and exchange*; another form which, **additionally**, can be characterised by the *ability to purposeful movement* The first we call **plants**, the second we call **animals** ∎ We shall, in this paper, not deal further with living species.

---

[1] The **RAISE** [19] Specification Language. **RSL** [18], as we use it in this paper, does not distinguish between *sorts* and *types*.

[2] This characterisation is the result of our study of relations between philosophy and computing science, notably influenced by Kai Sørlander's Philosophy. We refer to our research report [9].

2.1.3   Structures

By a **structure** we shall understand a discrete endurant which the domain engineer chooses to describe as consisting of one or more endurants, whether discrete or continuous, but to **not** endow with *internal qualities*: unique identifiers, mereology or attributes ■   We shall, in this paper, not deal further with the concept of structures.

2.2   Natural Parts and Artefacts

Physical parts are either *natural parts*, or are *artefacts*, i.e. man-made parts, which possess **internal qualities**: **unique identification, mereology**, and one or more **attributes** ■   For more on internal qualities, see Sect. 3.2.

2.2.1   Natural Parts

Natural parts are in *space* and *time*; are subject to the *laws of physics*, and also subject to the *principle of causality* and *gravitational pull* ■   **Examples:** an island, a mountain, a river, a lake, a granite rock, a gold lode ■

2.2.2   Artefacts

By an **artifact** we shall understand a *man-made physical part*. **Examples:** canals, road nets, **hub**s: road intersections, **link**s: roads between adjacent hubs, automobiles ■

2.3   Various Forms of Physical Parts

We now arrive at the point where **sorts** come into play. Natural parts are either **atomic**, or **composite**, and artefactual parts are either of **atomic** sort, or of **composite** sort, or of **set sort**.

2.3.1   Atomic Parts

Are those which, in a given context, are deemed to *not* consist of meaningful, separately observable proper *sub-parts*. A **sub-part** is a *part* ■   **Examples:** a hub, a link, a pipe, a valve, a wheel, an engine, a door, a window ■

2.3.2   Composite Parts

Are those which, in a given context, are deemed to *indeed* consist of meaningful, separately observable proper *sub-parts* ■ **Examples:** an automobile, a road net, a pipeline ■

2.3.3   Set Sort Parts

Are simplifications of components. A set sort part is a set of parts of the *same* sort ■   The domain analyser cum describer chooses to **indeed** endow components with **mereology**. **Examples:** Road nets are considered compositions of two parts. a hub aggregate and a link aggregate. The hub aggregate is a set sort part and consists of a set of hubs; the link aggregate is a set sort part and consists of a set of links ■   Set sort parts are pragmatic constructions.

2.4 Analysis and Description Prompts

Implicit in the "story" of Sects. 2.1–2.3 are the following **analysis prompts:**

⋆ is_entity	⋆ is_phys._part	⋆ is_atomic
⋆ is_endurant	⋆ is_liv._species	⋆ is_composite ∎
⋆ is_perdurant	⋆ is_structure	⋆ is_components ∎
⋆ is_discrete	⋆ is_natural_part	⋆ is_set_sort ∎
⋆ is_continuous	⋆ is_artefact	⋆ et cetera ∎

The ∎ boxes imply analysis states where the following **description prompts** are applicable:

⋆ observe_composite_sorts ⋆ observe_component_sorts ⋆ observe_set_sort

respectively. The description observers can be formalised:

---
type: observe_composite_sorts: E→**Text**

Narrative:
s. narrative text on sorts $E_1,\dots,E_n$
o. narrative text on observers obs_$E_1,\dots$,obs_E_n
p. narrative text on proof obligation: $\mathcal{P}$
Formalisation:
s. **type** $E_1,\dots,E_n$
o. **value** obs_E_1: E→$E_1,\dots$,obs_E_n: E→E_n
p. **proof obligation** $\mathcal{P}$: $\forall\ i{:}\{1..n\}\bullet\text{is\_}E_i(e)\equiv\bigwedge\{\sim E_j(e)|j{:}[\,1..n\,]\backslash\{i\}|j{:}[\,1..n\,]\}$

In any specific domain analysis & description the analyser cum describer chooses which subset of composite sorts to analyse & describe. That is: any one domain model emphasises certain aspects and leaves out many "other" aspects.

---
type: observe_set_sort: E→**Text**

Narratives:
s. narrative text on sort P
o. narrative text on observer obs_Ps
Formalisation:
s. **type**   P, Ps = P-**set**
o. **value** obs_Ps: E→P-**set**

Typically P may be a sort expression: P1|P2|...|Pn where Pi are sorts.

2.5 An Example: Road Transport

_____ External Qualities _____

1 The road transport system consists of two aggregates: a road net and automobiles.
2 The road net consists of aggregates of atomic hubs (street intersections) and atomic links (streets).
3 Hub aggregates are sets of hubs and link aggregates are sets of links.
4 Automobile aggregates are sets of automobiles.

type
1.   RTS, RN, AA
value
1.   obs_RN: RTS → RN
1.   obs_AA: RTS → AA
type
2.   AH, AL
value
2.   obs_AH: RN → AH
2.   obs_AL: RN → AL

type
3.   Hs = H-set, H
3.   Ls = L-set, L
value
3.   obs_Hs: AH → Hs
3.   obs_Ls: AL → Ls
type
4.   As = A-set, A
value
4.   obs_As: AA → As

3 Types

By a **type** we shall generally mean a named set of values which we, at the instance of introducing the type name, either define as an atomic **token** type, or as a *concrete* type. By an atomic token type we mean a set of further undefined atomic values. By a concrete type we shall here mean either a **set** of values of type **T**, i.e., **T-set**, or a **list** of values of type **T**, i.e., **T***, or a **map** from values of type **A** to values of type **B**, i.e., **A** $\overrightarrow{m}$ **B**, or a **Cartesian product** (a "record", a "structure") of **A, B, ..., C** typed values, i.e., **A**×**B**× · · · ×**C**. A type can also be a **union** type, that is, the set union of distinct types **A, B, ..., C**, i.e., **A|B|** · · · **|C**. **Tokens**, **Integers**, **Natural Numbers**, **Real**s, **Character**s, POINT, T, and TI, for the latter three, see Sect. 3.1, are base, or "atomic", types. Concrete types of common programming languages include **arrays** (**vector**s, **matrice**s, **tensor**s, etc.) and **record**s. Eventually it all ends up in atomic (i.e., base) types.

3.1 Space and Time

Space and time "fall" somewhat outside a "standard view" of types. Space and time can be explained by transcendental deductions based on purely logical reasoning. This is shown in [26–28]. We summarise [26–28] in Chap. 2 of [12]. We shall thus present a view of time different from that of either of [13, 16, 29].

3.1.1 Space

There is an abstract notion of (definite) SPACE(s) of further un-analysable points; and there is a notion of POINTs in SPACE. Space is not an attribute of endurants. Space is just there. So we do not define an observer, observe_space.

5 A point observer, observe_POINT, is a function which applies to a[ny] specific "location" on a physical endurant, e, and yields a point, ℓ : POINT.

value
5   obs_POINT: E → POINT

One can further define such notions as VOLUME, AREA, SURFACE, BORDER, etc.

3.1.2   Time
By a **definite time** we shall understand an abstract representation of time such as for example year, day, hour, minute, second, et cetera ■ We shall not be concerned with any representation of time. That is, we leave it to the domain analyser cum describer to choose an own representation [16]. But for domain analysis & description we need not be concerned about representation. Such concerns start arising when we "derive" requirements prescriptions from domain descriptions! (See Chap. 9 in [12].) Similarly we shall not be concerned with any representation of time intervals.[3]

6 So there is an abstract type $Time$,
7 and an abstract type TI: $TimeInterval$.
8 There is no $Time$ origin, but there is a "zero" TIme interval.
9 One can add (subtract) a time interval to (from) a time and obtain a time.
10 One can add and subtract two time intervals and obtain a time interval – with subtraction respecting that the subtrahend is smaller than or equal to the minuend.
11 One can subtract a time from another time obtaining a time interval respecting that the subtrahend is smaller than or equal to the minuend.
12 One can multiply a time interval with a real and obtain a time interval.
13 One can compare two times and two time intervals.

type
6 T
7 TI
value
8 0:TI
9 +,−: T × TI → T

10 +,−: TI × TI $\overset{\sim}{\to}$ TI
11 −: T × T → TI
12 *: TI × **Real** → TI
13 <,≤,=,≠,≥,>: T × T → **Bool**
13 <,≤,=,≠,≥,>: TI × TI → **Bool**
axiom
9 ∀ t:T • t+**0** = t

14 We define the signature of the meta-physical time observer.

---

[3] – but point out, that although a definite time interval may be referred to by number of years, number of days (less than 365), number of hours (less than 24), number of minutes (less than 60) number of seconds (less than 60), et cetera, this is not a time, but a time interval.

value
14 **record_TIME**(): **Unit** → $\mathbb{T}$

The time recorder applies to nothing and yields a time. **record_TIME**() can only occur in action, event and behavioural descriptions.

3.2 Internal Qualities

The internal qualities of endurants may include: unique identifiers, for physical parts and living species; mereologies, for atomic, composite, set sort and human parts; and attributes, for physical parts and living species.

3.2.1 Unique Identifiers

Every discrete endurant, $e{:}E$, is unique and can hence be ascribed a **unique identifier**; that identifier can be ascertained by applying the **uid_E** observer function to e.

3.2.2 Mereologies

Mereology is the study of parts and the wholes they form [15][4] ∎ We shall interpret the **mereology of a part**, p, here as as the topological and/or conceptual relations between that part and other parts. Typically we can express the mereology of p, i.e., **mereo_P**(p), in terms of the sets of unique identifiers of the other parts with which p is related. Generally, we can express that relationship as a triplet: **mereo_P**(p)=(ips,iops,ops) where ips is the set of unique identifiers of those parts "from" which p "receives input", whatever 'input' means (!); iops is the set of unique identifiers of those parts "with" which p mutually "shares" properties, whatever 'shares' means (!); ops is the set of unique identifiers of those parts "to" which p "delivers output", whatever 'output' means (!); and where the three sets are mutually disjoint.

3.2.3 Attributes

Part attributes form more "free-wheeling" sets of **internal qualities** than those of unique identifiers and mereologies.

Non-solids are typically recognised because of their spatial form and are otherwise characterised by their intangible, but measurable attributes. That is, whereas endurants, whether discrete (as are parts and components) or continuous (as are materials), are tangible, in the sense of being spatial [or being abstractions, i.e., concepts, of spatial endurants], attributes are intangible: cannot normally be touched, but can be objectively measured. Thus, in our quest for describing domains where humans play an active rôle, we rule out subjective "attributes": feelings, sentiments, moods. Thus we shall abstain, in our domain science also from matters of aesthetics.

---

[4] [15] builds on the concept of mereology as first studied [25] by the Polish philosopher and logician Stanisław Leśchniewski (1886–1939).

Thus, to any part and non-solid, e, we can associate one or more attributes A_1, A_2, ..., A_m, where A_i is an attribute type name and where **attr_A_i(e)** is the corresponding attribute observer.

3.2.4   Internal Quality Observers

We can summarise the observers for internal qualities while otherwise referring to [10] for details.

---

type observe_unique_identifier: P→**Text**

Narratives:
i.   text on unique identifier: UI
o.   text on unique identifier observer: uid_E
Formalisation:
i.   **type** UI
o.   **value** uid_E: E → UI

---

type observe_mereology: P→**Text**

Narratives:
m.   text on mereology: M
o.   text on mereology observer: mereo_E
Formalisation:
m.   **type** M = $\mathcal{E}(\text{UI}_a, ..., \text{UI}_c)$
o.   **value** mereo_E: E → M

For the expression of $\mathcal{E}(\text{UI}_a,...,\text{UI}_c)$ the domain analyser cum describer need not take into consideration any concern for possible "data structure efficiency" as we are not prescribing software requirements let alone specifying a software design. The choice of $\mathcal{E}(\text{UI}_a,...,\text{UI}_c)$, that is, of the mereology of any one sort $\mathcal{E}$, depends on the aspects of the domain that its analyser cum describer wishes to study. That is, "one and the same domain" may give rise to different models each emphasizing their aspects.

---

type observe_attributes: P→**Text**

Narratives:
a.   texts on attributes: A_i, ..., A_k
o.   texts on attribute observers: attr_A_i, ..., attr_A_k
Formalisation:
a.   **type** A_i [= $\mathcal{A}_i$], ..., A_k [= $\mathcal{A}_k$]
o.   **value**   attr_A_i: E → A_i, ..., attr_A_k: E → A_k

where [= $\mathcal{A}_j$] refer to an optional type expression.

In the expression of $\mathcal{A}_j$ the domain analyser cum describer need not take into consideration any concern for possible data structure efficiency as we, are not prescribing software requirements let alone specifying a software design.

One and "seemingly" the same domain may give rise to different analyses & descriptions. Each of these emphasize different aspects. **Example: Road Net:** In one model of a road net emphasis may be on automobile traffic (aiming, eventually, at a road pricing system). I another model of "the same" road net emphasis may be on the topological layout (aiming, eventually, at its construction). In yet a third model "over" a road net emphasis may be on traffic control ■   For each such "road net" model the domain analyser cum describer selects different overlapping sets of attributes.

3.2.5   Attribute Categories

Michael A. Jackson [22] has suggested a hierarchy of attribute categories: from static to dynamic values – and within the dynamic value category: inert values, reactive values, active values – and within the dynamic active value category: autonomous values, biddable values and programmable values. Endurant attribute values

Static: are constants, i.e., cannot change;

Dynamic: are variable, i.e., can change;

Inert: only change as the result of external stimuli where these stimuli prescribe new values;

Reactive: if they vary, change in response to external stimuli, where these stimuli either come from outside the domain of interest or from other endurants;

Active: change (also) of their own volition;

Autonomous: change only "on their own volition";

Biddable: are prescribed but may fail to be observed as such; and

Programmable: can be prescribed.

• • •

We can identify three kinds of attributes: (i) physics, (i) artefactual and (i) intentional.

3.3   Physics Attributes

Typically, when physicists write computer programs, intended for calculating physics behaviours, they "lump" observable properties into more-or-less continuous functions from TIME to some [atomic] quantity—which they then ascribe the **type Real**, thereby hiding some important physics 'dimensions'. In this section we shall review that which is missing !

The subject of physical dimensions in programming languages is rather decisively treated in David Kennedy's 1996 PhD Thesis [23]—so there really is no point in trying to cast new light on this subject other than to remind the reader of what these physical dimensions are all about.

3.3.1   SI: The International System of Quantities

In physics we operate on values of attributes of manifest, i.e., physical phenomena. The type of some of these attributes are recorded in well known tables, cf. Tables 1, 2 and 3. Table 1 shows the base units of physics.

Table 1. Base SI units

Base quantity	Name	Type
Length	meter	m
Mass	kilogram	kg
Time	second	s
Electric current	ampere	A
Thermodynamic temperature	kelvin	K
Amount of substance	mole	mol
Luminous intensity	candela	cd

Table 2. Derived SI units

Name	Type	Derived quantity	Derived type
radian	rad	angle	m/m
steradian	sr	solid angle	$m^2 \times m^{-2}$
Hertz	Hz	frequency	s^{-1}
newton	N	force, weight	$kg \times m \times s^{-2}$
pascal	Pa	pressure, stress	N/m^2
joule	J	energy, work, heat	$N \times m$
watt	W	power, radiant flux	J/s
coulomb	C	electric charge	$s \times A$
volt	V	electromotive force	$W/A \ (kg \times m^2 \times s^{-3} \times A^{-1})$
farad	F	capacitance	$C/V \ (kg^{-1} \times \cdot m^{-2} \times s^4 \times A^2)$
ohm	Ω	electrical resistance	$V/A \ (kg \times m^2 \times s^{-3} \times A^{-2})$
siemens	S	electrical conductance	$A/V \ (kg-1 \times m^{-2} \times s^3 \times A^2)$
weber	Wb	magnetic flux	$V \times s \ (kg \times m^2 \times s^{-2} \times A^{-1})$
tesla	T	magnetic flux density	$Wb/m^2 \ (kg \times s^{-2} \times A^{-1})$
henry	H	inductance	$Wb/A \ (kg \times m^2 \times s^{-2} \times A^2)$
degree Celsius	$^\circ C$	temp. rel. to 273.15 K	K
lumen	lm	luminous flux	$cd \times sr \ (cd)$
lux	lx	illuminance	$lm/m^2 \ (m^{-2} \times cd)$

Table 3. Further SI units

Name	Explanation	Derived type
area	square meter	m^2
volume	cubic meter	m^3
speed, velocity	meter per second	m/s
acceleration	meter per second squared	m/s^2
wave number	reciprocal meter	m-1
mass density	kilogram per cubic meter	kg/m^3
specific volume	cubic meter per kilogram	m3/kg
current density	ampere per square meter	A/m^2
magnetic field strength	ampere per meter	A/m
substance concentration	mole per cubic meter	mol/m3
luminance	candela per square meter	cd/m^2
mass fraction	kilogram per kilogram	kg/kg = 1

Table 4. SI units of measure and fractions

SI Units of measure						
Prefix name		deca	hecto	kilo	mega	giga
Prefix symbol		da	h	k	M	G
Factor	10^0	10^1	10^2	10^3	10^6	10^9
Prefix name		tera	peta	exa	zetta	yotta
Prefix symbol		T	P	E	Z	Y
Factor		10^{12}	10^{15}	10^{18}	10^{21}	10^{24}
Fractions						
Prefix name		deci	centi	milli	micro	nano
Prefix symbol		d	c	m	μ	n
Factor	10^0	10^{-1}	10^{-2}	10^{-3}	10^{-6}	10^{-9}
Prefix name		pico	femto	atto	zepto	yocto
Prefix symbol		p	f	a	z	y
Factor		10^{-12}	10^{-15}	10^{-18}	10^{-21}	10^{-24}

Table 2 shows the units of physics derived from the base units. Table 3 shows further units of physics derived from the base units. The upper half of Table 4 shows standard prefixes for SI units of measure and the lower half of Table 4 shows fractions of SI units.

●●●

The point in bringing this material is that when modelling, i.e., describing domains we must be extremely careful in not falling into the trap of modelling physics types, etc., as we do in programming – by simple **Real**s. We claim, without evidence, that many trivial programming mistakes are due to confusions between especially derived SI units, fractions and prefixes.

3.3.1.1 **Units are Atomic** A volt, $kg \times m^2 \times s^{-3} \times A^{-1}$, see Table 2, is atomic. It is not a composite structure of mass, length, time, and electric current – in some intricate relationship.

 Example 1: Physics attributes

Hub attributes:

15 number of lanes,
    surface,
    etc.;

type
15. NoL, SUR, ...
value
15. attr_NoL:H→NoL
15. attr_SUR:H→SUR, ...

Link attributes:

16 number of lanes,
    surface.
    etc.

value
16. attr_NoL:L→NoL
16. attr_SUR:L→SUR, ...

Automobile attributes:

17 Power,
    Fuel (Gasoline, Diesel, Electric, ...),
    Size, ...

18 Velocity,
    Acceleration, ...

type
17. $BHp = \mathbf{Nat:kg} \times m^{-2} \times s^{-3}$
17. Fuel
17. $Length = \mathbf{Nat:cm}$
17. $Width = \mathbf{Nat:cm}$
17. $Height = \mathbf{Nat:cm}$
18. $Vel = \mathbf{Real:m} \times s^{-1}$
18. $Acc = \mathbf{Real:m} \times s^{-2}$

value
17. attr_BHp: A→BHp
17. attr_Fuel: A→Fuel
17. attr_Length: A→Length
17. attr_Width: A→Width
17. attr_Height: A→Height
18. attr_Vel: A→Vel
18. attr_Acc: A→Acc

• • •

Physical attributes may ascribe mass and volume to endurants. But they do not reveal the substance, i.e., the material from which the endurant is made. That is done by chemical attributes.

3.3.2 Chemical Elements

The *mole*, mol, substance is about chemical molecules. A mole contains exactly $6.02214076 \times 10^{23}$ (the Avogadro number) constituent particles, usually atoms, molecules, or ions – of the elements, cf. Fig. 2.

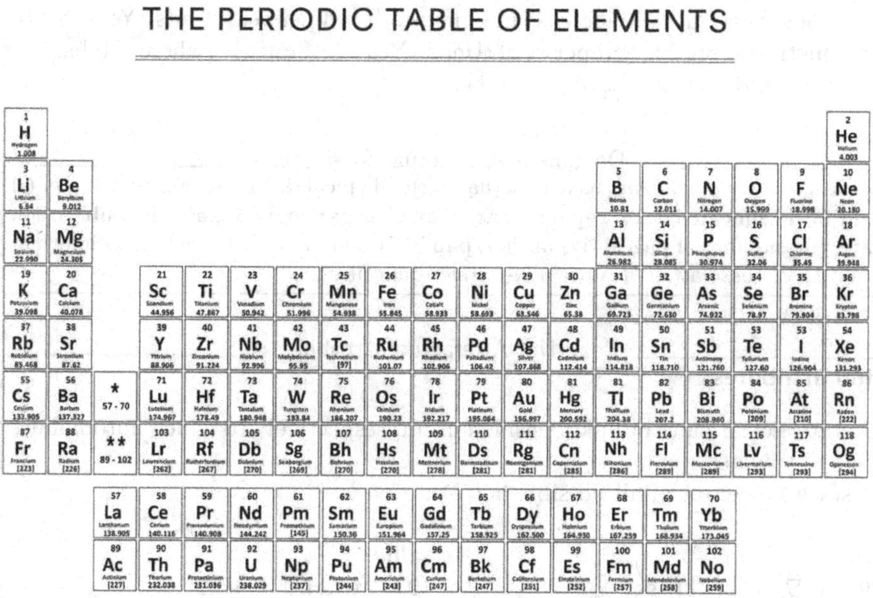

THE PERIODIC TABLE OF ELEMENTS

Fig. 2. Periodic table [https://www.postery.com/dk/periodic-table-poster]

Any specific molecule is then a compound of two or more elements, for example, calciumphosphat: Ca3(PO4)2.

Moles bring substance to endurants. The physics attributes may ascribe weight and volume to endurants, but they do not explain what it is that gives weight, i.e., fills out the volume.

3.4 Artefactual Attributes

3.4.1 Examples of Artefactual Attributes

We exemplify some artefactual attributes.

* **Designs.** Artefacts are man-made endurants. Hence "exhibit" a design. My three dimensional villa has floor plans, etc. The artefact attribute: *'design'* can thus be presented by the architect's or the construction engineer's CAD/CAM drawings.
* **States** of an artefact, such as, for example, a road intersection (or railway track) traffic signal; and
* **Currency**, e.g., Kr, $, £, €, ¥, et cetera, used as an attribute[5], say the cost of a train ticket.
* **Artefactual Dimensions.** Let the domain be that of industrial production whose attributes could then be: production: units produced per year,

---

[5] One could also consider a [10 €] bank note to be an artefact, i.e., a part.

Units/Year; growth: increase in units produced per year, Units×Year^{-2}; productivity: production per staff, Units×Year^{-1}×Staff^{-1}—where the base for units and staff are natural numbers.

_____ Document Artefactual Attributes _____

Let us consider *documents* as artefactual parts. Typical document attributes are: (i) kind of document: `book`, `report`, `pamphlet`, `letter` and `ticket`, (ii) publication date, (iii) number of pages, (iv) author/publisher and (v) possible colophon information. *All of these attributes are non-physics quantities.*

_____ Road Net Artefactual Attributes _____

Hub attributes:

19 state: set of pairs of link identifiers from, respectively to which automobiles may traverse the hub;
20 state space: set of all possible hub states.

type
19. $H\Sigma = (LI \times LI)$-**set**
20. $H\Omega = H\Sigma$-**set**

value
19. attr_$H\Sigma$:H→HΣ
20. attr_$H\Omega$:H→HΩ

Link attributes:

21 state: set of 0, 1, 2 or 3 pairs of adjacent hub identifiers, the link is closed, open in one direction (closed in the opposite), open in the other direction, or open in both directions; and
22 state space: set of all possible link states.

type
21. $L\Sigma = (LI \times LI)$-**set**
22. $L\Omega = L\Sigma$-**set**

value
21. attr_$L\Sigma$:L→LΣ
22. attr_$L\Omega$:L→LΩ

3.4.2 Continuous Function Attributes

Physicists, when appropriate, have no hesitance, in modelling natural phenomena in terms of continuous functions—often typically in the form of (possibly partial) differential equations. In domain engineering we shall necessarily see this practice continued. In the context of formal specification of software designs and of their requirements, there are, however, currently, some problems. The main issue is that of combining the classical discrete mathematics, that is, set theoretic and mathematical logic, modelling of software and requirements, with continuous functions. A mantra of discrete mathematics specifications is that of thereby being able to state and prove properties of software [requirements]. As long as we forego provability we can, of course, apply the language tools of continuous mathematics, e.g., differential equations and integrals, with those set theory and logic. Thus we shall be able to express a number of attributes.

─────────────── Pipelines ───────────────

23 The example is that of rather simplified pipelines. These pipelines consist of a sequence of pipe line units.
24 A pipe unit is either a well, a pipe, a pump, a valve or a sink. The first pipe unit is a well, the last is a sink, and all other units are either pipes, pumps, or valves.
25 A well and a sink contains, and pipe, pump, and valve pipe units conduct fluids, say oil.
26 We shall, in this simplified example, consider the following as attributes: volume [dynamic], the maximum laminar flow [static], the current flow [dynamic], the maximum laminar leak [static] and the current leak [dynamic] of fluid of a pipe line unit.
27 A valve is simplified to be either "fully open" or to be "fully closed" (shut) [programmable attribute].
28 A pump is simplified to be either "fully pumping" or to be "fully non-pumping" [programmable attribute] but allowing free flow.
29 Pipe, pump, and valve pipe line units have further attributes: diameter [static attribute], length [static attribute], [outside] temperature [dynamic attribute], etc., etc.
30 By the flow [history, dynamic attribute] of a pipe, pump, and valve pipeline unit we mean the volume of fluid passing through that unit per time interval, say second.

type
23.   PL = PU*
24.   PU == We | Pi | Pu | Va | Si
29.   LU = Pi | Pu | Va
26.   Vol, MaxLamFlow, CurFlow, MaxLamLeak, CurLeak
27.   ValveState == mkOpen(...) | mkClosed(...)
28.   PumpState == mkPumping(...) | mkNonPumping(...)
29.   Diam, Length, Temp, ...
30.   Flow = TIME → VolPerTI
axiom
24.   ∀ pl:PL • is_We(pl[1]) ∧ is_Si(pl[len pl]) ∧
24.   ∀ i:**Nat** • i ∈ **inds** pl\{1,len pl} ⇒ (is_Pi|is_Pu|is_Va)(pl[i])
value
25.   attr_Vol: (We|LU|Si)→Vol
26.   attr_...Flow: LU→...Vol, attr_...Leak: LU→...Leak
27.   attr_ValveState: LU→ValveState
28.   attr_PumpState: LU→PumpState
29.   attr_Diam: LU→Diam, attr_Length: LU→Length, attr_Temp: (We|LU|Si)→Temp, ...
30.   attr_Flow_History: LU$\xrightarrow{\sim}$Flow

Discussion: The volume, [instantaneous unit] flow, state, diameter, length and temperature attributes can be measured. Flow history is here considered an attribute. Flow history is a fact. We can speak about it. Hence it is an attribute. And, at any time we can measure it, But whether we do so is immaterial. Flow history TIME-dependency is shown as a partial function, $\xrightarrow{\sim}$. But that "partiality" does not reveal that the flow "starts" at "a definite time", say at the operational start of the pipeline, and ends at "the present time". Before 'the operational start' and after 'the present time' the flow history is undefined, i.e., **chaos** (!).

The formulas do not explain how fluid flow comes about.

To indicate that we elaborate on some perdurant-like properties of pipelines.

31 Pumps can be activated: set to pump, respectively reset to no longer pump;
32 and valves can be set to be fully open, respectively reset to be fully closed.

---

type
31. Pump_Act == Pump_Set | Pump_Reset
32. Valve_Act == Valve_Set | Valve_Reset

We do here model the perdurant actions and behaviours of pumps and valves. But now, having introduced that pumps and valves can be set and rest, we can model pump and valve histories.

33 Pump histories are discrete mappings from TIME to pump settings.
34 Valve histories are discrete mappings from TIME to valve settings.

type
33.   Pump_Hist = TIME $\overrightarrow{m}$ Pump_Act
34.   Valve_Hist = TIME $\overrightarrow{m}$ Valve_Act
valve
33.   attr_Pump_Hist: Pu → Pump_Hist
34.   attr_Valve_Hist: Va → Valve_Hist

Flow history is a partial function, $\overset{\sim}{\rightarrow}$, whereas pump and valve histories are discrete maps, $\overrightarrow{m}$. The former is the result of the combined settings of pumps and valves as well as of many additional physical phenomena, the latter is the result of actions performed on valve and pump behaviours.

Appendix A of [12] exemplifies a domain model of the endurants of general pipelines.

3.5   Intents

3.5.1   Expressing Intents
Artefacts are made with an **intent**: one or more purposes for which the parts are to serve. Usually intents involve two or more part sorts.

3.5.1.1   Examples of Intents

* **Road Transport:** roads are "made to accommodate" automobiles, and automobiles are "made to drive" on roads ■
* **Credit Card System:** credit cards are for "payment of purchased merchandise", and retailers are "there to sell merchandise" ■

3.5.2   Intent Modelling
We do not here suggest a formal way of expressing intents. That is, we do not formalise "made to accommodate", "made to drive", et cetera! Intents, instead, are expressed as **intentional pulls**, and these are then expressed in terms of "intent-related" attributes.

3.5.2.1   Examples of Intent-related Attributes The intent-related attributes are not based on physical evidence, but on what we can, but do not necessarily speak about.

───────── Example: Intentional Attributes ─────────

Road Transport:

35 Hub traversal history: the recording of which automobiles traversed a hub at which time.

36 Link traversal history: the recording of which automobiles traversed a link at which time.

37 Automobile history: the recording of which hubs and links were traversed at which time.

type	value
35. HHist=AI $\overrightarrow{m}$ T-set	35. attr_HHist:H→HHist
36. LHist=AI $\overrightarrow{m}$ T-set	36. attr_LHist:L→LHist
37. AHist=(HI|LI) $\overrightarrow{m}$ T-set	37. attr_AHist:A→AHist

All three history attributes are subject to constraints: the automobile, hub and link identifiers must be of automobiles, hubs and links of a (i.e., the) road net; the same automobile cannot be at two or more hubs and/or links at any one time (35–36) and the timed visits must be commensurate with the road net; et cetera.

Credit Card System:

38 Credit card histories X "records" Y^6, by time, the shop and the merchandise bought.

39 Shop histories "record", by time, the credit card and the merchandise sold.

type	value
38. CHist = $\mathbb{T}$ $\overrightarrow{m}$ (SI×MI)	38. attr_CHist: C → CHist
39. SHist = $\mathbb{T}$ $\overrightarrow{m}$ (CI×MI)	39. attr_SHist: S → SHist

The two history attributes are subject to constraints: the shop and credit card identifiers must be of shops and credit cards of the credit card system; and the merchandise identifier must be of a merchandise of the identified shop.

3.5.3 Intentional Pull

The term 'intentional pull' was first introduced in [10].

3.5.3.1 **An Aside: Road Transport System States** In order to express intentional pulls we need introduce a notion of states. In general, by a state, we shall mean any collection of parts each of which contains one or more dynamic attributes, that is, attributes whose values may change.

───────── Road Net States &c. ─────────

We shall consider the following states:

40 any road transport system;

41 the set of all its hubs;

42 the set of all its links; and

43 the set of all its automobiles.

───────────

[6] By "record" is meant: X "remembers" Y

value
40. rtn:RTN
41. hs:obs_Hs(obs_AH(rtn))

42. ls:obs_Ls(obs_AL(rtn))
43. as:obs_As(obs_AA(rtn))

44 From the set of hubs we can extract the map of hub histories:
   from hub identifiers to hub histories.

type
44. HHists=HI $\overrightarrow{m}$ (AI $\overrightarrow{m}$ T-**set**)
value
44. extr_HHists:H-**set**→HHists
44. extr_HHists(hs) ≡ [hi↦attr_HHist(h)|h:H•h ∈ hs ∧ hi=uid_H(h)]

45 From the set of links we can extract the map of link histories:
   from link identifiers to link histories.

type
45. LHists=LI $\overrightarrow{m}$ (AI $\overrightarrow{m}$ T-**set**)
value
45. extr_LHists:L-**set**→LHists
45. extr_LHists(ls) ≡ [li↦attr_LHist(l)|l:L•l ∈ ls ∧ li=uid_L(l)]

46 From the set of automobiles we can extract the map of automobile histories:
   from automobile identifiers to automobile histories.

type
46. • AHists=AI $\overrightarrow{m}$ ((HI|LI) $\overrightarrow{m}$ T-**set**)
value
46. extr_AHists:A-**set**→AHists
46. extr_AHists(as) ≡ [ai↦attr_AHist(a)|a:A•a ∈as ∧ ai=uid_A(a)]

47 We can merge the hub and link histories.

type
47. HLHists=(HI|LI) $\overrightarrow{m}$ (AI $\overrightarrow{m}$ T-**set**)
value
47. mergeHLHists:(HHists×LHists)→HLHists
47. mergeHLHists(hhists,lhists) ≡ hhists ∪ lhists

48 The ahists:AI $\overrightarrow{m}$ ((HI|LI) $\overrightarrow{m}$ T-**set**) can be "inverted":
   inv_ahists(ahists)[7] into hlhists:(HI|LI) $\overrightarrow{m}$ (AI $\overrightarrow{m}$ T-**set**)
49 and then "re-inverted":
   inv_hlhists(hlhists) into ahists':AI $\overrightarrow{m}$ ((HI|LI) $\overrightarrow{m}$ T-**set**)
50 to [re-]obtain ahists
   as no automobile can be in any two or more places at any one time.

value
48. inv_ahists: AHists → HLHists
48. inv_ahists(ahists) ≡
48.   [hli↦[ai'↦(ahists(ai'))(hli)|ai':Al•ai'∈ **dom** ahists∧hli∈ **dom** ahists(ai')]
48. |ai:Al,hli:(Hl|Ll)•ai∈ **dom** ahists∧hli∈ **dom** ahists(ai)]
assertion:
50. ∀ ahists:AHists • inv_hlhists(inv_ahists(ahists)) = ahists
where:
49. inv_hlhists: HLHists → AHists
49. inv_hlhists(hlhists) ≡ left to the reader

3.5.3.2 **Examples of Intentional Pulls** We present two examples.

Road Transport:

51 If an automobile history records that an automobile was at a hub or on a
link at some time,
then that hub, respectively link, history records that that automobile was
there at that time,
and vice versa—and only that.

Intentional Pull:
51. □ ∀ rtn:RTN, hs:Hs, ls:Ls, as:As•
51.   hs=obs_Hs(obs_AH(rtn)) ∧ ls=obs_Ls(obs_AL(rtn)) ∧ as=obs_As(obs_AA(rtn))
51.   ∧ **let** ahists=xtr_AHists(as), hlhists=xtr_HHists(hs)∪xtr_LHists(ls) **in**
51.   inv_AHists(ahists) = hlhists **end** ■

Credit Card System:

52 If a credit card history records that an purchase was made at a shop of some
merchandise and at
53 some time,
54 then that shop's history records that that such a purchase was made there
at that time,
55 and vice versa—and only that.

We leave the formalisation to the reader ■

4   Actions, Events, Behaviours

By a **transcendental deduction** [10] we shall interpret discrete endurants as
behaviours. Behaviours are sets of sequences of actions, events and behaviours.
Behaviours communicate, for example, by means of CSP channels and out-
put/input commands [21].

---

[7] Note the subtle use of free and bound variables in the map comprehension expressions.

4.1 Actions

Actions are functions which purposefully are initiated by behaviours and potentially changes a state. Actions apply to behaviour arguments and yield updates to these.

4.2 Events

Events are functions which surreptitiously "occur" to behaviours, typically instigated by "some outside", and usually changes a state. Events updates behaviour arguments. Events can be expressed as CSP [21] inputs.

4.3 Behaviours

To every part we shall, in principle, associate a behaviour. The behaviour is unique identified by the unique identifier of the part. The behaviour communicates with such other parts as are identified by the mereology of the parts. The behaviour otherwise depends on arguments: the unique part identifier, the part mereology, the part attributes separated into the static attributes, i.e., those with constant values, the programmable attributes, and the remaining dynamic attributes. The programmable attributes are those whose values are set by the behaviour, i.e., its actions.

4.4 Summary

The "miracle" of transcendental deduction is fundamental to domain analysis & description. It "ties" sorts: their external and internal qualities strongly to the dynamics of domains. Details on transcendental deductions, actions, events and behaviours are given in [10].

5   Conclusion

The sort, type and intent concepts of the domain analysis & description method covered in [10] has been studied in further detail. Although, as also illustrated by Fig. 1, the method includes the analysis of natural and living species, it is primarily aimed at artefacts and domains dominated by such. We refer to [11] for a dozen or so examples of medium-scale domain analysis & description case studies. You will see from those examples that they are all rather frugal with respect to ascribing attributes. That is: An endurant may have very many attributes, but in any one domain description in which it is present the analyser cum describer may have chosen to "abstract some out (!)", that is, to not consider some—often very many of these—of these attributes.

5.1   Sort Versus Types

"Sorts are not recursive !" That is, endurant parts of sort S do not contain proper endurant sub-parts of same sort S. For a discussion of this see [12, Sect. 4.18.2].

5.1.1   Pragmatics

In this paper we have used the terms 'sorts' and 'types' as follows. **Sorts** are used to describe external qualities of endurants: whether discrete or continuous (solids or non-solids), whether physical parts, living species or structures, whether natural parts or artefacts, and whether atomic, composite, components or set sorts. **Types** are used to describe internal qualities of endurants: unique identifiers, mereologies, and attributes.

5.1.2   Syntactics

Sorts are defined by simple identifiers:

   ⋆ **type** S.

Types are defined either by base type definitions **type** T = BTE, where BTE is an atomic type expression, for example either of,

⋆ **Intg**[:Dim],   ⋆ **Real**[:Dim],   ⋆ **Token**,   ⋆ $\mathbb{T}, \mathbb{TI}$.
⋆ **Nat**[:Dim],   ⋆ **Char**[:Dim],   ⋆ $\mathbb{POINT}$ and

where [:Dim] is either absent or some standard prefix and fraction SI unit. Or types are defined by composite type expressions, **type** T = CTE, for example of the form:

   CTE = A-**set** | B×C×...×D | E $\overrightarrow{m}$ F | etc.

where A, B, C, ..., D, E, F, etc., are type expressions – where [recursive] T is allowed.

5.1.3   Semantics

We start with types. **Types** are sets of either base (type) values, or structures over these: sets of sets (of etc.), sets of Cartesians (of etc.), sets of maps (from etc.), et cetera. **Sorts** are sets of endurants as characterised by their being discrete or continuous (solids or non-solids), physical parts, living species or structures, natural parts or artefacts, and atomic, composite, components or set sorts; and as furthermore characterised by the types of their possible unique identifiers, possible mereologies (components have no mereologies), and attributes.

5.2 Domain Oriented Programming Languages

I found out about Kennedy's work from [20]. My own interest in the subject goes back to the early 1980s. Around year 2000 I had an MSc student work out formal specifications and compilers for two "small" programming languages: one for senior high school [student] physics and one for business college [student] accounting. I otherwise refer to [2, Exercise 9.4, Page 235].

One could, rather easily, augment standard programming languages, for use in physics calculations, to feature a refined type system that reflects the SI units, simple and composite, as well as standard SI prefixes and fractions.

We refer to the very elegant domain-specific actuarial programming language, **Actulus**, [14] for life insurance and pensions.

Our *Domain Specific Language* **dogma** is this: **the design (and semantics) of any DSL must be based on a carefully analysed and both informally and formally described domain.**

5.3 Attributes of Living Species

The Swedish botanist, zoologist, and physician, *Carl von Linné*, is the father of modern taxonomy: the science that finds, describes, classifies, and names living things, published [30, in 1748]. In domain analysing & describing living species one, of course, cannot really contribute much new. So we leave that area to the living species taxonomists – while referring to [17, *Formal Concept Analysis— Mathematical Foundations*]. See also [6, Sect. 1.8].

Acknowledgements. It is a pleasure to acknowledge my collaboration over recent years with Klaus Havelund.

References

1. Bjørner, D.: Domain models of "The Market" – in preparation for E-transaction systems. In: Kilov, H., Baclawski, K. (eds.), Practical Foundations of Business and System Specifications, Kluwer Academic Press, Amsterdam. http://www2.imm.dtu.dk/~dibj/themarket.pdf
2. Bjørner, D.: Software Engineering, Vol. 2: Specification of Systems and Languages. Texts in Theoretical Computer Science, the EATCS Series. Springer, Berlin (2006). https://doi.org/10.1007/978-3-540-33193-3
3. Bjørner, D.: Domain engineering. In: Boca, P., Bowen, J. (eds.) Formal Methods: State of the Art and New Directions, pp. 1–42. Springer, London (2010). https://doi.org/10.1007/978-3-642-36654-3
4. Bjørner, D.: Domain science & engineering - from computer science to the sciences of informatics, Part I of II: the engineering part. Kibernetika i sistemny analiz **2**(4), 100–116 (2010)
5. Bjørner, D.: Domain Science & Engineering - From Computer Science to The Sciences of Informatics Part II of II: The Science Part. Kibernetika i sistemny analiz **2**(3), 100–120 (2011)

6. Bjørner. D.: Manifest domains: analysis & description. Formal Aspect. Comput. **29**(2), 175–225 (2017)

7. Bjørner, D.: Domain analysis & description - the implicit and explicit semantics problem. In: Laleau, R., Méry, D., Nakajima, S., Troubitsyna, E. (eds.) Proceedings Joint Workshop on Handling IMPlicit and EXplicit Knowledge in Formal System Development (IMPEX) and Formal and Model-Driven Techniques for Developing Trustworthy Systems (FM&MDD), Xi'An, China, 16th November 2017, vol. 271 of Electronic Proceedings in Theoretical Computer Science, pp. 1–23. Open Publishing Association (2018)

8. Bjørner, D.: Domain facets: analysis & description. Technical report, Technical University of Denmark, Fredsvej 11, DK-2840 Holte, Denmark, May 2018. Extensive revision of [3]. `imm.dtu.dk/~ibj/2016/facets/faoc-facets.pdf`

9. Bjørner, D.: Domain analysis & description - a philosophy basis. Technical report, Technical University of Denmark, Fredsvej 11, DK-2840 Holte, Denmark, November 2019. `imm.dtu.dk/~dibj/2019/filo/main2.pdf`

10. Bjørner, D.: Domain analysis & description - principles, techniques and modelling languages. ACM Trans. Softw. Eng. Method. **29**(2), April 2019. `imm.dtu.dk/~dibj/2018/tosem/Bjorner-TOSEM.pdf`

11. Bjørner, D.: Domain Case Studies (`imm.dtu.dk/~db/`). 2021: Shipping Lines, March–April, `2021/ral/ral.pdf`. 2021: Rivers and Canals, Februrary, `2021/Graphs/Rivers-and-Canals.pdf`. 2021: Retailers, January, `2021/Retailer/BjornerHeraklit27January2021.pdf`. 2019: Container Line, ECNU, Shanghai, China, `container-paper.pdf`. 2018: Documents, TongJi Univ., Shanghai, China, `2017/docs/docs.pdf`. 2017: Urban Planning, TongJi Univ., Shanghai, China, `2017/up/urban-planning.pdf`. 2017: Swarms of Drones, ISCAS, `2017/swarms/swarm-paper.pdf`. 2013: Road Transport, Techn. Univ. of Denmark, `road-p.pdf` . 2012: Credit Cards, Uppsala, Sweden `2016/credit/accs.pdf`. 2012: Weather Information, Bergen, Norway, `2016/wis/wis-p.pdf`. 2010: Web-based Transaction Processing, Techn. Univ. of Vienna, Austria `wfdftp.pdf`. 2010: The Tokyo Stock Exchange, Tokyo Univ., Japan, `todai/tse-1.pdf`, `todai/tse-2.pdf`. 2009: Pipelines, Techn. Univ. of Graz, Austria, `ipipe-p.pdf`. 2007: A Container Line Industry Domain, Techn. Univ. of Denmark, `container-paper.pdf` . 2002: The Market, Techn. Univ. of Denmark, `themarket.pdf`, [1]. 1995–2004: Railways, Techn. Univ. of Denmark - a compendium, `train-book.pdf`. Experimental research reports, Technical University of Denmark, Fredsvej 11, DK-2840 Holte, Denmark

12. Bjørner, D.:Domain science & engineering - a foundation for software development. In: EATCS Monographs in Theoretical Computer Science. Springer, Cham (2021). DOIurl10.1007/978-3-030-73484-8

13. Blizard, W.D.: A formal theory of objects, space and time. J. Symbol. Logic **55**(1), 74–89 (1990)

14. Christiansen, D.R., Grue, K., Niss, H., Sestoft, P., Sigtryggsson, K.S.: Actulus modeling language - an actuarial programming language for life insurance and pensions. Technical Report (2015). `edlund.dk/sites/default/files/Downloads/paper_actulus-modeling-language.pdf`, Edlund A/S, Denmark. http://www.edlund.dk/en/insights/scientific-papers

15. Casati, R., Varzi, A.C.: Parts and Places: The Structures of Spatial Representation. MIT Press, Cambridge (1999)

16. Furia, C.A., Mandrioli, D., Morzenti,, A., Rossi, A.: Modeling Time in Computing. Monographs in Theoretical Computer Science. Springer, Berlin (2012). https://doi.org/10.1007/978-3-642-32332-4
17. Ganter, B., Wille, R.: Formal Concept Analysis – Mathematical Foundations. Springer-Verlag, Berlin, January 1999. https://doi.org/10.1007/978-3-642-59830-2
18. Chris, W.G., et al.: The RAISE Specification Language. The BCS Practitioner Series. Prentice-Hall, Hemel Hampstead (1992)
19. Chris, W.G., et al.: The RAISE Development Method. The BCS Practitioner Series. Prentice-Hall, Hemel Hampstead, (1995)
20. Gibson, J.S., Méry, D.: Explicit modelling of physical measures: from event-b to java. In: Laleau, R., Méry, D., Nakajima, S., Troubitsyna, E. (eds.) Proceedings Joint Workshop on Handling IMPlicit and EXplicit knowledge in formal system development (IMPEX) and Formal and Model-Driven Techniques for Developing Trustworthy Systems (FM&MDD), Xi'An, China, 16th November 2017, vol. 271 of Electronic Proceedings in Theoretical Computer Science, pp. 64–79. Open Publishing Association (2018)
21. Anthony, C., Hoare, R.: Communicating Sequential Processes. C.A.R. Hoare Series in Computer Science. Prentice-Hall International 1985. Published electronically: usingcsp.com/cspbook.pdf (2004)
22. Jackson, M.A.: Software Requirements & Specifications: A Lexicon of Practice, Principles and Prejudices. ACM Press. Addison-Wesley, Reading (1995)
23. Kennedy. A.: Programming languages and dimensions. PhD thesis, University of Cambridge, Computer Laboratory, 149 p. April 1996. cl.cam.ac.uk/tech reports/UCAM-CL-TR-391.pdf. Technical report UCAM-CL-TR-391, ISSN 1476-298
24. Little, W., Fowler, H.W., Coulson, J., Onions, C.T.: The Shorter Oxford English Dictionary on Historical Principles. vol. 2, Clarendon Press, Oxford (1973, 1987)
25. Luschei, E.C.: The Logical Systems of Leśniewksi. North Holland, Amsterdam (1962)
26. Sørlander, K.: Det Uomgængelige - Filosofiske Deduktioner [The Inevitable - Philosophical Deductions, with a foreword by Georg Henrik von Wright]. 168 p. Munksgaard · Rosinante (1994)
27. Sørlander, K.: Under Evighedens Synsvinkel [Under the viewpoint of eternity]. Munksgaard · Rosinante, 200 p (1997)
28. Sørlander, K.: Indføring i Filosofien [Introduction to The Philosophy]. Informations Forlag, 233 p (2016)
29. van Benthem, J.: The Logic of Time. In: Hintika. J. Synthese Library: Studies in Epistemology, Logic, Methhodology, and Philosophy of Science, 2nd edn. 1983, vol. 156. Kluwer Academic Publishers, Dordrecht (1991)
30. von Linné, C.: An Introduction to the Science of Botany. Lipsiae [Leipzig]: Impensis Godofr. Kiesewetteri (1748)
31. WanLing, X., ShuangQing, X., HuiBiao, Z.: A UTP approach for rTiMo. Formal Aspect. Comput. **30**(6), 713–738 (2018)
32. WanLing, X., HuiBiao, Z., QiWen, X.: A process calculus BigrTiMo of mobile systems and its formal semantics. Formal Aspect. Comput. **33**(2), 207–249 (2021)

Dynamic interval analysis
by abstract interpretation[*]

Patrick Cousot[1 (0000-0003-0101-9953)]

CS, CIMS, NYU, New York, NY, USA, pcousot@cims.nyu.edu, visiting IMDEA
Software, Madrid, Spain

Dedicated to Klaus Havelund
for his 65th birthday

Abstract. Interval arithmetic introduced by Ramon E. Moore in scientific computing to put bounds on rounding errors in floating point
computations was a very first example of dynamic program analysis. We
show that it can be formalized by abstract interpretation.

Keywords: Abstract interpretation · Dynamic analysis · Interval Arithmetics · Soundness.

1   Introduction

Ramon E. Moore [31,32,33] may have introduced the first dynamic analysis ever
to put bounds on rounding (or roundoff) errors in floating point computations
[24,37]. Similar to static analyses, this can be formalized and proved sound (but
incomplete) by abstract interpretation [6,8].

   Given the formal structural trace semantics of a C-subset on reals, the interval
abstraction provides the best abstraction of these execution traces on reals into
execution traces on float intervals. Unfortunately, this best interval abstraction is
not implementable since it is not inductive and requires computations on reals to
guarantee that the interval abstraction is the best possible (i.e. the float intervals
are the smallest possible that include the real computation).

   By calculus, we design a formal structural trace semantics of this C-subset
on float interval which over-approximates the best abstraction of real traces
into float interval traces. All computations on reals are over-approximated by
performing the computation on two ends of an interval [l, h] where l and h are
floating point numbers so that this abstract interval semantics is implementable.
For tests and loops both true and false alternatives may be taken while only one
would be taken with reals. Although incomplete and sometimes imprecise, this
is sound.

   The difference with dynamic analysis [21] is that, interval arithmetics collects
interval information about real executions but does not check this collected information for a specification. Instead, it is used to replace the real computation. But

---

[*] Supported by NSF Grant CCF-1617717.

© Springer Nature Switzerland AG 2021
E. Bartocci et al. (Eds.): Havelund Festschrift, LNCS 13065, pp. 61–86, 2021.
https://doi.org/10.1007/978-3-030-87348-6_4

the formalization by abstract interpretation is exactly the same. As discussed in the conclusion, abstraction is used to relate the original and the instrumented semantics as well as the instrumented semantics and the specification and so the original semantics and the specification via a monitor [5].

2 Syntax and Trace Semantics of the Programming Language

Syntax Programs are a subset of C with the following context-free syntax.

$x, y, \ldots \in \mathcal{X}$	variable ($\mathcal{X}$ not empty)
$A \in \mathcal{A} ::= 0.1 \mid x \mid A_1 - A_2$	arithmetic expression
$B \in \mathcal{B} ::= A_1 < A_2 \mid B_1 \text{ nand } B_2$	boolean expression
$S \in \mathcal{S} ::=$	statement
$\quad x = A ;$	assignment
$\quad \mid \, ;$	skip
$\quad \mid \text{ if } (B) \text{ S} \mid \text{ if } (B) \text{ S else S}$	conditionals
$\quad \mid \text{ while } (B) \text{ S} \mid \text{ break } ;$	iteration and break
$\quad \mid \{ \text{ Sl } \}$	compound statement
$Sl \in \mathcal{Sl} ::= Sl \ S \mid \epsilon$	statement list
$P \in \mathcal{P} ::= Sl$	program

The float constant 0.1 is $0.000(1100)^{\infty}$ in binary so has no exact finite binary representation. It is approximated as 0.1.000000014901161193847656562500.... A break exits the closest enclosing loop, if none this is a syntactic error. If P is a program then int main (void) { P } is a valid C program (after adding variable declarations that we omit for concision). We call "[program] component" $S \in Pc \triangleq \mathcal{S} \cup \mathcal{Sl} \cup \mathcal{P}$ either a statement, a statement list, or a program. We let $\lhd$ be the syntactic relation between immediate syntactic components. For example, if $S = \text{if } (B) \, S_t \text{ else } S_f$ then $B \lhd S$, $S_t \lhd S$, and $S_f \lhd S$.

Program labels Labels $\ell \in \mathbb{L}$ are not part of the language, but useful to discuss program points reached during execution. For each program component S, we define

at⟦S⟧   the program point at which execution of S starts;

aft⟦S⟧   the program exit point after S, at which execution of S is supposed to normally terminate, if ever;

esc⟦S⟧   a boolean indicating whether or not the program component S contains a break ; statement escaping out of that component S;

brk-to⟦S⟧   the program point at which execution of the program component S goes to when a break ; statement escapes out of that component S;

brks-of⟦S⟧   the set of labels of all break ; statements that can escape out of S;

in⟦S⟧   the set of program points inside S (including at⟦S⟧ but excluding aft⟦S⟧ and brk-to⟦S⟧);

labs⟦S⟧   the potentially reachable program points while executing S either at, in, or after the statement, or resulting from a break.

Here is an example,

$\ell_0 = \text{at}[\![S]\!] = \text{aft}[\![S_4]\!]$, $\ell_1 = \text{at}[\![S_1]\!] = \text{at}[\![S_b]\!]$, $\ell_2 = \text{at}[\![S_2]\!] = \text{aft}[\![S_1]\!]$, $\ell_3 = \text{at}[\![S_3]\!]$,
$\ell_5 = \text{at}[\![S_5]\!] = \text{brk-to}[\![S_b]\!] = \text{aft}[\![S]\!]$, $\text{esc}[\![S_b]\!] = \text{tt}$, $\text{brks-of}[\![S_b]\!] = \{\ell_2, \ell_3\}$, $\text{esc}[\![S]\!] = \text{ff}$,
$\text{in}[\![S_b]\!] = \{\ell_1, \ldots, \ell_2, \ldots, \ell_3, \ldots\}$, $\text{in}[\![S]\!] = \text{labs}[\![S_b]\!] = \{\ell_0, \ell_1, \ldots, \ell_2, \ldots, \ell_3, \ldots\}$,
$\text{labs}[\![S]\!] = \{\ell_0, \ell_1, \ldots, \ell_2, \ldots, \ell_3, \ldots, \ell_5\}$

Float intervals Let $\mathbb{F}^1$ be the set of floating point numbers (including $-\infty$ and $+\infty$, but excluding NaN (Not a Number)[2] and $-0, +0^3$). The float intervals are

$$\mathbb{I} \triangleq \begin{array}{l} \{\varnothing\} \cup \{[\underline{x}, \overline{x}] \mid \underline{x}, \overline{x} \in \mathbb{F} \setminus \{-\infty, +\infty\} \wedge \underline{x} \leqslant \overline{x}\} \\ \cup \\ \{[-\infty, \overline{x}] \mid \overline{x} \in \mathbb{F} \setminus \{-\infty\}\} \cup \{[\underline{x}, +\infty] \mid \underline{x} \in \mathbb{F} \setminus \{+\infty\}\} \end{array}$$

with the empty interval $\varnothing$ and the intervals $[-\infty, -\infty] \notin \mathbb{I}$ and $[\infty, \infty] \notin \mathbb{I}$ are excluded.

The order on intervals is $\varnothing \sqsubseteq^i \varnothing \sqsubseteq^i [\underline{x}, \overline{x}] \sqsubseteq^i [\underline{y}, \overline{y}]$ if and only if $\underline{y} \leqslant \underline{x} \leqslant \overline{x} \leqslant \overline{y}$. We have the complete lattice $\langle \mathbb{I}, \sqsubseteq^i, \varnothing, [-\infty, +\infty], \bigsqcap^i, \bigsqcup^i \rangle$.

Values Programs compute on values $\mathbb{V}$. Values can be reals $\mathbb{R}$, floating point numbers $(\mathbb{F} \setminus \{\text{NaN}, -0, +0\}) \cup \{0\}^4)$, or float intervals $\mathbb{I}$. For simplicity, we assume that execution stops in case of error (*e.g.* when dividing by zero).

Traces A trace π is a non-empty sequence of states where states $\langle \ell, \rho \rangle \in \mathbb{S}_\mathbb{V} \triangleq (\mathbb{L} \times \text{Ev}_\mathbb{V})$ are pairs of a program label $\ell \in \mathbb{L}$ designating the next action to be executed in the program and an environment $\rho \in \text{Ev}_\mathbb{V} \triangleq \mathbb{X} \to \mathbb{V}$ assigning values $\rho(x) \in \mathbb{V}$ to variables $x \in \mathbb{X}$. A trace π can be finite $\pi \in \mathbb{S}_\mathbb{V}^+$ or infinite $\pi \in \mathbb{S}_\mathbb{V}^\infty$ (recording a non-terminating computation) so $\mathbb{S}_\mathbb{V}^{+\infty} \triangleq \mathbb{S}_\mathbb{V}^+ \cup \mathbb{S}_\mathbb{V}^\infty$. We let $|\pi| = n \in \mathbb{N}_*$ be the length of a finite trace $\pi = \overset{n-1}{\underset{i=0}{\frown}} \pi_i = \pi_0 \ldots \pi_{n-1} \in \mathbb{S}_\mathbb{V}^+$ and $|\pi| = \infty$ for infinite traces $\pi = \underset{i \in \mathbb{N}}{\frown} \pi_i = \pi_0 \ldots \pi_n \ldots \in \mathbb{S}_\mathbb{V}^\infty$. Trace concatenation $\frown$ is defined as follows

---

[1] For simplicity, we consider only one category of floats say of type `float` in C, ignoring `double`, `long double`, *etc.*

[2] For simplicity, we ignore NaN and assume that execution stops in case a NaN would be returned when executing an expression.

[3] For simplicity, we ignore $-0, +0$ used to determine whether $+\infty$ or $-\infty$ is returned when dividing a nonzero number by a zero.

[4] Therefore $+0 = -0 = 0$ and 0 is positive for the rule of signs

$\pi_1\sigma_1 \frown \sigma_2\pi_2$ undefined if $\sigma_1 \neq \sigma_2$ | $\pi_1 \frown \sigma_2\pi_2 \triangleq \pi_1$ if $\pi_1 \in \mathbb{S}_\mathbb{V}^\infty$ is infinite
$\pi_1\sigma_1 \frown \sigma_1\pi_2 \triangleq \pi_1\sigma_1\pi_2$ if $\pi_1 \in \mathbb{S}_\mathbb{V}^+$ is finite

In pattern matching, we sometimes need the empty trace $\ni$. For example the match $\sigma\pi\sigma' = \sigma$ holds when $\pi = \ni$ and $\sigma = \sigma'$.

Formal definition of the real and float prefix trace semantics The prefix trace semantics $\mathcal{S}_\mathbb{V}^*[\![S]\!]$ for reals $\mathbb{V} = \mathbb{R}$ or float $\mathbb{V} = \mathbb{F}$ is defined below. The definition is structural (by induction on the syntax) using fixpoints for the iteration. $\mathcal{S}_\mathbb{R}^*[\![S]\!]$ and $\mathcal{S}_\mathbb{F}^*[\![S]\!]$ will be abstracted in the prefix trace interval semantics $\mathcal{S}_\mathbb{I}^*[\![S]\!]$ in Section **7**.

• *The value of an arithmetic expression* A *in environment* $\rho \in \mathbb{Ev}_\mathbb{V} \triangleq X \to \mathbb{V}$ *is* $\mathcal{A}_\mathbb{V}[\![A]\!]\rho \in \mathbb{V}$:

$$\mathcal{A}_\mathbb{V}[\![0.1]\!]\rho \triangleq 0.1_\mathbb{V} \quad \mathcal{A}_\mathbb{V}[\![x]\!]\rho \triangleq \rho(x) \quad \mathcal{A}_\mathbb{V}[\![A_1 - A_2]\!]\rho \triangleq \mathcal{A}_\mathbb{V}[\![A_1]\!]\rho -_\mathbb{V} \mathcal{A}_\mathbb{V}[\![A_2]\!]\rho \quad (1)$$

where $0.1_\mathbb{V}$ denotes the real 0.1 and $-_\mathbb{V}$ the difference in $\mathbb{V}$. For example $-_\mathbb{F}$ is the difference found on IEEE-754 machines and must take rounding mode (and the machine specificities [30]) into account.

• *The prefix traces of an assignment statement* S ::= ℓ x = A ; (*where* at$[\![S]\!] = \ell$) either stops in an initial state $\langle \ell, \rho \rangle$ or is this initial state $\langle \ell, \rho \rangle$ followed by the next state $\langle$aft$[\![S]\!], \rho[x \leftarrow \mathcal{A}_\mathbb{V}[\![A]\!]\rho]\rangle$ recording the assignment of the value $\mathcal{A}_\mathbb{V}[\![A]\!]\rho$ of the arithmetic expression to variable x when reaching the label aft$[\![S]\!]$ after the assignment[5].

$$\mathcal{S}_\mathbb{V}^*[\![S]\!] = \{\langle \ell, \rho \rangle \mid \rho \in \mathbb{Ev}_\mathbb{V}\} \cup \{\langle \ell, \rho \rangle \langle \text{aft}[\![S]\!], \rho[x \leftarrow \mathcal{A}_\mathbb{V}[\![A]\!]\rho]\rangle \mid \rho \in \mathbb{Ev}_\mathbb{V}\} \quad (2)$$

• *The prefix trace semantics of a break statement* S ::= ℓ **break** ; *either stops at* ℓ *or goes on to the break label* brk-to$[\![S]\!]$ (*which is defined syntactically as the exit label of the closest enclosing iteration*).
$$\mathcal{S}_\mathbb{V}^*[\![S]\!] \triangleq \{\langle \ell, \rho \rangle \mid \rho \in \mathbb{Ev}_\mathbb{V}\} \cup \{\langle \ell, \rho \rangle \langle \text{brk-to}[\![S]\!], \rho \rangle \mid \rho \in \mathbb{Ev}_\mathbb{V}\} \quad (3)$$

• *The value of an boolean expression* B *in environment* ρ *is the boolean* $\mathcal{B}_\mathbb{V}[\![B]\!]\rho \in \mathbb{B} \triangleq \{\text{tt}, \text{ff}\}$:
$$\mathcal{B}_\mathbb{V}[\![A_1 < A_2]\!]\rho \triangleq \mathcal{A}_\mathbb{V}[\![A_1]\!]\rho < \mathcal{A}_\mathbb{V}[\![A_2]\!]\rho \quad (4)$$
$$\mathcal{B}_\mathbb{V}[\![B_1 \text{ nand } B_2]\!]\rho \triangleq \mathcal{B}_\mathbb{V}[\![B_1]\!]\rho \uparrow \mathcal{B}_\mathbb{V}[\![B_2]\!]\rho$$

where < is strictly less than on reals and floats while $\uparrow$ is the "not and" boolean operator.
• *The prefix trace semantics of a conditional statement* S ::= if ℓ (B) S_t *is*
  • either the trace $\langle \ell, \rho \rangle$ when the observation of the execution stops on entry ℓ = at$[\![S]\!]$ of the program component S for initial environment ρ;

---

[5] If we had NaNs and $\mathcal{A}_\mathbb{V}[\![A]\!]\rho$ returns a NaN, the second term would include a condition $\mathcal{A}_\mathbb{V}[\![A]\!]\rho \neq$ NaN to terminate execution on error.

- or, when the value of the boolean expression B for ρ is false ff, the initial state $\langle \ell, \rho \rangle$ followed by the state $\langle \text{aft}[\![\mathsf{S}]\!], \rho \rangle$ at the label $\text{aft}[\![\mathsf{S}]\!]$ after the conditional statement;
- or finally, when the value of the boolean expression B for ρ is true tt, the initial state $\langle \ell, \rho \rangle$ followed by a prefix trace of S_t starting $\text{at}[\![\mathsf{S}_t]\!]$ in environment ρ (and possibly ending $\text{aft}[\![\mathsf{S}_t]\!] = \text{aft}[\![\mathsf{S}]\!]$).

$$\mathcal{S}^*_{\mathsf{V}}[\![\mathsf{S}]\!] \triangleq \quad \{\langle \ell, \rho \rangle \mid \rho \in \mathbb{E}\mathsf{v}_{\mathsf{V}}\} \cup \{\langle \ell, \rho \rangle \langle \text{aft}[\![\mathsf{S}]\!], \rho \rangle \mid \mathcal{B}_{\mathsf{V}}[\![\mathsf{B}]\!]\rho = \text{ff}\} \tag{5}$$
$$\cup \{\langle \ell, \rho \rangle \langle \text{at}[\![\mathsf{S}_t]\!], \rho \rangle \pi \mid \mathcal{B}_{\mathsf{V}}[\![\mathsf{B}]\!]\rho = \text{tt} \wedge \langle \text{at}[\![\mathsf{S}_t]\!], \rho \rangle \pi \in \mathcal{S}^*_{\mathsf{V}}[\![\mathsf{S}_t]\!]\}$$

Observe that definition (5) includes the case of termination of the true branch S_t and so also of termination of the conditional S since $\text{aft}[\![\mathsf{S}]\!] = \text{aft}[\![\mathsf{S}_t]\!]$. Moreover, if the conditional S is within an iteration and contains a break statement in the true branch S_t then $\text{brk-to}[\![\mathsf{S}]\!] = \text{brk-to}[\![\mathsf{S}_t]\!]$, so from $\langle \text{at}[\![\mathsf{S}_t]\!], \rho \rangle \pi \langle \text{brk-to}[\![\mathsf{S}_t]\!], \rho' \rangle \in \mathcal{S}^*_{\mathsf{V}}[\![\mathsf{S}_t]\!]$ and $\mathcal{B}_{\mathsf{V}}[\![\mathsf{B}]\!]\rho = \text{tt}$, we infer that $\langle \text{at}[\![\mathsf{S}]\!], \rho \rangle \langle \text{at}[\![\mathsf{S}_t]\!], \rho \rangle \pi \langle \text{brk-to}[\![\mathsf{S}]\!], \rho' \rangle \in \mathcal{S}^*_{\mathsf{V}}[\![\mathsf{S}]\!]$.

- *The prefix trace semantics of the empty statement list* $\mathsf{Sl} = \epsilon$ is reduced to the states at that empty statement (which is also after that empty statement since $\text{at}[\![\mathsf{Sl}]\!] = \text{aft}[\![\mathsf{Sl}]\!]$).

$$\mathcal{S}^*_{\mathsf{V}}[\![\mathsf{Sl}]\!] \triangleq \{\langle \text{at}[\![\mathsf{Sl}]\!], \rho \rangle \mid \rho \in \mathbb{E}\mathsf{v}_{\mathsf{V}}\} \tag{6}$$

- The prefix traces of the *prefix trace semantics of a non-empty statement list* $\mathsf{Sl} ::= \mathsf{Sl}' \, \mathsf{S}$ are the prefix traces of Sl' or the finite maximal traces of Sl' followed by a prefix trace of S.

$$\mathcal{S}^*_{\mathsf{V}}[\![\mathsf{Sl}]\!] \triangleq \mathcal{S}^*_{\mathsf{V}}[\![\mathsf{Sl}']\!] \cup \mathcal{S}^*_{\mathsf{V}}[\![\mathsf{Sl}']\!] \frown \mathcal{S}^*_{\mathsf{V}}[\![\mathsf{S}]\!] \tag{7}$$
$$\mathcal{S} \frown \mathcal{S}' \triangleq \{\pi \frown \pi' \mid \pi \in \mathcal{S} \wedge \pi' \in \mathcal{S}' \wedge \pi \frown \pi' \text{ is well-defined}\}$$

Notice that if $\pi \in \mathcal{S}^*_{\mathsf{V}}[\![\mathsf{Sl}']\!]$, $\pi' \in \mathcal{S}^*_{\mathsf{V}}[\![\mathsf{S}]\!]$, and $\pi \frown \pi' \in \mathcal{S}^*_{\mathsf{V}}[\![\mathsf{Sl}]\!]$ then the last state of π must be the first state of π' and this state is $\text{at}[\![\mathsf{S}]\!] = \text{aft}[\![\mathsf{Sl}']\!]$ and so the trace π must be a maximal terminating execution of Sl' *i.e.* S is executed if and only if Sl' terminates.

- *The prefix finite trace semantic definition* $\mathcal{S}^*_{\mathsf{V}}[\![\mathsf{S}]\!]$ (8) *of an iteration statement of the form* $\mathsf{S} ::= \texttt{while} \, \ell \, (\texttt{B}) \, \mathsf{S}_b$ where $\ell = \text{at}[\![\mathsf{S}]\!]$ is the $\subseteq$-least solution $\text{lfp}^{\subseteq} \mathcal{F}^*_{\mathsf{V}}[\![\mathsf{S}]\!]$ to the equation $X = \mathcal{F}^*_{\mathsf{V}}[\![\mathsf{S}]\!](X)$. Since $\mathcal{F}^*_{\mathsf{V}}[\![\mathsf{S}]\!] \in \wp(\mathbb{S}^+) \to \wp(\mathbb{S}^+)$ is $\subseteq$-monotone (if $X \subseteq X'$ then $\mathcal{F}^*_{\mathsf{V}}[\![\mathsf{S}]\!](X) \subseteq \mathcal{F}^*_{\mathsf{V}}[\![\mathsf{S}]\!](X')$ and $\langle \wp(\mathbb{S}^+), \subseteq, \varnothing, \mathbb{S}^+, \cup, \cap \rangle$ is a complete lattice, $\text{lfp}^{\subseteq} \mathcal{F}^*_{\mathsf{V}}[\![\mathsf{S}]\!]$ exists by Tarski's fixpoint theorem and can be defined as the limit of iterates [7]. In definition (8) of the transformer $\mathcal{F}^*_{\mathsf{V}}[\![\mathsf{S}]\!]$, case (8.a) corresponds to a loop execution observation stopping on entry, (8.b) corresponds to an observation of a loop exiting after 0 or more iterations, and (8.c) corresponds to a loop execution observation that stops anywhere in the body S_b after 0 or more iterations. This last case covers the case of an iteration terminated by a break statement (to $\text{aft}[\![\mathsf{S}]\!]$ after the iteration statement). This last case also covers the case of termination of the loop body S_b at label $\text{aft}[\![\mathsf{S}_b]\!] = \text{at}[\![\texttt{while} \, \ell \, (\texttt{B}) \, \mathsf{S}_b]\!] = \ell$ so that the iteration goes on.

$$\mathcal{S}^*_{\mathsf{V}}[\![\texttt{while} \, \ell \, (\texttt{B}) \, \mathsf{S}_b]\!] = \text{lfp}^{\subseteq} \mathcal{F}^*_{\mathsf{V}}[\![\texttt{while} \, \ell \, (\texttt{B}) \, \mathsf{S}_b]\!] \tag{8}$$

$$\mathcal{F}_\mathbb{V}^*[\![\mathtt{while}\ \ell\ (\mathtt{B})\ \mathtt{S}_b]\!]\ X \triangleq \{\langle \ell, \rho \rangle \mid \rho \in \mathbb{Ev}_\mathbb{V}\} \tag{8.a}$$

$$\cup\ \{\pi_2\langle \ell', \rho\rangle\langle \mathtt{aft}[\![\mathtt{S}]\!], \rho\rangle \mid \pi_2\langle \ell', \rho\rangle \in X \wedge \mathcal{B}[\![\mathtt{B}]\!]\rho = \mathtt{ff} \wedge \ell' = \ell\}^6 \tag{8.b}$$

$$\cup\ \{\pi_2\langle \ell', \rho\rangle\langle \mathtt{at}[\![\mathtt{S}_b]\!], \rho\rangle\pi_3 \mid \pi_2\langle \ell', \rho\rangle \in X \wedge \mathcal{B}[\![\mathtt{B}]\!]\rho = \mathtt{tt} \wedge \tag{8.c}$$
$$\langle \mathtt{at}[\![\mathtt{S}_b]\!], \rho\rangle\pi_3 \in \mathcal{S}_\mathbb{V}^*[\![\mathtt{S}_b]\!] \wedge \ell' = \ell\}$$

- The other cases are similar.
- Observe than the only difference between real ($\mathbb{V} = \mathbb{R}$) and float ($\mathbb{V} = \mathbb{F}$) computations is the constant $0.1_\mathbb{V}$ and the difference $-_\mathbb{V}$, which for floats depends on the rounding mode (round-to $+\infty$, round-to $-\infty$, round-to 0, or round-to-nearest). For simplicity, we assume that the rounding mode is fixed, not changed during execution, and correctly taken into account by these operations.

Maximal trace semantics Let $\mathbb{V}$ be $\mathbb{R}$, $\mathbb{F}$, or $\mathbb{I}$. The maximal trace semantics $\mathcal{S}_\mathbb{V}^{+\infty}[\![\mathtt{S}]\!] = \mathcal{S}_\mathbb{V}^+[\![\mathtt{S}]\!] \cup \mathcal{S}_\mathbb{V}^\infty[\![\mathtt{S}]\!]$ is derived from the prefix trace semantics $\mathcal{S}_\mathbb{V}^*[\![\mathtt{S}]\!]$ by keeping the longest finite traces $\mathcal{S}_\mathbb{V}^+[\![\mathtt{S}]\!]$ and passing to the limit $\mathcal{S}_\mathbb{V}^\infty[\![\mathtt{S}]\!]$ of prefix-closed traces for infinite traces.

$$\mathcal{S}_\mathbb{V}^+[\![\mathtt{S}]\!] \triangleq \{\pi\ell \in \mathcal{S}_\mathbb{V}^*[\![\mathtt{S}]\!] \mid (\ell = \mathtt{aft}[\![\mathtt{S}]\!]) \vee (\mathtt{esc}[\![\mathtt{S}]\!] \wedge \ell = \mathtt{brk\text{-}to}[\![\mathtt{S}]\!])\} \tag{9}$$

$$\mathcal{S}_\mathbb{V}^\infty[\![\mathtt{S}]\!] \triangleq \lim(\mathcal{S}_\mathbb{V}^*[\![\mathtt{S}]\!]) \tag{10}$$

where the limit is $\lim \mathcal{T} \triangleq \{\pi \in \mathbb{S}_\mathbb{V}^\infty \mid \forall n \in \mathbb{N}\ .\ \pi[0..n] \in \mathcal{T}\}$. $\tag{11}$

The intuition for (11) is the following. Let $\mathtt{S}$ be an iteration. $\pi \in \mathcal{S}_\mathbb{V}^\infty[\![\mathtt{S}]\!] = \lim \mathcal{S}_\mathbb{V}^*[\![\mathtt{S}]\!]$ where π is infinite if and only if, whenever we take a prefix $\pi[0..n]$ of π, it is a possible finite observation of the execution of $\mathtt{S}$ and so belongs to the prefix trace semantics $\pi[0..n] \in \mathcal{S}_\mathbb{V}^*[\![\mathtt{S}]\!]$.

3 Float intervals

Let $\lceil x$ (which may be $-\infty$) be the largest float smaller than or equal to $x \in \mathbb{R}$ (or $\lceil x = x$ for $x \in \mathbb{F}$) and $x\rceil$ (which may be $+\infty$) be the smallest float greater than or equal to $x \in \mathbb{R}$ (or $x\rceil = x$ for $x \in \mathbb{F}$). We let $\lceil x$ be the largest floating-point number strictly less than $x \in \mathbb{F}$ (which may be $-\infty$) and $x\rceil$ be the smallest floating-point number strictly larger than $x \in \mathbb{F}$ (which may be $+\infty$). We assume that

$$\lceil x -_\mathbb{F} y\rceil \leqslant \lceil(x -_\mathbb{V} y) \qquad\qquad (\mathbb{V}\text{ is }\mathbb{R}\text{ or }\mathbb{F}) \tag{12}$$
$$x\rceil -_\mathbb{F} \lceil y \geqslant (x -_\mathbb{V} y)\rceil$$

$$(x \in [\underline{x}, \overline{x}] \wedge y \in [\underline{y}, \overline{y}] \wedge x < y) \Rightarrow (x \in [\underline{x}, \min(\overline{x}, \overline{y})] \wedge y \in [\max(\underline{x}, \underline{y}), \overline{y}]) \tag{13}$$

$$(x \in [\underline{x}, \overline{x}] \wedge y \in [\underline{y}, \overline{y}] \wedge x < y) \Rightarrow (x \in [\underline{x}, \min(\overline{x}, \overline{y}\rceil)] \wedge y \in [\max(\lceil\underline{x}, \underline{y}), \overline{y}]) \tag{13.bis}$$

---

⁶ A definition of the form $d(\vec{x}) \triangleq \{f(\vec{x}') \mid P(\vec{x}', \vec{x})\}$ has the variables $\vec{x}'$ in $P(\vec{x}', \vec{x})$ bound to those of $f(\vec{x}')$ whereas $\vec{x}$ is free in $P(\vec{x}', \vec{x})$ since it appears neither in $f(\vec{x}')$ nor (by assumption) under quantifiers in $P(\vec{x}', \vec{x})$. The $\vec{x}$ of $P(\vec{x}', \vec{x})$ is therefore bound to the $\vec{x}$ of $d(\vec{x})$.

Machine implementations of IEEE-754 floating point arithmetics [24] are sometimes incorrect [14,30]. So the above hypotheses (12) and (13) on floats must be adjusted accordingly, for example replacing (13) by (13.bis). In particular (13.bis) follows the recommendation of [30, Sect. 6.1.2]. If $x < y$ then the value of x is smaller than its maximal value $\overline{x}$ and the maximal $\overline{y}$ value of y, by precaution, certainly smaller or equal to the next float greater that $\overline{y}$.

4   Abstraction of real traces by float interval traces

Given a real trace semantics *i.e.* a set $\Pi \in \wp(\mathbb{S}_\mathbb{R}^{+\infty})$, we define a float interval trace semantics by abstracting the real $x \in \mathbb{R}$ values by an interval $[\lceil x, x \rceil]$. More precisely, since abstract interpretation is about the abstraction of properties, the strongest property $\{x\} \in \wp(\mathbb{R})$ of this value is over-approximated by a weaker interval property, that is $\{x\} \subseteq [\lceil x, x \rceil]$, or equivalently $x \in [\lceil x, x \rceil]$. Formally

$$\alpha^{\mathbb{I}}(x) \triangleq [\lceil x, x \rceil] \qquad \text{real abstraction by float interval} \quad (14)$$

$$\gamma^{\mathbb{I}}([\underline{x}, \overline{x}]) \triangleq \{x \in \mathbb{R} \mid \underline{x} \leqslant x \leqslant \overline{x}\}$$

$$\dot{\alpha}^{\mathbb{I}}(\rho) \triangleq \lambda x \in \mathcal{X} \cdot \alpha^{\mathbb{I}}(\rho(x)) \qquad \text{environment abstraction}$$

$$\dot{\gamma}^{\mathbb{I}}(\overline{\rho}) \triangleq \{\rho \in \mathcal{X} \to \mathbb{R} \mid \forall x \in \mathcal{X} . \rho(x) \in \gamma^{\mathbb{I}}(\overline{\rho}(x))\}$$

$$\ddot{\alpha}^{\mathbb{I}}(\langle \ell, \rho \rangle) \triangleq \langle \ell, \dot{\alpha}^{\mathbb{I}}(\rho)\rangle \qquad \text{state abstraction}$$

$$\ddot{\gamma}^{\mathbb{I}}(\langle \ell, \overline{\rho} \rangle) \triangleq \{\langle \ell, \rho \rangle \mid \rho \in \dot{\gamma}^{\mathbb{I}}(\overline{\rho})\}$$

$$\vec{\alpha}^{\mathbb{I}}(\pi_1 \dots \pi_n \dots) \triangleq \ddot{\alpha}^{\mathbb{I}}(\pi_1) \dots \ddot{\alpha}^{\mathbb{I}}(\pi_n) \dots \qquad \text{[in]finite trace abstraction}$$

$$\vec{\gamma}^{\mathbb{I}}(\overline{\pi}_1 \dots \overline{\pi}_n \dots) \triangleq \{\pi_1 \dots \pi_n \dots \mid |\pi| = |\overline{\pi}| \wedge \forall i = 1, \dots, n, \dots . \pi_i \in \ddot{\gamma}^{\mathbb{I}}(\overline{\pi}_i)\}$$

$$\dot{\alpha}^{\mathbb{I}}(\Pi) \triangleq \{\vec{\alpha}^{\mathbb{I}}(\pi) \mid \pi \in \Pi\} \qquad \text{set of traces abstraction}$$

$$\dot{\gamma}^{\mathbb{I}}(\overline{\Pi}) \triangleq \{\pi \mid \vec{\alpha}^{\mathbb{I}}(\pi) \in \overline{\Pi}\} = \bigcup \{\vec{\gamma}^{\mathbb{I}}(\overline{\pi}) \mid \overline{\pi} \in \overline{\Pi}\}$$

Because the floats are a subset of the reals, we can use $\alpha^{\mathbb{I}}$ to abstract both real and float traces in (14) (*i.e.* $\mathbb{R}$ becomes $\mathbb{V}$ standing for $\mathbb{R}$ or $\mathbb{F}$).

$$\langle \wp(\mathbb{S}_\mathbb{V}^{+\infty}), \subseteq \rangle \xleftrightarrow[\dot{\alpha}^{\mathbb{I}}]{\dot{\gamma}^{\mathbb{I}}} \langle \wp(\mathbb{S}_\mathbb{I}^{+\infty}), \subseteq \rangle \qquad (15)$$

Proof (of (15)).

$$\dot{\alpha}^{\mathbb{I}}(\Pi) \subseteq \overline{\Pi}$$

$$\Leftrightarrow \{\vec{\alpha}^{\mathbb{I}}(\pi) \mid \pi \in \Pi\} \subseteq \overline{\Pi} \qquad \qquad \wr\text{def. (14) of } \dot{\alpha}^{\mathbb{I}}\wr$$

$$\Leftrightarrow \forall \pi \in \Pi . \vec{\alpha}^{\mathbb{I}}(\pi) \in \overline{\Pi} \qquad \qquad \wr\text{def. } \subseteq\wr$$

$$\Leftrightarrow \Pi \subseteq \{\pi \mid \vec{\alpha}^{\mathbb{I}}(\pi) \in \overline{\Pi}\} \qquad \qquad \wr\text{def. } \subseteq\wr$$

$$\Leftrightarrow \Pi \subseteq \dot{\gamma}^{\mathbb{I}}(\overline{\Pi}) \qquad \qquad \wr\text{by defining } \dot{\gamma}^{\mathbb{I}}(\overline{\Pi}) \triangleq \{\pi \mid \vec{\alpha}^{\mathbb{I}}(\pi) \in \overline{\Pi}\}\wr$$

where

$$\vec{\alpha}^{\mathbb{I}}(\pi) \in \overline{\Pi}$$

$$\Leftrightarrow \exists \overline{\pi} \in \overline{\Pi} . \vec{\alpha}^{\mathbb{I}}(\pi) = \overline{\pi} \qquad \qquad \wr\text{def. } \in\wr$$

$$\Leftrightarrow \exists \overline{\pi} \in \overline{\Pi} . \pi \in \overline{\gamma}^{\mathrm{II}}(\overline{\pi}) \qquad\qquad \langle\mathrm{def.}\ \vec{\alpha}^{\mathrm{II}}(\pi)\ \mathrm{and}\ \vec{\gamma}^{\mathrm{II}}(\overline{\pi})\rangle$$

$$\Leftrightarrow \pi \in \bigcup_{\overline{\pi} \in \overline{\Pi}} \vec{\gamma}^{\mathrm{II}}(\overline{\pi}) \qquad\qquad\qquad\qquad \langle\mathrm{def.}\ \bigcup\rangle$$

and therefore

$$\vec{\gamma}^{\mathrm{II}}(\overline{\Pi})$$

$$\triangleq \{\pi \mid \vec{\alpha}^{\mathrm{II}}(\pi) \in \overline{\Pi}\} \qquad\qquad\qquad\qquad\qquad \langle\mathrm{def.}\ \gamma^{\mathrm{II}}\rangle$$

$$= \{\pi \mid \pi \in \bigcup_{\overline{\pi}\in\overline{\Pi}} \vec{\gamma}^{\mathrm{II}}(\overline{\pi})\} = \bigcup\{\vec{\gamma}^{\mathrm{II}}(\overline{\pi}) \mid \overline{\pi} \in \overline{\Pi}\} \qquad \langle\mathrm{as\ shown\ above}\rangle \quad \square$$

5   Sound over-approximation in the concrete

Let $\Pi = \{\langle \ell_1,\ x = 0.1_{\mathbb{R}}\rangle\langle \ell_2,\ x = 2.1_{\mathbb{R}}\rangle, \langle \ell_1,\ x = -0.1_{\mathbb{R}}\rangle\langle \ell_2,\ x = 1.9_{\mathbb{R}}\rangle\}$. Assume that $\overline{\Pi}_1 = \alpha^{\mathrm{II}}(\Pi) = \{\langle \ell_1,\ x = [0.09, 0.11]\rangle\langle \ell_2,\ x = [2.09, 2.11]\rangle, \langle \ell_1,\ x = [-0.11, -0.09]\rangle\langle \ell_2,\ x = [1.89, 1.91]\rangle\}$ where each trace π of Π is over-approximated by a trace $\vec{\alpha}^{\mathrm{II}}(\pi)$ of $\overline{\Pi}_1$ with a ± 0.01 rounding interval. We have $\Pi \subseteq \vec{\gamma}^{\mathrm{II}}(\overline{\Pi}_1)$ so $\overline{\Pi}_1$ is a sound over-approximation of Π. But $\overline{\Pi}_2 = \{\langle \ell_1,\ x = [-0.11, 0.11]\rangle\langle \ell_2,\ x = [1.89, 2.11]\rangle\}$ is also a sound over-approximation of Π since $\Pi \subseteq \vec{\gamma}^{\mathrm{II}}(\overline{\Pi}_2)$. Although $\overline{\Pi}_1 \in \wp(\mathbb{S}_{\mathrm{II}}^{+\infty})$ is more precise than $\overline{\Pi}_2 \in \wp(\mathbb{S}_{\mathrm{II}}^{+\infty})$, they are not comparable as abstract elements of $\langle \wp(\mathbb{S}_{\mathrm{II}}^{+\infty}),\ \subseteq\rangle$ in (15). The intuition that $\overline{\Pi}_1$ is more precise than $\overline{\Pi}_2$ is by comparison in the concrete that is $\vec{\gamma}^{\mathrm{II}}(\overline{\Pi}_1) \subseteq \vec{\gamma}^{\mathrm{II}}(\overline{\Pi}_2)$. We now express this preorder relation $\sqsubseteq^i$ between $\overline{\Pi}_1$ and $\overline{\Pi}_2$ which will allow us to over-approximate intervals when needed.

$$\overline{\Pi} \sqsubseteq^i \overline{\Pi}' \triangleq \vec{\gamma}^{\mathrm{II}}(\overline{\Pi}) \subseteq \vec{\gamma}^{\mathrm{II}}(\overline{\Pi}') \qquad\qquad\qquad\qquad\qquad (16)$$

$$= \forall \overline{\pi} \in \overline{\Pi} . \forall \pi \in \vec{\gamma}^{\mathrm{II}}(\overline{\pi}) . \exists \overline{\pi}' \in \overline{\Pi}' . \pi \in \vec{\gamma}^{\mathrm{II}}(\overline{\pi}')$$

Proof (of (16)).

$$\overline{\Pi} \sqsubseteq^i \overline{\Pi}'$$

$$\triangleq \vec{\gamma}^{\mathrm{II}}(\overline{\Pi}) \subseteq \vec{\gamma}^{\mathrm{II}}(\overline{\Pi}') \qquad\qquad\qquad\qquad\qquad \langle(16)\rangle$$

$$= \bigcup\{\vec{\gamma}^{\mathrm{II}}(\overline{\pi}) \mid \overline{\pi} \in \overline{\Pi}\} \subseteq \bigcup\{\vec{\gamma}^{\mathrm{II}}(\overline{\pi}) \mid \overline{\pi} \in \overline{\Pi}'\} \qquad \langle(14)\ \mathrm{for\ sets\ of\ traces}\rangle$$

$$= \forall \overline{\pi} \in \overline{\Pi} . \vec{\gamma}^{\mathrm{II}}(\overline{\pi}) \subseteq \bigcup\{\vec{\gamma}^{\mathrm{II}}(\overline{\pi}) \mid \overline{\pi} \in \overline{\Pi}'\} \qquad\qquad \langle\mathrm{def.}\ \subseteq\rangle$$

$$= \forall \overline{\pi} \in \overline{\Pi} . \forall \pi \in \vec{\gamma}^{\mathrm{II}}(\overline{\pi}) . \pi \in \bigcup\{\vec{\gamma}^{\mathrm{II}}(\overline{\pi}') \mid \overline{\pi}' \in \overline{\Pi}'\} \qquad \langle\mathrm{def.}\ \subseteq\rangle$$

$$= \forall \overline{\pi} \in \overline{\Pi} . \forall \pi \in \vec{\gamma}^{\mathrm{II}}(\overline{\pi}) . \exists \overline{\pi}' \in \overline{\Pi}' . \pi \in \vec{\gamma}^{\mathrm{II}}(\overline{\pi}') \qquad\qquad \langle\mathrm{def.}\ \bigcup\rangle \quad \square$$

It follows that we have a Galois connection (note that the abstract preorder and concretization are different from (15))

$$\langle\wp(\mathbb{S}_{\mathrm{V}}^{+\infty}),\ \subseteq\rangle \xrightarrow[\substack{\alpha^{\mathrm{II}}}]{\substack{\mathring{\gamma}}} \langle\wp(\mathbb{S}_{\mathrm{II}}^{+\infty}),\ \sqsubseteq^i\rangle \qquad\qquad\qquad\qquad (17)$$

Proof (of (17)).

$$\mathring{\alpha}^{\mathrm{II}}(\Pi) \sqsubseteq^i \overline{\Pi}$$

$$\Leftrightarrow \{\vec{\alpha}^{\mathrm{II}}(\pi) \mid \pi \in \Pi\} \sqsubseteq^i \overline{\Pi} \qquad\qquad\qquad\qquad\qquad \langle\mathrm{def.}\ (14)\ \mathrm{of}\ \mathring{\alpha}^{\mathrm{II}}\rangle$$

$$\Leftrightarrow \forall \bar{\pi} \in \{\bar{\alpha}^{\mathbb{I}}(\pi') \mid \pi' \in \Pi\} . \forall \pi \in \bar{\gamma}^{\mathbb{I}}(\bar{\pi}) . \exists \bar{\pi}' \in \overline{\Pi} . \pi \in \bar{\gamma}^{\mathbb{I}}(\bar{\pi}') \qquad \langle \text{def. (16) of } \dot{\sqsubseteq}^i \rangle$$

$$\Leftrightarrow \forall \pi' \in \Pi . \forall \pi \in \bar{\gamma}^{\mathbb{I}}(\bar{\alpha}^{\mathbb{I}}(\pi')) . \exists \bar{\pi}' \in \overline{\Pi} . \pi \in \bar{\gamma}^{\mathbb{I}}(\bar{\pi}') \qquad \langle \text{def. } \in \rangle$$

$$\Leftrightarrow \Pi \subseteq \{\pi' \mid \forall \pi \in \bar{\gamma}^{\mathbb{I}}(\bar{\alpha}^{\mathbb{I}}(\pi')) . \exists \bar{\pi}' \in \overline{\Pi} . \pi \in \bar{\gamma}^{\mathbb{I}}(\bar{\pi}')\} \qquad \langle \text{def. } \subseteq \rangle$$

$$\Leftrightarrow \Pi \subseteq \overset{\circ}{\bar{\gamma}}(\overline{\Pi})$$

by defining $\overset{\circ}{\bar{\gamma}}(\overline{\Pi}) \triangleq \{\pi' \mid \forall \pi \in \bar{\gamma}^{\mathbb{I}}(\bar{\alpha}^{\mathbb{I}}(\pi')) . \exists \bar{\pi}' \in \overline{\Pi} . \pi \in \bar{\gamma}^{\mathbb{I}}(\bar{\pi}')\}$. $\qquad \square$

Soundness is now $\bar{\alpha}^{\mathbb{I}}(\mathcal{S}^*_{\mathbb{V}}[\![\mathsf{S}]\!]) \dot{\sqsubseteq}^i \mathcal{S}^*_{\mathbb{I}}[\![\mathsf{S}]\!]$ or equivalently $\mathcal{S}^*_{\mathbb{V}}[\![\mathsf{S}]\!] \subseteq \overset{\circ}{\bar{\gamma}}(\mathcal{S}^*_{\mathbb{I}}[\![\mathsf{S}]\!])$. Our objective is to calculate $\mathcal{S}^*_{\mathbb{I}}[\![\mathsf{S}]\!]$ by $\dot{\sqsubseteq}^i$-over approximation of $\bar{\alpha}^{\mathbb{I}}(\mathcal{S}^*_{\mathbb{V}}[\![\mathsf{S}]\!])$. However $\dot{\sqsubseteq}^i$ in (16) is impractical since it is defined by concretization to $\wp(\mathbb{S}^{+\infty}_{\mathbb{V}})$. We look for a definition $\dot{\check{\sqsubseteq}}^i$ in the abstract only that provides a sufficient soundness condition $(\overline{\Pi} \dot{\check{\sqsubseteq}}^i \overline{\Pi}') \Rightarrow (\overline{\Pi} \dot{\sqsubseteq}^i \overline{\Pi}')$.

6   Sound over-approximation in the abstract

We define $\overline{\Pi} \dot{\check{\sqsubseteq}}^i \overline{\Pi}'$ so that the traces of $\overline{\Pi}'$ have the same control as the traces of $\overline{\Pi}$ but intervals are larger (and $\overline{\Pi}'$ may contain extra traces due to the imprecision of interval tests).

Formally, the interval order $\sqsubseteq^i$ is extended pointwise $\dot{\sqsubseteq}^i$ to environments, and to states $\dot{\check{\sqsubseteq}}^i$ with same control points/program labels. Then it is extended $\dot{\check{\sqsubseteq}}^i$ to traces of same length with same control but larger intervals, and finally to sets of traces, by Hoare preorder [41].

$$[\underline{x}, \bar{x}] \sqsubseteq^i [\underline{y}, \bar{y}] \triangleq \underline{y} \leqslant \underline{x} \leqslant \bar{x} \leqslant \bar{y} \tag{18}$$

$$\rho \dot{\sqsubseteq}^i \rho' \triangleq \forall x \in \mathcal{X} . \rho(x) \sqsubseteq^i \rho'(x)$$

$$\langle \ell, \rho \rangle \dot{\check{\sqsubseteq}}^i \langle \ell', \rho' \rangle \triangleq (\ell = \ell') \wedge (\rho \dot{\sqsubseteq}^i \rho')$$

$$\pi \dot{\check{\sqsubseteq}}^i \pi' \triangleq (|\pi| = |\pi'|) \wedge (\forall i \in [0, |\pi|[. \pi_i \dot{\check{\sqsubseteq}}^i \pi'_i)$$

$$\overline{\Pi} \dot{\check{\sqsubseteq}}^i \overline{\Pi}' \triangleq \forall \pi \in \overline{\Pi} . \exists \bar{\pi}' \in \overline{\Pi}' . \pi \dot{\check{\sqsubseteq}}^i \pi'$$

Lemma 1. $(\overline{\Pi} \dot{\check{\sqsubseteq}}^i \overline{\Pi}') \Rightarrow (\overline{\Pi} \dot{\sqsubseteq}^i \overline{\Pi}')$. $\qquad \square$

Proof (of Lem. 1). By (14) and (18), we have $[\underline{x}, \bar{x}] \sqsubseteq^i [\underline{y}, \bar{y}]$ implies $\gamma^{\mathbb{I}}([\underline{x}, \bar{x}]) \subseteq \gamma^{\mathbb{I}}([\underline{y}, \bar{y}])$ and so $\rho \dot{\sqsubseteq}^i \rho'$ implies $\dot{\gamma}^{\mathbb{I}}(\rho) \subseteq \dot{\gamma}^{\mathbb{I}}(\rho')$ and therefore $\langle \ell, \rho \rangle \dot{\check{\sqsubseteq}}^i \langle \ell', \rho' \rangle$ implies $\gamma^{\mathbb{I}}(\langle \ell, \rho \rangle) \subseteq \gamma^{\mathbb{I}}(\langle \ell', \rho' \rangle)$ so that finally $\pi \dot{\check{\sqsubseteq}}^i \pi'$ implies $\bar{\gamma}^{\mathbb{I}}(\bar{\pi}) \subseteq \bar{\gamma}^{\mathbb{I}}(\bar{\pi}')$. It follows that

$$\overline{\Pi} \dot{\check{\sqsubseteq}}^i \overline{\Pi}'$$

$$\Leftrightarrow \forall \bar{\pi} \in \overline{\Pi} . \exists \bar{\pi}' \in \overline{\Pi}' . \pi \dot{\check{\sqsubseteq}}^i \pi' \qquad \langle \text{def. (18) of } \dot{\check{\sqsubseteq}}^i \rangle$$

$$\Rightarrow \forall \bar{\pi} \in \overline{\Pi} . \exists \bar{\pi}' \in \overline{\Pi}' . \bar{\gamma}^{\mathbb{I}}(\bar{\pi}) \subseteq \bar{\gamma}^{\mathbb{I}}(\bar{\pi}') \qquad \langle \text{since } \pi \dot{\check{\sqsubseteq}}^i \pi' \text{ implies } \bar{\gamma}^{\mathbb{I}}(\bar{\pi}) \subseteq \bar{\gamma}^{\mathbb{I}}(\bar{\pi}') \rangle$$

$$\Rightarrow \forall \bar{\pi} \in \overline{\Pi} . \exists \bar{\pi}' \in \overline{\Pi}' . \forall \pi \in \bar{\gamma}^{\mathbb{I}}(\bar{\pi}) . \pi \in \bar{\gamma}^{\mathbb{I}}(\bar{\pi}') \qquad \langle \text{def. } \subseteq \rangle$$

$\Rightarrow \forall \overline{\pi} \in \overline{\Pi} . \forall \pi \in \check{\gamma}^{\mathbb{I}}(\overline{\pi}) . \exists \overline{\pi}'' \in \overline{\Pi}' . \pi \in \check{\gamma}^{\mathbb{I}}(\overline{\pi}'')$

$\qquad\qquad\qquad\qquad\qquad\qquad\qquad$ $\{$choosing the same $\overline{\pi}'' = \overline{\pi}'$ for all $\pi\}$

$\Leftrightarrow \overline{\Pi} \sqsubseteq^i \overline{\Pi}'$ $\qquad\qquad\qquad\qquad\qquad\qquad\qquad\qquad$ $\{(16)\}$ □

It follows that we have a Galois connection (note that the abstract preorder and concretization are different from both (15) and (17))

$$\langle \wp(\mathbb{S}_V^{+\infty}), \subseteq \rangle \xleftrightarrow[\check{\alpha}^{\mathbb{I}}]{\overset{\circ}{\check{\gamma}}} \langle \wp(\mathbb{S}_{\mathbb{I}}^{+\infty}), \overset{\circ}{\sqsubseteq}^i \rangle \tag{19}$$

Proof (of (19)).

$\check{\alpha}^{\mathbb{I}}(\Pi) \overset{\circ}{\sqsubseteq}^i \overline{\Pi}$

$\Leftrightarrow \{\check{\alpha}^{\mathbb{I}}(\pi) \mid \pi \in \Pi\} \overset{\circ}{\sqsubseteq}^i \overline{\Pi}$ $\qquad\qquad\qquad\qquad$ $\{$def. (14) of $\check{\alpha}^{\mathbb{I}}\}$

$\Leftrightarrow \forall \overline{\pi} \in \{\check{\alpha}^{\mathbb{I}}(\pi) \mid \pi \in \Pi\} . \exists \overline{\pi}' \in \overline{\Pi} . \overline{\pi} \sqsubseteq^i \overline{\pi}'$ $\qquad$ $\{$def. (18) of $\sqsubseteq^i\}$

$\Leftrightarrow \forall \pi \in \Pi . \exists \overline{\pi}' \in \overline{\Pi} . \check{\alpha}^{\mathbb{I}}(\pi) \sqsubseteq^i \overline{\pi}'$ $\qquad\qquad\qquad\qquad$ $\{$def. $\in\}$

$\Leftrightarrow \Pi \subseteq \{\pi \mid \exists \overline{\pi}' \in \overline{\Pi} . \check{\alpha}^{\mathbb{I}}(\pi) \sqsubseteq^i \overline{\pi}'\}$ $\qquad\qquad\qquad\qquad$ $\{$def. $\subseteq\}$

$\Leftrightarrow \Pi \subseteq \overset{\circ}{\check{\gamma}}(\overline{\Pi})$

by defining $\overset{\circ}{\check{\gamma}}(\overline{\Pi}) \triangleq \{\pi \mid \exists \overline{\pi}' \in \overline{\Pi} . \check{\alpha}^{\mathbb{I}}(\pi) \sqsubseteq^i \overline{\pi}'\}$. $\qquad\qquad\qquad$ □

7 Calculational design of the float interval trace semantics

The float interval trace semantics $\mathcal{S}_{\mathbb{I}}^*[\![S]\!]$ of a program component S replaces concrete real or float traces (as defined by $\mathcal{S}_V^*[\![S]\!]$) by interval traces. It is sound if and only if the concrete traces are included in the abstract traces that is $\mathcal{S}_V^*[\![S]\!] \subseteq \check{\gamma}^{\mathbb{I}}(\mathcal{S}_{\mathbb{I}}^*[\![S]\!])$ or, equivalently, by (15), $\check{\alpha}^{\mathbb{I}}(\mathcal{S}_V^*[\![S]\!]) \subseteq \mathcal{S}_{\mathbb{I}}^*[\![S]\!]$.

Although, the soundness condition $\check{\alpha}^{\mathbb{I}}(\mathcal{S}_V^*[\![S]\!]) \subseteq \mathcal{S}_{\mathbb{I}}^*[\![S]\!]$ allows the abstract semantics $\mathcal{S}_{\mathbb{I}}^*[\![S]\!]$ to contain more traces, including with larger intervals, it requires the abstract traces in $\check{\alpha}^{\mathbb{I}}(\mathcal{S}_V^*[\![S]\!])$ (which are the best float interval abstractions of real computations) to all belong to the abstract semantics $\mathcal{S}_{\mathbb{I}}^*[\![S]\!]$.

We introduced $\sqsubseteq^i$ in (18) to relax this requirement about the presence of best interval trace abstractions of real computations in the abstract semantics. The weaker requirement $\check{\alpha}^{\mathbb{I}}(\mathcal{S}_V^*[\![S]\!]) \overset{\circ}{\sqsubseteq}^i \mathcal{S}_{\mathbb{I}}^*[\![S]\!])$ implies, by Lem. 1, that $\check{\alpha}^{\mathbb{I}}(\mathcal{S}_V^*[\![S]\!]) \sqsubseteq^i \mathcal{S}_{\mathbb{I}}^*[\![S]\!]$ so that, by (16), $\check{\gamma}^{\mathbb{I}}(\check{\alpha}^{\mathbb{I}}(\mathcal{S}_V^*[\![S]\!])) \subseteq \check{\gamma}^{\mathbb{I}}(\mathcal{S}_{\mathbb{I}}^*[\![S]\!])$, which, together with $\mathcal{S}_V^*[\![S]\!] \subseteq \check{\gamma}^{\mathbb{I}}(\check{\alpha}^{\mathbb{I}}(\mathcal{S}_V^*[\![S]\!]))$ from the Galois connection (15) yields, by transitivity, that $\mathcal{S}_V^*[\![S]\!] \subseteq \check{\gamma}^{\mathbb{I}}(\mathcal{S}_{\mathbb{I}}^*[\![S]\!])$.

This weaker soundness requirement $\check{\alpha}^{\mathbb{I}}(\mathcal{S}_V^*[\![S]\!]) \overset{\circ}{\sqsubseteq}^i \mathcal{S}_{\mathbb{I}}^*[\![S]\!])$ yields a calculational design method where $\check{\alpha}^{\mathbb{I}}(\mathcal{S}_V^*[\![S]\!])$ is $\overset{\circ}{\sqsubseteq}^i$-over-approximated so as to eliminate any reference to the concrete semantics $\mathcal{S}_V^*[\![S]\!]$. We proceed by structural induction on $\lhd$, assuming $\check{\alpha}^{\mathbb{I}}(\mathcal{S}_V^*[\![S']\!]) \overset{\circ}{\sqsubseteq}^i \mathcal{S}_{\mathbb{I}}^*[\![S']\!]$ for all $S' \lhd S$.

To design $\mathcal{S}_{\mathbb{I}}^*[\![S]\!]$ such that $\alpha^{\mathbb{I}}(\mathcal{S}_R[\![S]\!]) \overset{\circ}{\sqsubseteq}^i \mathcal{S}_{\mathbb{I}}^*[\![S]\!]$ by structural induction, we will need to prove a stronger result stating that any interval overapproximation of an initial state of a real computation can be extended into an interval computation abstracting this real computation. Formally, we have

$$\forall \langle \text{at}[\![\mathsf{S}]\!], \, \rho \rangle \pi \in X \, . \, \forall \bar{\rho} \in \mathbb{Ev}_{\mathbb{I}} \, . \tag{20}$$

$$(\dot{\alpha}^{\mathbb{I}}(\rho) \sqsubseteq^i \bar{\rho}) \Rightarrow (\exists \bar{\pi} \, . \, \alpha^{\mathbb{I}}(\pi) \sqsubseteq^i \bar{\pi} \wedge \langle \text{at}[\![\mathsf{S}]\!], \, \bar{\rho} \rangle \bar{\pi} \in \overline{X})$$

which we will use for $X = \mathcal{S}^*_{\mathbb{V}}[\![\mathsf{S}]\!]$ and $\overline{X} = \mathcal{S}^*_{\mathbb{I}}[\![\mathsf{S}]\!]$ is well as for the concrete X and abstract $\overline{X}$ fixpoint iterates in (8) for iteration statements.

Interval abstraction of an arithmetic expression Given $\rho \in \mathbb{Ev}_{\mathbb{V}}$ (where $\mathbb{V}$ is $\mathbb{R}$ or $\mathbb{F}$), let us evaluate $\alpha^{\mathbb{I}}(\mathcal{A}_{\mathbb{V}}[\![\mathsf{A}]\!]\rho)$ by structural induction on A and define $\mathcal{A}_{\mathbb{I}}[\![\mathsf{A}]\!]$ such that

$$\alpha^{\mathbb{I}}(\mathcal{A}_{\mathbb{V}}[\![\mathsf{A}]\!]\rho) \sqsubseteq^i \mathcal{A}_{\mathbb{I}}[\![\mathsf{A}]\!]\dot{\alpha}^{\mathbb{I}}(\rho). \tag{21}$$

— $\alpha^{\mathbb{I}}(\mathcal{A}_{\mathbb{V}}[\![\texttt{0.1}]\!]\rho)$

$= \alpha^{\mathbb{I}}(\texttt{0.1}_{\mathbb{V}})$ $\wr$def. $\mathcal{A}_{\mathbb{V}}$ in (1)$\wr$

$= [\mathopen{}^\lceil\texttt{0.1}_{\mathbb{V}}, \texttt{0.1}_{\mathbb{V}}\mathclose{}^\rceil]$ $\wr$real abstraction by float interval in (14)$\wr$

$\triangleq \mathcal{A}_{\mathbb{I}}[\![\texttt{0.1}]\!](\dot{\alpha}^{\mathbb{I}}(\rho))$ $\wr$by defining $\mathcal{A}_{\mathbb{I}}[\![\texttt{0.1}]\!]\bar{\rho} \triangleq [\mathopen{}^\lceil\texttt{0.1}_{\mathbb{V}}, \texttt{0.1}_{\mathbb{V}}\mathclose{}^\rceil]\wr$

— $\alpha^{\mathbb{I}}(\mathcal{A}_{\mathbb{V}}[\![\mathsf{x}]\!]\rho)$

$= \alpha^{\mathbb{I}}(\rho(\mathsf{x}))$ $\wr$def. $\mathcal{A}_{\mathbb{V}}$ in (1)$\wr$

$= \dot{\alpha}^{\mathbb{I}}(\rho)(\mathsf{x})$ $\wr$def. environment abstraction in (14)$\wr$

$\triangleq \mathcal{A}_{\mathbb{I}}[\![\mathsf{x}]\!](\dot{\alpha}^{\mathbb{I}}(\rho))$ $\wr$by defining $\mathcal{A}_{\mathbb{I}}[\![\mathsf{x}]\!]\bar{\rho} \triangleq \bar{\rho}(\mathsf{x})\wr$

— $\alpha^{\mathbb{I}}(\mathcal{A}_{\mathbb{V}}[\![\mathsf{A}_1 - \mathsf{A}_2]\!]\rho)$

$= \alpha^{\mathbb{I}}(\mathcal{A}_{\mathbb{V}}[\![\mathsf{A}_1]\!]\rho -_{\mathbb{V}} \mathcal{A}_{\mathbb{V}}[\![\mathsf{A}_2]\!]\rho)$ $\wr$def. $\mathcal{A}_{\mathbb{V}}$ in (1)$\wr$

$= [\mathopen{}^\lceil(\mathcal{A}_{\mathbb{V}}[\![\mathsf{A}_1]\!]\rho -_{\mathbb{V}} \mathcal{A}_{\mathbb{V}}[\![\mathsf{A}_2]\!]\rho), (\mathcal{A}_{\mathbb{V}}[\![\mathsf{A}_1]\!]\rho -_{\mathbb{V}} \mathcal{A}_{\mathbb{V}}[\![\mathsf{A}_2]\!]\rho)\mathclose{}^\rceil]$

$\wr$value abstraction by float interval in (14)$\wr$

$\sqsubseteq^i [\mathopen{}^\lceil(\mathcal{A}_{\mathbb{V}}[\![\mathsf{A}_1]\!]\rho) -_{\mathbb{F}} (\mathcal{A}_{\mathbb{V}}[\![\mathsf{A}_2]\!]\rho)\mathclose{}^\rceil), (\mathcal{A}_{\mathbb{V}}[\![\mathsf{A}_1]\!]\rho)\mathclose{}^\rceil -_{\mathbb{F}} \mathopen{}^\lceil(\mathcal{A}_{\mathbb{V}}[\![\mathsf{A}_2]\!]\rho)]$

$\wr$(18) and hyp. (12)$\wr$

$\sqsubseteq^i$ let $[\underline{x}, \overline{x}] = \mathcal{A}_{\mathbb{I}}[\![\mathsf{A}_1]\!]\dot{\alpha}^{\mathbb{I}}(\rho)$ and $[\underline{y}, \overline{y}] = \mathcal{A}_{\mathbb{I}}[\![\mathsf{A}_2]\!]\dot{\alpha}^{\mathbb{I}}(\rho)$ in $[\underline{x} -_{\mathbb{F}} \overline{y}, \overline{x} -_{\mathbb{F}} \underline{y}]$

$\wr$By ind. hyp. $[\mathopen{}^\lceil\mathcal{A}_{\mathbb{V}}[\![\mathsf{A}_i]\!]\rho, \mathcal{A}_{\mathbb{V}}[\![\mathsf{A}_i]\!]\rho\mathclose{}^\rceil] = \alpha^{\mathbb{I}}(\mathcal{A}_{\mathbb{V}}[\![\mathsf{A}_i]\!]\rho) \sqsubseteq^i \mathcal{A}_{\mathbb{I}}[\![\mathsf{A}_i]\!]\dot{\alpha}^{\mathbb{I}}(\rho)$,

$i = 1, 2.\wr$

$= \mathcal{A}_{\mathbb{I}}[\![\mathsf{A}_1]\!]\dot{\alpha}^{\mathbb{I}}(\rho) -_{\mathbb{I}} \mathcal{A}_{\mathbb{I}}[\![\mathsf{A}_2]\!]\dot{\alpha}^{\mathbb{I}}(\rho)$ $\wr$by defining $[\underline{x}, \overline{x}] -_{\mathbb{I}} [\underline{y}, \overline{y}] \triangleq [\underline{x} -_{\mathbb{F}} \overline{y}, \overline{x} -_{\mathbb{F}} \underline{y}]\wr$

$\triangleq \mathcal{A}_{\mathbb{I}}[\![\mathsf{A}_1 - \mathsf{A}_2]\!]\dot{\alpha}^{\mathbb{I}}(\rho)$ $\wr$by defining $\mathcal{A}_{\mathbb{I}}[\![\mathsf{A}_1 - \mathsf{A}_2]\!]\bar{\rho} \triangleq \mathcal{A}_{\mathbb{I}}[\![\mathsf{A}_1]\!]\bar{\rho} -_{\mathbb{I}} \mathcal{A}_{\mathbb{I}}[\![\mathsf{A}_2]\!]\bar{\rho}\wr$

We observe that $\mathcal{A}_{\mathbb{I}}[\![\mathsf{A}]\!]$ is $\sqsubseteq^i$-increasing. $\square$

If we had a division, we would have to handle NaN. A simple way is to stop execution, by choosing $\mathcal{A}_{\mathbb{I}}[\![\texttt{1/0}]\!]\bar{\rho} \triangleq \varnothing$. Another way would be to include the NaN in the abstraction by considering $\mathsf{N}[\underline{x}, \overline{x}]$ meaning a float between the bounds while $\mathsf{NaN}[\underline{x}, \overline{x}]$ would mean a float between the bounds or NaN. We chose the first alternative, which is simpler.

Interval trace semantics of an assignment statement We can now abstract the semantics of real ($\mathbb{V} = \mathbb{R}$) or float ($\mathbb{V} = \mathbb{F}$) assignments by float intervals.

$$\dot{\alpha}^{\mathbb{I}}(\mathcal{S}^*_{\mathbb{V}}[\![\mathsf{S}]\!]) \qquad\qquad\qquad\qquad \wr\text{where } \mathsf{S} = \ell\ \mathsf{x} = \mathsf{A}\ ; \wr$$

$$= \{\alpha^{\mathbb{I}}(\pi) \mid \pi \in \mathcal{S}^*_{\mathbb{V}}[\![\ell\ \mathsf{x} = \mathsf{A}\ ;]\!]\} \qquad\qquad \wr\text{set of traces abstraction (14)}\wr$$

$$= \{\alpha^{\mathbb{I}}(\pi) \mid \pi \in \{\langle \ell, \rho\rangle \mid \rho \in \mathbb{Ev}_{\mathbb{V}}\} \cup \{\langle \ell, \rho\rangle\langle \mathsf{aft}[\![\mathsf{S}]\!], \rho[\mathsf{x} \leftarrow \mathcal{A}_{\mathbb{V}}[\![\mathsf{A}]\!]\rho]\rangle \mid \rho \in \mathbb{Ev}_{\mathbb{V}}\}\}$$
$$\wr\text{def. } \mathcal{S}^*_{\mathbb{V}}[\![\ell\ \mathsf{x} = \mathsf{A}\ ;]\!] \text{ in (2)}\wr$$

$$= \{\langle \ell, \dot{\alpha}^{\mathbb{I}}(\rho)\rangle \mid \rho \in \mathbb{Ev}_{\mathbb{V}}\} \cup \{\langle \ell, \dot{\alpha}^{\mathbb{I}}(\rho)\rangle\langle \mathsf{aft}[\![\mathsf{S}]\!], \alpha^{\mathbb{I}}(\rho[\mathsf{x} \leftarrow \mathcal{A}_{\mathbb{V}}[\![\mathsf{A}]\!]\rho])\rangle \mid \rho \in \mathbb{Ev}_{\mathbb{V}}\}$$
$$\wr\text{def. (14) of trace abstraction}\wr$$

$$= \{\langle \ell, \dot{\alpha}^{\mathbb{I}}(\rho)\rangle \mid \rho \in \mathbb{Ev}_{\mathbb{V}}\} \cup \{\langle \ell, \dot{\alpha}^{\mathbb{I}}(\rho)\rangle\langle \mathsf{aft}[\![\mathsf{S}]\!], \dot{\alpha}^{\mathbb{I}}(\rho)[\mathsf{x} \leftarrow \alpha^{\mathbb{I}}(\mathcal{A}_{\mathbb{V}}[\![\mathsf{A}]\!]\rho])\rangle \mid \rho \in \mathbb{Ev}_{\mathbb{V}}\}$$
$$\wr\text{def. (14) of environment abstraction}\wr$$

$$\stackrel{\circ}{\sqsubseteq}^i \{\langle \ell, \dot{\alpha}^{\mathbb{I}}(\rho)\rangle \mid \rho \in \mathbb{Ev}_{\mathbb{V}}\} \cup \{\langle \ell, \dot{\alpha}^{\mathbb{I}}(\rho)\rangle\langle \mathsf{aft}[\![\mathsf{S}]\!], \dot{\alpha}^{\mathbb{I}}(\rho)[\mathsf{x} \leftarrow \mathcal{A}_{\mathbb{I}}[\![\mathsf{A}]\!]\dot{\alpha}^{\mathbb{I}}(\rho)]\rangle \mid \rho \in \mathbb{Ev}_{\mathbb{V}}\}$$
$$\wr\text{def. (18) of } \stackrel{\circ}{\sqsubseteq}^i \text{ and (21)}\wr$$

$$\stackrel{\circ}{\sqsubseteq}^i \{\langle \ell, \overline{\rho}\rangle \mid \overline{\rho} \in \mathbb{Ev}_{\mathbb{I}}\} \cup \{\langle \ell, \overline{\rho}\rangle\langle \mathsf{aft}[\![\mathsf{S}]\!], \overline{\rho}[\mathsf{x} \leftarrow \mathcal{A}_{\mathbb{I}}[\![\mathsf{A}]\!]\overline{\rho}]\rangle \mid \overline{\rho} \in \mathbb{Ev}_{\mathbb{I}}\}$$
$$\wr\{\dot{\alpha}^{\mathbb{I}}(\rho) \mid \rho \in \mathbb{Ev}_{\mathbb{V}}\} \subseteq \mathbb{Ev}_{\mathbb{I}} \text{ by (14) for environment abstraction}\wr$$

$$\triangleq \mathcal{S}^*_{\mathbb{I}}[\![\ell\ \mathsf{x} = \mathsf{A}\ ;]\!] \qquad\qquad \wr\text{by defining } \mathcal{S}^*_{\mathbb{I}}[\![\ell\ \mathsf{x} = \mathsf{A}\ ;]\!] \text{ as in (2) for } \mathbb{V} = \mathbb{I}\wr$$

(20) follows from $\mathcal{A}_{\mathbb{I}}[\![\mathsf{A}]\!]$ is $\sqsubseteq^i$-increasing. $\qquad\qquad\qquad\qquad\qquad\qquad\square$

Interval trace semantics of a break statement

$$\dot{\alpha}^{\mathbb{I}}(\mathcal{S}^*_{\mathbb{R}}[\![\mathsf{S}]\!]) \qquad\qquad\qquad\qquad \wr\text{where } \mathsf{S} = \ell\ \textbf{break}\ ; \wr$$

$$\triangleq \dot{\alpha}^{\mathbb{I}}(\{\langle \ell, \rho\rangle \mid \rho \in \mathbb{Ev}_{\mathbb{V}}\} \cup \{\langle \ell, \rho\rangle\langle \mathsf{brk\text{-}to}[\![\mathsf{S}]\!], \rho\rangle \mid \rho \in \mathbb{Ev}_{\mathbb{R}}\}) \qquad\qquad \wr(3)\wr$$

$$= \dot{\alpha}^{\mathbb{I}}(\{\langle \ell, \rho\rangle \mid \rho \in \mathbb{Ev}_{\mathbb{R}}\}) \cup \alpha^{\mathbb{I}}(\{\langle \ell, \rho\rangle\langle \mathsf{brk\text{-}to}[\![\mathsf{S}]\!], \rho\rangle \mid \rho \in \mathbb{Ev}_{\mathbb{R}}\})$$
$$\wr\text{the abstraction preserves joins in the Galois connection (15)}\wr$$

$$= \{\langle \ell, \dot{\alpha}^{\mathbb{I}}(\rho)\rangle \mid \rho \in \mathbb{Ev}_{\mathbb{R}}\} \cup \{\langle \ell, \dot{\alpha}^{\mathbb{I}}(\rho)\rangle\langle \mathsf{brk\text{-}to}[\![\mathsf{S}]\!], \dot{\alpha}^{\mathbb{I}}(\rho)\rangle \mid \rho \in \mathbb{Ev}_{\mathbb{R}}\}$$
$$\wr\text{def. (14) of } \dot{\alpha}^{\mathbb{I}}\wr$$

$$\stackrel{\circ}{\sqsubseteq}^i \{\langle \ell, \overline{\rho}\rangle \mid \overline{\rho} \in \mathbb{Ev}_{\mathbb{I}}\} \cup \{\langle \ell, \overline{\rho}\rangle\langle \mathsf{brk\text{-}to}[\![\mathsf{S}]\!], \overline{\rho}\rangle \mid \overline{\rho} \in \mathbb{Ev}_{\mathbb{I}}\} \quad \wr\{\dot{\alpha}^{\mathbb{I}}(\rho) \mid \overline{\rho} \in \mathbb{Ev}_{\mathbb{V}}\} \subseteq \mathbb{Ev}_{\mathbb{I}}\wr$$

$$\triangleq \mathcal{S}^*_{\mathbb{I}}[\![\mathsf{S}]\!] \qquad\qquad\qquad \wr\text{by defining } \mathcal{S}^*_{\mathbb{I}}[\![\mathsf{S}]\!] \text{ as in (3) for } \mathbb{V} = \mathbb{I}\wr$$

(20) follows from $\overline{\rho} \in \mathbb{Ev}_{\mathbb{I}}$ and $\overline{\rho} \sqsubseteq^i \overline{\rho}'$ implies $\overline{\rho}' \in \mathbb{Ev}_{\mathbb{I}}$. $\qquad\qquad\qquad\square$

Interval trace semantics of the statement list Given sets of traces $\Pi_1, \Pi_2 \in \wp(\mathbb{S}^*_{\mathbb{V}})$, let us calculate

$$\alpha^{\mathbb{I}}(\Pi_1 \frown \Pi_2)$$

$$= \alpha^{\mathbb{I}}(\{\pi_1 \sigma \pi_2 \mid \pi_1 \sigma \in \Pi_1 \wedge \sigma \pi_2 \in \Pi_2\} \qquad\qquad\qquad \wr\text{def. } \frown\wr$$

$$= \{\alpha^{\mathbb{I}}(\pi_1 \sigma \pi_2) \mid \pi_1 \sigma \in \Pi_1 \wedge \sigma \pi_2 \in \Pi_2\} \qquad\qquad\qquad \wr\text{def. } \alpha^{\mathbb{I}}\wr$$

$$= \{\alpha^{\mathbb{I}}(\pi_1 \sigma) \frown \alpha^{\mathbb{I}}(\sigma \pi_2) \mid \pi_1 \sigma \in \Pi_1 \wedge \sigma \pi_2 \in \Pi_2\} \qquad\qquad \wr\text{def. } \frown\wr$$

$$= \{\overline{\pi_1 \sigma} \frown \overline{\sigma}\,\overline{\pi}_2 \mid \overline{\pi_1\,\sigma} \in \alpha^{\mathbb{I}}(\Pi_1) \wedge \overline{\sigma\pi}_2 \in \alpha^{\mathbb{I}}(\Pi_2)\}$$
$$\wr\text{letting } \overline{\pi_1\sigma} = \alpha^{\mathbb{I}}(\pi_1\sigma) \text{ and } \overline{\sigma}\,\overline{\pi}_2 = \alpha^{\mathbb{I}}(\sigma\pi_2)\wr$$

$$= \alpha^{\mathbb{I}}(\Pi_1) \mathbin{\widetilde{}} \alpha^{\mathbb{I}}(\Pi_2) \qquad\qquad\qquad\qquad\qquad \wr\text{def.} \mathbin{\widetilde{}}\wr$$

The case of an empty statement list $\mathsf{Sl} ::= \epsilon$ is trivial and we get $\mathcal{S}_{\mathbb{I}}^*[\![\mathsf{Sl}]\!] \triangleq \{\langle \mathrm{at}[\![\mathsf{Sl}]\!], \overline{\rho}\rangle \mid \overline{\rho} \in \mathbb{Ev}_{\mathbb{I}}\}$. For a non-empty statement list $\mathsf{Sl} ::= \mathsf{Sl'}\ \mathsf{S}$, we have

$$\mathring{\alpha}^{\mathbb{I}}(\mathcal{S}_{\mathbb{R}}^*[\![\mathsf{Sl}]\!])$$

$$\triangleq \mathring{\alpha}^{\mathbb{I}}(\mathcal{S}_{\mathbb{R}}^*[\![\mathsf{Sl'}]\!] \cup \mathcal{S}_{\mathbb{R}}^*[\![\mathsf{Sl'}]\!] \mathbin{\widetilde{}} \mathcal{S}_{\mathbb{R}}^*[\![\mathsf{S}]\!]) \qquad\qquad\qquad \wr(7)\wr$$

$$= \mathring{\alpha}^{\mathbb{I}}(\mathcal{S}_{\mathbb{R}}^*[\![\mathsf{Sl'}]\!]) \cup \mathring{\alpha}^{\mathbb{I}}(\mathcal{S}_{\mathbb{R}}^*[\![\mathsf{Sl'}]\!] \mathbin{\widetilde{}} \mathcal{S}_{\mathbb{R}}^*[\![\mathsf{S}]\!])$$

$$\wr\text{the abstraction preserves joins in the Galois connection (15)}\wr$$

$$= \mathring{\alpha}^{\mathbb{I}}(\mathcal{S}_{\mathbb{R}}^*[\![\mathsf{Sl'}]\!]) \cup \mathring{\alpha}^{\mathbb{I}}(\mathcal{S}_{\mathbb{R}}^*[\![\mathsf{Sl'}]\!]) \mathbin{\widetilde{}} \mathring{\alpha}^{\mathbb{I}}(\mathcal{S}_{\mathbb{R}}^*[\![\mathsf{S}]\!]) \qquad\qquad \wr\text{as shown above}\wr$$

$$\mathbin{\mathring{\sqsubseteq}}^i \mathcal{S}_{\mathbb{I}}^*[\![\mathsf{Sl'}]\!] \cup \mathcal{S}_{\mathbb{I}}^*[\![\mathsf{Sl'}]\!] \mathbin{\widetilde{}} \mathcal{S}_{\mathbb{I}}^*[\![\mathsf{S}]\!]$$

$$\wr\text{hyp. ind., } (\overline{\Pi}_0 \mathbin{\mathring{\sqsubseteq}}^i \overline{\Pi}_0' \wedge \overline{\Pi}_1 \mathbin{\mathring{\sqsubseteq}}^i \overline{\Pi}_1') \text{ implies } (\overline{\Pi}_0 \mathbin{\widetilde{}} \overline{\Pi}_1 \mathbin{\mathring{\sqsubseteq}}^i \overline{\Pi}_0' \mathbin{\widetilde{}} \overline{\Pi}_1') \text{ and}$$
$$(\overline{\Pi}_0 \cup \overline{\Pi}_1 \mathbin{\mathring{\sqsubseteq}}^i \overline{\Pi}_0' \cup \overline{\Pi}_1')\wr$$

(20) follows by ind. hyp. and def. $\mathbin{\widetilde{}}$. $\qquad\qquad\qquad\qquad\qquad\qquad\qquad\qquad$ □

Interval abstraction of a boolean expression The situation is more complicated for conditionals. While a test is true or false for $\mathbb{V} = \mathbb{R}$ and $\mathbb{V} = \mathbb{F}$, it might be true for part of a float interval and false for another part of this interval when $\mathbb{V} = \mathbb{I}$. Moreover in case of uncertainty (*e.g.* $<$ is handled as $\leqslant$) the two part may overlap.

Therefore we assume that the abstract interpretation $\mathcal{B}_{\mathbb{I}}[\![\mathsf{B}]\!]$ of a boolean expression B is defined such that

$$\text{let } \langle \overline{\rho}_{\mathrm{tt}}, \overline{\rho}_{\mathrm{ff}}\rangle = \mathcal{B}_{\mathbb{I}}[\![\mathsf{B}]\!]\mathring{\alpha}^{\mathbb{I}}(\rho) \text{ in} \qquad\qquad\qquad\qquad (22)$$

$$\mathring{\alpha}^{\mathbb{I}}(\rho) \mathbin{\mathring{\sqsubseteq}}^i \overline{\rho}_{\mathrm{tt}} \qquad\qquad \text{if } \mathcal{B}_{\mathbb{V}}[\![\mathsf{B}]\!]\rho = \mathrm{tt}$$

$$\mathring{\alpha}^{\mathbb{I}}(\rho) \mathbin{\mathring{\sqsubseteq}}^i \overline{\rho}_{\mathrm{ff}} \qquad\qquad \text{if } \mathcal{B}_{\mathbb{V}}[\![\mathsf{B}]\!]\rho = \mathrm{ff}$$

$$\text{and } (\langle \overline{\rho}_{\mathrm{tt}}, \overline{\rho}_{\mathrm{ff}}\rangle = \mathcal{B}_{\mathbb{I}}[\![\mathsf{B}]\!]\overline{\rho}) \Rightarrow (\overline{\rho}_{\mathrm{tt}} \mathbin{\mathring{\sqsubseteq}}^i \overline{\rho} \wedge \overline{\rho}_{\mathrm{ff}} \mathbin{\mathring{\sqsubseteq}}^i \overline{\rho})$$

stating that no concrete state passing the test is omitted in the abstract and that the postcondition $\overline{\rho}_{\mathrm{tt}}$ or $\overline{\rho}_{\mathrm{ff}}$ is stronger than the precondition $\overline{\rho}$ since, in absence of side effects, the test cannot introduce any new state. Examples of def. of $\mathcal{B}_{\mathbb{V}}$ are found *e.g.* in [3]. If $\mathcal{B}_{\mathbb{V}}[\![\mathsf{B}]\!]\rho = \mathrm{tt}$ (respectively ff), there is no constraint on $\overline{\rho}_{\mathrm{ff}}$ (respectively $\overline{\rho}_{\mathrm{tt}}$), the best choice being the $\mathbin{\mathring{\sqsubseteq}}^i$-infimum empty interval environment $\mathring{\varnothing}$.

Interval trace semantics of a conditional statement We can now abstract the semantics of real tests using float intervals.

$$\mathring{\alpha}^{\mathbb{I}}(\mathcal{S}_{\mathbb{R}}^*[\![\mathtt{if}\ \ell\ (\mathsf{B})\ \mathsf{S}_t]\!])$$

$$\triangleq \mathring{\alpha}^{\mathbb{I}}(\{\langle \ell, \rho\rangle \mid \rho \in \mathbb{Ev}_{\mathbb{R}}\} \cup \{\langle \ell, \rho\rangle\langle \mathrm{aft}[\![\mathsf{S}]\!], \rho\rangle \mid \mathcal{B}_{\mathbb{V}}[\![\mathsf{B}]\!]\rho = \mathrm{ff}\} \cup \{\langle \ell, \rho\rangle\langle \mathrm{at}[\![\mathsf{S}_t]\!], \rho\rangle\pi \mid$$
$$\mathcal{B}_{\mathbb{V}}[\![\mathsf{B}]\!]\rho = \mathrm{tt} \wedge \langle \mathrm{at}[\![\mathsf{S}_t]\!], \rho\rangle\pi \in \mathcal{S}_{\mathbb{R}}^*[\![\mathsf{S}_t]\!]\}) \qquad\quad \wr\text{def. } \mathcal{S}_{\mathbb{R}}^*[\![\mathtt{if}\ \ell\ (\mathsf{B})\ \mathsf{S}_t]\!] \text{ in (5)}\wr$$

$$= \{\langle \ell, \mathring{\alpha}^{\mathbb{I}}(\rho)\rangle \mid \rho \in \mathbb{Ev}_{\mathbb{R}}\} \cup \{\langle \ell, \mathring{\alpha}^{\mathbb{I}}(\rho)\rangle\langle \mathrm{aft}[\![\mathsf{S}]\!], \mathring{\alpha}^{\mathbb{I}}(\rho)\rangle \mid \mathcal{B}_{\mathbb{V}}[\![\mathsf{B}]\!]\rho = \mathrm{ff}\} \cup \{\langle \ell, \mathring{\alpha}^{\mathbb{I}}(\rho)\rangle\langle \mathrm{at}[\![\mathsf{S}_t]\!],$$
$$\mathring{\alpha}^{\mathbb{I}}(\rho)\rangle\alpha^{\mathbb{I}}(\pi) \mid \mathcal{B}_{\mathbb{V}}[\![\mathsf{B}]\!]\rho = \mathrm{tt} \wedge \langle \mathrm{at}[\![\mathsf{S}_t]\!], \rho\rangle\pi \in \mathcal{S}_{\mathbb{R}}^*[\![\mathsf{S}_t]\!]\} \qquad\qquad \wr(14)\wr$$

$\stackrel{\circ i}{\sqsubseteq} \{\langle \ell, \overline{\rho} \rangle \mid \overline{\rho} \in \mathbb{Ev}_{\mathbb{I}}\} \cup \{\langle \ell, \overline{\rho} \rangle \langle \text{aft}[\![S]\!], \overline{\rho}_{\text{ff}} \rangle \mid \exists \overline{\rho}_{\text{tt}} . \mathcal{B}_{\mathbb{I}}[\![B]\!]\overline{\rho} = \langle \overline{\rho}_{\text{tt}}, \overline{\rho}_{\text{ff}} \rangle \wedge \overline{\rho}_{\text{ff}} \neq \dot{\varnothing}\} \cup \{\langle \ell,$
$\overline{\rho} \rangle \langle \text{at}[\![S_t]\!], \overline{\rho}_{\text{tt}} \rangle \overline{\pi} \mid \exists \overline{\rho}_{\text{ff}} . \mathcal{B}_{\mathbb{I}}[\![B]\!]\overline{\rho} = \langle \overline{\rho}_{\text{tt}}, \overline{\rho}_{\text{ff}} \rangle \wedge \overline{\rho}_{\text{tt}} \neq \dot{\varnothing} \wedge \langle \text{at}[\![S_t]\!], \overline{\rho}_{\text{tt}} \rangle \overline{\pi} \in \mathcal{S}^*_{\mathbb{I}}[\![S_t]\!]\}$

≀— For the first term, by def. (18) of $\stackrel{\circ i}{\sqsubseteq}$, we must prove that $\forall \rho . \exists \overline{\rho} . \langle \ell,$
$\dot{\alpha}^{\mathbb{I}}(\rho) \rangle \stackrel{i}{\sqsubseteq} \langle \ell, \overline{\rho} \rangle$. Since $\{\dot{\alpha}^{\mathbb{I}}(\rho) \mid \rho \in \mathbb{Ev}_{\mathbb{R}}\} \subseteq \mathbb{Ev}_{\mathbb{I}}$, we can simply choose
$\overline{\rho} = \dot{\alpha}^{\mathbb{I}}(\rho)$.

— The second term may be empty, in which case $\overline{\rho}_{\text{ff}} = \dot{\varnothing}$. Otherwise, by
def. (18) of $\stackrel{\circ i}{\sqsubseteq}$, we must prove that $\forall \rho . \exists \overline{\rho} . \langle \ell, \dot{\alpha}^{\mathbb{I}}(\rho) \rangle \langle \text{at}[\![S_t]\!], \dot{\alpha}^{\mathbb{I}}(\rho) \rangle \stackrel{i}{\sqsubseteq}$
$\langle \ell, \overline{\rho} \rangle \langle \text{aft}[\![S]\!], \overline{\rho}_{\text{ff}} \rangle$. The control abstraction is the same. We can choose
$\overline{\rho} = \dot{\alpha}^{\mathbb{I}}(\rho)$ so that $\mathcal{B}_{\vee}[\![B]\!]\rho = \text{ff}$ implies, by (22), that $\dot{\alpha}^{\mathbb{I}}(\rho) \sqsubseteq^i \overline{\rho}_{\text{ff}}$.

— The third term may be empty, in which case $\overline{\rho}_{\text{tt}} = \dot{\varnothing}$. Otherwise,
by def. (18) of $\sqsubseteq^i$, we must prove that $\forall \rho, \pi . \exists \overline{\rho}, \overline{\pi} . \langle \ell, \dot{\alpha}^{\mathbb{I}}(\rho) \rangle \langle \text{at}[\![S_t]\!],$
$\dot{\alpha}^{\mathbb{I}}(\rho) \rangle \alpha^{\mathbb{I}}(\pi) \sqsubseteq^i \langle \ell, \overline{\rho} \rangle \langle \text{at}[\![S_t]\!], \overline{\rho}_{\text{tt}} \rangle \overline{\pi}$ where $\mathcal{B}_{\vee}[\![B]\!]\rho = \text{tt}, \langle \text{at}[\![S_t]\!], \rho \rangle \pi \in$
$\mathcal{S}^*_{\mathbb{R}}[\![S_t]\!], \mathcal{B}_{\mathbb{I}}[\![B]\!]\overline{\rho} = \langle \overline{\rho}_{\text{tt}}, \overline{\rho}_{\text{ff}} \rangle$, and $\langle \text{at}[\![S_t]\!], \overline{\rho}_{\text{tt}} \rangle \overline{\pi} \in \mathcal{S}^*_{\mathbb{I}}[\![S_t]\!]$.

The control abstraction is the same. We can choose $\overline{\rho} = \dot{\alpha}^{\mathbb{I}}(\rho)$ so that
$\mathcal{B}_{\vee}[\![B]\!]\rho = \text{tt}$ implies, by (22), that $\dot{\alpha}^{\mathbb{I}}(\rho) \sqsubseteq^i \overline{\rho}_{\text{tt}} \sqsubseteq^i \overline{\rho}$ so that $\dot{\alpha}^{\mathbb{I}}(\rho) = \overline{\rho}_{\text{tt}}$
since $\overline{\rho} = \dot{\alpha}^{\mathbb{I}}(\rho)$.

It remains to find $\overline{\pi}$ such that $\alpha^{\mathbb{I}}(\pi) \stackrel{i}{\sqsubseteq} \overline{\pi}$ and $\langle \text{at}[\![S_t]\!], \overline{\rho}_{\text{tt}} \rangle \overline{\pi} \in \mathcal{S}^*_{\mathbb{I}}[\![S_t]\!]$.
It is given by (20) where $\langle \text{at}[\![S_t]\!], \rho \rangle \pi \in \mathcal{S}^*_{\mathbb{R}}[\![S_t]\!]$ implies for $\overline{\rho} = \dot{\alpha}^{\mathbb{I}}(\rho)$ that
$\exists \overline{\pi} . \alpha^{\mathbb{I}}(\pi) \stackrel{i}{\sqsubseteq} \overline{\pi} \wedge \langle \text{at}[\![S]\!], \dot{\alpha}^{\mathbb{I}}(\rho) \rangle \overline{\pi} \in \mathcal{S}^*_{\mathbb{I}}[\![S]\!]$. It follows that $\alpha^{\mathbb{I}}(\pi) \stackrel{i}{\sqsubseteq} \overline{\pi}$ and
$\langle \text{at}[\![S_t]\!], \overline{\rho}_{\text{tt}} \rangle \overline{\pi} \in \mathcal{S}^*_{\mathbb{I}}[\![S_t]\!]$ since $\overline{\rho} = \dot{\alpha}^{\mathbb{I}}(\rho)$. ∫

$\triangleq \mathcal{S}^*_{\mathbb{I}}[\![\text{if } \ell \text{ (B) } S_t]\!]$

≀since the above term involves only computations in $\mathbb{S}_{\mathbb{I}}$ and none in $\mathbb{S}_{\vee}$∫

It remains to show that $\mathcal{S}^*_{\mathbb{I}}[\![\text{if } \ell \text{ (B) } S_t]\!]$ satisfies (20), which is trivial for the first
two terms. For the third term, this follows from the induction hypothesis.   □

By calculational design, we have got the interval test as follows

$$\mathcal{S}^*_{\mathbb{I}}[\![S]\!] \triangleq \{\langle \ell, \overline{\rho} \rangle \mid \overline{\rho} \in \mathbb{Ev}_{\mathbb{I}}\} \qquad \text{(5bis)}$$
$$\cup \{\langle \ell, \overline{\rho} \rangle \langle \text{aft}[\![S]\!], \overline{\rho}_{\text{ff}} \rangle \mid \exists \overline{\rho}_{\text{tt}} . \mathcal{B}_{\mathbb{I}}[\![B]\!]\overline{\rho} = \langle \overline{\rho}_{\text{tt}}, \overline{\rho}_{\text{ff}} \rangle \wedge \rho_{\text{ff}} \neq \dot{\varnothing}\}$$
$$\cup \{\langle \ell, \overline{\rho} \rangle \langle \text{at}[\![S_t]\!], \overline{\rho}_{\text{tt}} \rangle \pi \mid \exists \overline{\rho}_{\text{ff}} . \mathcal{B}_{\mathbb{I}}[\![B]\!]\overline{\rho} = \langle \overline{\rho}_{\text{tt}}, \overline{\rho}_{\text{ff}} \rangle \wedge \rho_{\text{tt}} \neq \dot{\varnothing} \wedge$$
$$\langle \text{at}[\![S_t]\!], \overline{\rho}_{\text{tt}} \rangle \pi \in \mathcal{S}^*_{\mathbb{I}}[\![S_t]\!]\}$$

Most libraries raise an error exception in case of split (or chose only one branch)
which we can formalize as an undefined behavior, à la C, where any behavior is
possible.

$$\mathcal{S}^*_{\mathbb{I}}[\![S]\!] \triangleq \cdots \qquad \text{(5.ter)}$$
$$\cup \{\langle \ell, \overline{\rho} \rangle \pi \mid \exists \overline{\rho}_{\text{tt}}, \overline{\rho}_{\text{ff}} . \mathcal{B}_{\mathbb{I}}[\![B]\!]\overline{\rho} = \langle \overline{\rho}_{\text{tt}}, \overline{\rho}_{\text{ff}} \rangle \wedge \rho_{\text{tt}} \sqcap^i \rho_{\text{ff}} \neq \dot{\varnothing} \wedge \pi \in \mathbb{S}^{+\infty}_{\mathbb{I}}\}$$

Fixpoint approximation For the iteration statement, we rely on the following
fixpoint abstraction theorem (adapted from the more general [9, Prop. 2]).

Theorem 1 (least fixpoint over-approximation in a cpo). *Assume that*
$\langle C, \sqsubseteq, \bot, \sqcup \rangle$ *is a cpo,* $f \in C \xrightarrow{uc} C$ *is* $\sqcup$-*upper continuous,* $\mathcal{I} \in \wp(C)$ *contains the*

iterates $f^0(\bot) = \bot$ *and* $f^{n+1}(\bot) = f(f^n(\bot))$ *of* f *from* $\bot$, $\langle \mathcal{A}, \preccurlyeq, 0, \curlyvee \rangle$ *is a cpo,* $\overline{f} \in \mathcal{A} \xrightarrow{uc} \mathcal{A}$ *is* $\curlyvee$*-upper continuous,* $\trianglelefteq$ *is a preorder on* $\mathcal{A}$, $\alpha \in C \to \mathcal{A}$, $\alpha(\bot) \trianglelefteq 0$, $\forall x \in \mathcal{1}, y \in \mathcal{A} . (\alpha(x) \trianglelefteq y) \Rightarrow (\alpha(f(x)) \trianglelefteq \overline{f}(y))$, *and for all* $\sqsubseteq$*-increasing chains* $\langle x^i,$ $i \in \mathbb{N} \rangle$ *of* $\mathcal{1}$ *and* $\preccurlyeq$*-increasing chains* $\langle y^i, i \in \mathbb{N} \rangle$ *of* $\mathcal{A}$, $\alpha(\bigsqcup_{i \in \mathbb{N}} x^i) \trianglelefteq \bigcurlyvee_{i \in \mathbb{N}} y^i$. *Then* $\alpha(\mathsf{lfp}^{\sqsubseteq} f) \trianglelefteq \mathsf{lfp}^{\preccurlyeq} \overline{f}$. $\square$

Remark 1. If $\overline{f}$ is $\trianglelefteq$-increasing, and $\forall x \in \mathcal{1} . \alpha \circ f(x) \trianglelefteq \overline{f} \circ \alpha(x)$ (semi-commutativity) then $\forall x \in \mathcal{1} . \alpha(x) \trianglelefteq y \Rightarrow \overline{f}(\alpha(x)) \trianglelefteq \overline{f}(y) \Rightarrow \alpha(f(x)) \trianglelefteq \overline{f}(y)$. Since, in general, this property does not hold for all $x \in C$ and it is used for the iterates of f only, $\mathcal{1} \in \wp(C)$ can be used to restrict the elements of C for which the property is required to hold. $\square$

Proof (of Th. 1). By Scott-Kleene fixpoint, $f \in C \xrightarrow{uc} C$ is $\sqcup$-continuous function on a cpo $\langle C, \sqsubseteq, \bot, \sqcup \rangle$ so f has a least fixpoint $\mathsf{lfp}^{\sqsubseteq} f = \bigsqcup_{n \in \mathbb{N}} f^n(\bot)$. Similarly, $\mathsf{lfp}^{\preccurlyeq} \overline{f} = \bigcurlyvee_{n \in \mathbb{N}} \overline{f}^n(0)$. We have $\alpha(f^0(\bot)) = \alpha(\bot) \trianglelefteq 0 = \overline{f}^0(0)$. Then $f^n(\bot) \in \mathcal{1}$ and $\alpha(f^n(\bot)) \trianglelefteq \overline{f}^n(0)$ by ind. hyp. so that $\alpha(f^{n+1}(\bot)) = \alpha(f(f^n(\bot))) \trianglelefteq \overline{f}(\overline{f}^n(0)) = \overline{f}^{n+1}(0)$. By recurrence $\forall n \in \mathbb{N} . \alpha(f^n(\bot)) \trianglelefteq \overline{f}^n(0)$. Since the fixpoint iterates are increasing, it follows, by hypothesis, that $\alpha(\mathsf{lfp}^{\sqsubseteq} f) = \alpha(\bigsqcup_{n \in \mathbb{N}} f^n(\bot)) = \bigcurlyvee_{n \in \mathbb{N}} \overline{f}^n(0) = \mathsf{lfp}^{\preccurlyeq} \overline{f}$. $\square$

Interval trace semantics of the iteration statement We define $\mathcal{1}$ in Th. 1 by assuming that iterate X satisfies the induction hypothesis (20), which is trivially satisfied by the first iterate $\varnothing$.

$\dot{\alpha}^{\mathbb{I}}(\mathcal{F}_{\mathbb{V}}^*[\![\mathtt{while}\, \ell\, \mathtt{(B)}\, \mathsf{S}_b]\!]\, X)$

$= \dot{\alpha}^{\mathbb{I}}(\{\langle \ell, \rho \rangle \mid \rho \in \mathbb{E}\mathsf{v}_{\mathbb{R}}\} \cup \{\pi_2\langle \ell', \rho \rangle\langle \mathsf{aft}[\![\mathsf{S}]\!], \rho \rangle \mid \pi_2\langle \ell', \rho \rangle \in X \wedge \mathcal{B}[\![\mathsf{B}]\!]\, \rho = \mathsf{ff} \wedge \ell' = \ell\} \cup \{\pi_2\langle \ell', \rho \rangle\langle \mathsf{at}[\![\mathsf{S}_b]\!], \rho \rangle\pi_3 \mid \pi_2\langle \ell', \rho \rangle \in X \wedge \mathcal{B}[\![\mathsf{B}]\!]\, \rho = \mathsf{tt} \wedge \langle \mathsf{at}[\![\mathsf{S}_b]\!], \rho \rangle\pi_3 \in \mathcal{S}_{\mathbb{R}}^*[\![\mathsf{S}_b]\!] \wedge \ell' = \ell\})$ $\wr$def (8) of $\mathcal{F}_{\mathbb{V}}^*[\![\mathtt{while}\, \ell\, \mathtt{(B)}\, \mathsf{S}_b]\!]\wr$

$= \dot{\alpha}^{\mathbb{I}}(\{\langle \ell, \rho \rangle \mid \rho \in \mathbb{E}\mathsf{v}_{\mathbb{R}}\}) \cup \dot{\alpha}^{\mathbb{I}}(\{\pi_2\langle \ell', \rho \rangle\langle \mathsf{aft}[\![\mathsf{S}]\!], \rho \rangle \mid \pi_2\langle \ell', \rho \rangle \in X \wedge \mathcal{B}[\![\mathsf{B}]\!]\, \rho = \mathsf{ff} \wedge \ell' = \ell\}) \cup \dot{\alpha}^{\mathbb{I}}(\{\pi_2\langle \ell', \rho \rangle\langle \mathsf{at}[\![\mathsf{S}_b]\!], \rho \rangle\pi_3 \mid \pi_2\langle \ell', \rho \rangle \in X \wedge \mathcal{B}[\![\mathsf{B}]\!]\, \rho = \mathsf{tt} \wedge \langle \mathsf{at}[\![\mathsf{S}_b]\!], \rho \rangle\pi_3 \in \mathcal{S}_{\mathbb{R}}^*[\![\mathsf{S}_b]\!] \wedge \ell' = \ell\})$ $\wr$join preservation in the Galois connection (15)$\wr$

The first two terms have already been handled in the case of a conditional statement $\mathtt{if}\, \ell\, \mathtt{(B)}\, \mathsf{S}_t$. It remains the third term (simplified with $\ell' = \ell$), which, in the non-empty case is as follows.

$\dot{\alpha}^{\mathbb{I}}(\{\pi_2\langle \ell, \rho \rangle\langle \mathsf{at}[\![\mathsf{S}_b]\!], \rho \rangle\pi_3 \mid \pi_2\langle \ell, \rho \rangle \in X \wedge \mathcal{B}[\![\mathsf{B}]\!]\, \rho = \mathsf{tt} \wedge \langle \mathsf{at}[\![\mathsf{S}_b]\!], \rho \rangle\pi_3 \in \mathcal{S}_{\mathbb{R}}^*[\![\mathsf{S}_b]\!]\})$

$= \{\alpha^{\mathbb{I}}(\pi_2)\langle \ell \rangle\langle \dot{\alpha}^{\mathbb{I}}(\rho) \rangle\langle \mathsf{at}[\![\mathsf{S}_b]\!], \dot{\alpha}^{\mathbb{I}}(\rho) \rangle\alpha^{\mathbb{I}}(\pi_3) \mid \pi_2\langle \ell, \rho \rangle \in X \wedge \mathcal{B}[\![\mathsf{B}]\!]\, \rho = \mathsf{tt} \wedge \langle \mathsf{at}[\![\mathsf{S}_b]\!], \rho \rangle\pi_3 \in \mathcal{S}_{\mathbb{R}}^*[\![\mathsf{S}_b]\!]\}$ $\wr$def. (14) of $\dot{\alpha}^{\mathbb{I}}\wr$

$\sqsubseteq^i \{\overline{\pi}_2\langle \ell, \overline{\rho} \rangle\langle \mathsf{at}[\![\mathsf{S}_b]\!], \overline{\rho}_{\mathsf{tt}} \rangle\overline{\pi}_3) \mid \overline{\pi}_2\langle \ell, \overline{\rho} \rangle \in \alpha^{\mathbb{I}}(X) \wedge \exists \overline{\rho}_{\mathsf{ff}} . \mathcal{B}_{\mathbb{I}}[\![\mathsf{B}]\!]\overline{\rho} = \langle \overline{\rho}_{\mathsf{tt}}, \overline{\rho}_{\mathsf{ff}} \rangle \wedge \langle \mathsf{at}[\![\mathsf{S}_b]\!], \overline{\rho}_{\mathsf{tt}} \rangle\overline{\pi}_3 \in \mathcal{S}_{\mathbb{I}}^*[\![\mathsf{S}_b]\!]\}$

⟨By def. (18) of $\overset{\circ}{\sqsubseteq}^i$, we must prove that $\vec{\alpha}^{\mathbb{I}}(\pi_2)\langle \ell,\ \dot{\alpha}^{\mathbb{I}}(\rho)\rangle\langle\text{at}[\![S_b]\!],$ $\dot{\alpha}^{\mathbb{I}}(\rho)\rangle\vec{\alpha}^{\mathbb{I}}(\pi_3) \sqsubseteq^i \overline{\pi}_2\langle\ell,\ \overline{\rho}\rangle\langle\text{at}[\![S_b]\!],\ \overline{\rho}\rangle\overline{\pi}_3)$ where $\mathcal{B}_{\mathbb{V}}[\![B]\!]\rho = \text{tt},\ \langle\text{at}[\![S_b]\!],$ $\rho\rangle\pi_3 \in \mathcal{S}_{\mathbb{R}}^*[\![S_b]\!]$, $\mathcal{B}_{\mathbb{I}}[\![B]\!]\overline{\rho} = \langle\overline{\rho}_{\text{tt}},\ \overline{\rho}_{\text{ff}}\rangle$, and $\langle\text{at}[\![S_b]\!],\ \overline{\rho}\rangle\overline{\pi}_3 \in \mathcal{S}_{\mathbb{I}}^*[\![S_b]\!]$.

The control abstraction is the same. We can choose $\overline{\rho} = \dot{\alpha}^{\mathbb{I}}(\rho)$ so that $\mathcal{B}_{\mathbb{V}}[\![B]\!]\rho = \text{tt}$ implies, by (22), that $\dot{\alpha}^{\mathbb{I}}(\rho) \sqsubseteq^i \overline{\rho}_{\text{tt}} \sqsubseteq^i \overline{\rho}$ so that $\dot{\alpha}^{\mathbb{I}}(\rho) = \overline{\rho}_{\text{tt}}$ since $\overline{\rho} = \dot{\alpha}^{\mathbb{I}}(\rho)$.

We choose $\overline{\pi}_2 = \vec{\alpha}^{\mathbb{I}}(\pi_2)$ so that $\pi_2\langle\ell,\ \rho\rangle \in X$ implies, by def. (14) of $\alpha^{\mathbb{I}}$, that $\overline{\pi}_2\langle\ell,\ \overline{\rho}\rangle \in \dot{\alpha}^{\mathbb{I}}(X)$ with $\vec{\alpha}^{\mathbb{I}}(\pi_2\langle\ell,\ \rho\rangle) \sqsubseteq^i \overline{\pi}_2\langle\ell,\ \overline{\rho}\rangle$ since $\overline{\rho} = \dot{\alpha}^{\mathbb{I}}(\rho)$ and $\sqsubseteq^i$ is reflexive.

It remains to find $\overline{\pi}_3$ such that $\vec{\alpha}^{\mathbb{I}}(\pi_3) \sqsubseteq^i \overline{\pi}_3$ and $\langle\text{at}[\![S_t]\!],\ \overline{\rho}_{\text{tt}}\rangle\overline{\pi}_3 \in \mathcal{S}_{\mathbb{I}}^*[\![S_t]\!]$. It is given by (20) where $\langle\text{at}[\![S_t]\!],\ \rho\rangle\pi_3 \in \mathcal{S}_{\mathbb{R}}^*[\![S_b]\!]$ implies for $\overline{\rho} = \dot{\alpha}^{\mathbb{I}}(\rho)$ that $\exists\overline{\pi}_3 \,.\, \vec{\alpha}^{\mathbb{I}}(\pi_3) \sqsubseteq^i \overline{\pi}_3 \wedge \langle\text{at}[\![S]\!],\ \dot{\alpha}^{\mathbb{I}}(\rho)\rangle\overline{\pi}_3 \in \mathcal{S}_{\mathbb{I}}^*[\![S]\!]$. It follows that $\vec{\alpha}^{\mathbb{I}}(\pi_3) \sqsubseteq^i \overline{\pi}_3$ and $\langle\text{at}[\![S_t]\!],\ \overline{\rho}_{\text{tt}}\rangle\overline{\pi}_3 \in \mathcal{S}_{\mathbb{I}}^*[\![S_b]\!]$ since $\overline{\rho} = \dot{\alpha}^{\mathbb{I}}(\rho)$ ⟩

Since the above terms involves only computations in $\mathbb{S}_{\mathbb{I}}$ and none in $\mathbb{S}_{\mathbb{V}}$, we can define (again an undefined behavior can be introduced for overlapping tests)

$$\mathcal{F}_{\mathbb{I}}^*[\![\text{while }\ell\text{ (B) }S_b]\!]\,X \triangleq \{\langle\ell,\ \overline{\rho}\rangle \mid \overline{\rho} \in \mathbb{Ev}_{\mathbb{I}}\} \tag{8bis}$$

$$\cup\ \{\overline{\pi}_2\langle\ell',\ \overline{\rho}\rangle\langle\text{aft}[\![S]\!],\ \overline{\rho}_{\text{ff}}\rangle \mid$$

$$\overline{\pi}_2\langle\ell',\ \overline{\rho}\rangle \in X \wedge \exists\overline{\rho}_{\text{tt}} \,.\, \mathcal{B}_{\mathbb{I}}[\![B]\!]\overline{\rho} = \langle\overline{\rho}_{\text{tt}},\ \overline{\rho}_{\text{ff}}\rangle \wedge \overline{\rho}_{\text{ff}} \neq \varnothing \wedge \ell' = \ell\}$$

$$\cup\ \{\overline{\pi}_2\langle\ell',\ \overline{\rho}\rangle\langle\text{at}[\![S_b]\!],\ \overline{\rho}\rangle\overline{\pi}_3 \mid \overline{\pi}_2\langle\ell',\ \overline{\rho}\rangle \in X \wedge$$

$$\exists\overline{\rho}_{\text{ff}} \,.\, \mathcal{B}_{\mathbb{I}}[\![B]\!]\overline{\rho} = \langle\overline{\rho}_{\text{tt}},\ \overline{\rho}_{\text{ff}}\rangle \wedge \overline{\rho}_{\text{tt}} \neq \varnothing \wedge \langle\text{at}[\![S_b]\!],\ \overline{\rho}\rangle\overline{\pi}_3 \in \mathcal{S}_{\mathbb{I}}^*[\![S_b]\!] \wedge \ell' = \ell\}$$

so that $\dot{\alpha}^{\mathbb{I}}(\mathcal{F}_{\mathbb{R}}^*[\![\text{while }\ell\text{ (B) }S_b]\!]X) = \mathcal{F}_{\mathbb{I}}^*[\![\text{while }\ell\text{ (B) }S_b]\!](\alpha^{\mathbb{I}}(X))$. We have to show that the next iterate $\mathcal{F}_{\mathbb{I}}^*[\![\text{while }\ell\text{ (B) }S_b]\!]\,X$ satisfies (20), which is trivial for the first two terms. For the third term this follows from the induction hypothesis. It follows that

$$\mathcal{S}_{\mathbb{I}}^*[\![\text{while }\ell\text{ (B) }S_b]\!] = \dot{\alpha}^{\mathbb{I}}(\mathcal{S}_{\mathbb{R}}^*[\![\text{while }\ell\text{ (B) }S_b]\!]) \qquad\qquad \text{⟨by def.⟩} \quad (23)$$

$$= \dot{\alpha}^{\mathbb{I}}(\text{lfp}^{\subseteq}\,\mathcal{F}_{\mathbb{R}}^*[\![\text{while }\ell\text{ (B) }S_b]\!]) \qquad\qquad \text{⟨by (8)⟩}$$

$$\sqsubseteq^i \text{lfp}^{\subseteq}\,\mathcal{F}_{\mathbb{I}}^*[\![\text{while }\ell\text{ (B) }S_b]\!] \qquad\qquad \text{⟨by Th. 1⟩}$$

It remains to show that $\mathcal{S}_{\mathbb{I}}^*[\![\text{while }\ell\text{ (B) }S_b]\!]$ satisfies (20). We have shown that it holds for all fixpoint iterates. Moreover, it is trivially preserved by trace set union. □

In conclusion of this section, $\mathcal{S}_{\mathbb{I}}^*$ is similar to $\mathcal{S}_{\mathbb{V}}^*$ in (2)—(7) except for statements involving tests for which we have (5bis) or (5ter) and (8bis).

8   On floating point computations

Unfortunately real computations are usually performed using floating point arithmetics. One computes only one floating point value hoping it is not too far from the real one. This problem has been deeply studied in static analysis [10,11,13,15,16,18,19,20,17,29]. Another dynamic analysis solution is to check the precision with an interval analysis.

Consider the execution with reals (at least their semantics), floats and float intervals, maybe with different possible execution traces for float intervals due to the nondeterminacy of tests. These interval executions abstract both the real and float executions.

If there is only one interval execution trace or we can prove that the real and float executions follow exactly the same control path then the real execution is in the join of the interval executions to which the float execution belongs to, when projected on all program points.

Otherwise, the real and float executions may have followed different paths but both are guaranteed to belong to the union of all interval executions projected on all program points.

In both cases this provides an estimate of the rounding error of the float execution compared to the ideal real execution. Of course the estimate might be rough since specific properties of the computation are not taken into account (*e.g.* [25, pp. 91–94]).

9   Abstraction to a transition system

One could argue that a sound maximal trace semantics of interval arithmetics does not describe an implementation. However, we can abstract to a small-step operational semantics that is a transition system describing elementary steps of an implementation.

A transition system is a triple $\langle \Sigma, I, \xrightarrow{\tau} \rangle$ where Σ is a non-empty set of states σ, $I \subseteq \Sigma$ is a set of initial states, and $\xrightarrow{\tau} \in \wp(\Sigma \times \Sigma)$ is a transition relation between a state and its possible successors.

A transition system $\langle \Sigma, I, \xrightarrow{\tau} \rangle$ can be used to define a state prefix trace semantics as follows.

$$\gamma^\tau(\langle \Sigma, I, \xrightarrow{\tau} \rangle) \triangleq \{\pi_0 \cdots \cdots \pi_n \mid n \in \mathbb{N} \wedge \pi_0 \in I \wedge \forall i \in [0, n[\,.\, \pi_i \xrightarrow{\tau} \pi_{i+1}\} \quad (24)$$

(where $\sigma \xrightarrow{\tau} \sigma'$ is a shorthand for $\langle \sigma, \sigma' \rangle \in \xrightarrow{\tau}$.)

Conversely a prefix trace semantics S can be abstracted in a transition system

$$\alpha^\tau(S) \triangleq \langle \Sigma, I, \xrightarrow{\tau} \rangle \quad (25)$$

where

$$\Sigma \triangleq \{\pi_i \mid \exists n \in \mathbb{N}, \pi_0, \dots, \pi_{i-1}, \pi_{i+1}, \dots, \pi_n \,.\, \pi_0 \cdots \pi_n \in S\} \qquad (\text{or } \mathbb{S})$$

$$I \triangleq \{\pi_0 \mid \exists n \in \mathbb{N}, \pi_1, \dots, \pi_n \,.\, \pi_0 \cdots \pi_n \in S\}$$

$$\xrightarrow{\tau} \triangleq \{\pi_i \to \pi_{i+1} \mid \exists n \in \mathbb{N}_*, \pi_0, \dots, \pi_{i-1}, \pi_{i+2}, \dots, \pi_n \,.\, \pi_0 \cdots \pi_n \in S\}$$

This is a Galois connection

$$\langle \wp(\mathbb{T}^+), \subseteq \rangle \xleftarrow{\quad \gamma^\tau \quad}_{\xrightarrow{\quad \alpha^\tau \quad}} \langle \{\langle \Sigma, I, \xrightarrow{\tau} \rangle \mid \Sigma \in \wp(\mathbb{S}) \wedge I \subseteq \Sigma \wedge \xrightarrow{\tau} \subseteq \Sigma \times \Sigma\}, \subseteq \rangle$$

In general information is lost by the abstraction of a prefix trace semantics to a transition system (take for example $\Pi = \{a, aa\}$ so that $\gamma^\tau \circ \alpha^\tau(\Pi) = a^+$ is the set of all non-empty finite sequences of "a"s). However, this is not the case since the maximal semantics has been defined as the limit of prefix-closed traces, finite maximal final traces are not strict prefixes of any other trace, and so, final states have no possible successor.

Notice that the abstraction of the prefix trace semantics of a program into a transition system will only comprehend reachable states. So the transition semantics for a language is the join of all transition systems of the prefix trace semantics of all programs in the semantics. This may still be a strict overapproximation.

The transition semantics of the programming language P with program components Pc is

$$\alpha^\tau(\boldsymbol{S}^*_\lor[\![S]\!]) = \langle \mathbb{S}, \{\langle \mathsf{at}[\![S]\!], \rho\rangle \mid S \in Pc \land \rho \in \mathbb{Ev}\}, \widehat{\boldsymbol{S}}^\tau_\lor[\![S]\!]\rangle$$

defined by structural induction on program components $S \in Pc$ as follows.

9.1   Transition semantics of an assignment statement $S ::= \ell\, x = A$;

$$\widehat{\boldsymbol{S}}^\tau_\lor[\![S]\!] = \{\langle \ell, \rho\rangle \longrightarrow \langle \mathsf{aft}[\![S]\!], \rho[x \leftarrow \mathscr{A}[\![A]\!]\rho]\rangle \mid \rho \in \mathbb{Ev}_\lor\} \tag{26}$$

Proof (of (26)).

$\widehat{\boldsymbol{S}}^\tau_\lor[\![S]\!]$

$= \{\pi_i \longrightarrow \pi_{i+1} \mid \exists n \in \mathbb{N}_*, \pi_0, \dots, \pi_{i-1}, \pi_{i+2}, \dots, \pi_n . \pi_0 \cdots \pi_n \in \boldsymbol{S}^*_\lor[\![S]\!]\}$ $\wr(25)\wr$

$= \{\langle \ell, \rho\rangle \longrightarrow \langle \mathsf{aft}[\![S]\!], \rho[x \leftarrow \mathscr{A}[\![A]\!]\rho]\rangle \mid \rho \in \mathbb{Ev}_\lor\}$ $\wr(2)\wr$ □

9.2   Transition semantics of a statement list $Sl ::= Sl'\, S$

$$\widehat{\boldsymbol{S}}^\tau_\lor[\![Sl]\!] = \widehat{\boldsymbol{S}}^\tau_\lor[\![Sl']\!] \cup \widehat{\boldsymbol{S}}^\tau_\lor[\![S]\!] \tag{27}$$

Proof (of (27)).

$\widehat{\boldsymbol{S}}^\tau_\lor[\![Sl]\!]$

$= \{\pi_i \longrightarrow \pi_{i+1} \mid \exists n \in \mathbb{N}_*, \pi_0, \dots, \pi_{i-1}, \pi_{i+2}, \dots, \pi_n . \pi_0 \cdots \pi_n \in \boldsymbol{S}^*_\lor[\![Sl]\!]\}$ $\wr(25)\wr$

$= \{\pi_i \longrightarrow \pi_{i+1} \mid \exists n \in \mathbb{N}_*, \pi_0, \dots, \pi_{i-1}, \pi_{i+2}, \dots, \pi_n . \pi_0 \cdots \pi_n \in \boldsymbol{S}^*_\lor[\![Sl']\!] \cup \{\pi \cdot \langle \mathsf{at}[\![S]\!], \rho\rangle \cdot \pi' \mid \pi \cdot \langle \mathsf{at}[\![S]\!], \rho\rangle \in \boldsymbol{S}^*_\lor[\![Sl']\!] \land \langle \mathsf{at}[\![S]\!], \rho\rangle \cdot \pi' \in \boldsymbol{S}^*_\lor[\![S]\!]\}\}$ $\wr$def. (7) of $\boldsymbol{S}^*_\lor[\![Sl]\!]\wr$

$= \{\pi_i \longrightarrow \pi_{i+1} \mid \exists n \in \mathbb{N}_*, \pi_0, \dots, \pi_{i-1}, \pi_{i+2}, \dots, \pi_n . \pi_0 \cdots \pi_n \in \boldsymbol{S}^*_\lor[\![Sl']\!]\} \cup \{\pi_i \longrightarrow \pi_{i+1} \mid \exists n \in \mathbb{N}_*, \pi_0, \dots, \pi_{i-1}, \pi_{i+2}, \dots, \pi_n . \pi_0 \cdots \pi_n \in \{\pi \cdot \langle \mathsf{at}[\![S]\!], \rho\rangle \cdot \pi' \mid \pi \cdot \langle \mathsf{at}[\![S]\!], \rho\rangle \in \boldsymbol{S}^*_\lor[\![Sl']\!] \land \langle \mathsf{at}[\![S]\!], \rho\rangle \cdot \pi' \in \boldsymbol{S}^*_\lor[\![S]\!]\}\}$ $\wr$def. $\cup\wr$

$= \{\pi_i \longrightarrow \pi_{i+1} \mid \exists n \in \mathbb{N}_*, \pi_0, \dots, \pi_{i-1}, \pi_{i+2}, \dots, \pi_n . \pi_0 \cdots \pi_n \in \boldsymbol{S}^*_\lor[\![Sl']\!]\} \cup \{\pi_i \longrightarrow \pi_{i+1} \mid \exists n \in \mathbb{N}_*, \pi_0, \dots, \pi_{i-1}, \pi_{i+2}, \dots, \pi_n . \pi_0 \cdots \pi_n \in \{\langle \mathsf{at}[\![S]\!], \rho\rangle \cdot \pi' \mid \langle \mathsf{at}[\![S]\!], \rho\rangle \cdot \pi' \in \boldsymbol{S}^*_\lor[\![S]\!]\}\}$

$(\text{since all transitions originating from } \pi \cdot \langle \text{at}[\![S]\!], \rho \rangle = \pi \cdot \langle \text{aft}[\![Sl']\!], \rho \rangle \in$
$\boldsymbol{\mathcal{S}}^*_\mathbb{V}[\![Sl']\!] \text{ have already been collected in the first term of the } \cup)$

$= \{\pi_i \longrightarrow \pi_{i+1} \mid \exists n \in \mathbb{N}_*, \pi_0, \dots, \pi_{i-1}, \pi_{i+2}, \dots, \pi_n \cdot \pi_0 \cdots \pi_n \in \boldsymbol{\mathcal{S}}^*_\mathbb{V}[\![Sl']\!]\} \cup \{\pi_i \longrightarrow$
$\pi_{i+1} \mid \exists n \in \mathbb{N}_*, \pi_0, \dots, \pi_{i-1}, \pi_{i+2}, \dots, \pi_n \cdot \pi_0 \cdots \pi_n \in \boldsymbol{\mathcal{S}}^*_\mathbb{V}[\![S]\!]\}$

$(\text{since all traces of } \boldsymbol{\mathcal{S}}^*_\mathbb{V}[\![S]\!] \text{ start with state } \langle \text{at}[\![S]\!], \rho \rangle)$

$= \widehat{\boldsymbol{\mathcal{S}}}^\tau_\mathbb{V}[\![Sl']\!] \cup \widehat{\boldsymbol{\mathcal{S}}}^\tau_\mathbb{V}[\![S]\!]$ $(\text{(25) and ind. hyp.})$ □

9.3 Transition semantics of an iteration statement S ::= while ℓ (B) S_b and a break statement S ::= ℓ break ;

Real ($\mathbb{V} = \mathbb{R}$) and float ($\mathbb{V} = \mathbb{F}$) semantics.

$$\widehat{\boldsymbol{\mathcal{S}}}^\tau_\mathbb{V}[\![\text{while } \ell \text{ (B) } S_b]\!] = \{\langle \ell, \rho \rangle \longrightarrow \langle \text{aft}[\![S]\!], \rho \rangle \mid \boldsymbol{\mathcal{B}}[\![B]\!]\rho = \text{ff}\} \tag{28}$$
$$\cup \{\langle \ell, \rho \rangle \longrightarrow \langle \text{at}[\![S_b]\!], \rho \rangle \mid \boldsymbol{\mathcal{B}}[\![B]\!]\rho = \text{tt}\} \cup \widehat{\boldsymbol{\mathcal{S}}}^\tau_\mathbb{V}[\![S_b]\!]$$
$$\widehat{\boldsymbol{\mathcal{S}}}^\tau_\mathbb{V}[\![\text{break ;}]\!] = \{\langle \ell, \rho \rangle \longrightarrow \langle \text{brk-to}[\![S]\!], \rho \rangle \mid \rho \in \mathbb{Ev}_\mathbb{V}\} \tag{29}$$

By definition of $\text{aft}[\![S_b]\!] = \text{at}[\![\text{while } \ell \text{ (B) } S_b]\!] = \ell$, there is no need for a transition from after the loop body S_b to the start ℓ of the loop.

Float interval ($\mathbb{V} = \mathbb{I}$) semantics. For float intervals, the transition is non-deterministic.

$$\widehat{\boldsymbol{\mathcal{S}}}^\tau_\mathbb{I}[\![\text{while } \ell \text{ (B) } S_b]\!] = \{\langle \ell, \overline{\rho} \rangle \longrightarrow \langle \text{aft}[\![S]\!], \overline{\rho}_{\text{ff}} \rangle \mid \exists \overline{\rho}_{\text{tt}} \cdot \boldsymbol{\mathcal{B}}_\mathbb{I}[\![B]\!]\overline{\rho} = \langle \overline{\rho}_{\text{tt}}, \overline{\rho}_{\text{ff}} \rangle\} \tag{30}$$
$$\cup \{\langle \ell, \overline{\rho} \rangle \longrightarrow \langle \text{at}[\![S_b]\!], \overline{\rho}_{\text{tt}} \rangle \mid \exists \overline{\rho}_{\text{ff}} \cdot \boldsymbol{\mathcal{B}}_\mathbb{I}[\![B]\!]\overline{\rho} = \langle \overline{\rho}_{\text{tt}}, \overline{\rho}_{\text{ff}} \rangle\} \cup \widehat{\boldsymbol{\mathcal{S}}}^\tau_\mathbb{I}[\![S_b]\!]$$

Proof (of (30)). (The proof of (28) and (29) is similar).

$\widehat{\boldsymbol{\mathcal{S}}}^\tau_\mathbb{V}[\![S]\!]$ $(\text{where S ::= while } \ell \text{ (B) } S_b)$

$= \{\pi_i \longrightarrow \pi_{i+1} \mid \exists n \in \mathbb{N}_*, \pi_0, \dots, \pi_{i-1}, \pi_{i+2}, \dots, \pi_n \cdot \pi_0 \cdots \pi_n \in \boldsymbol{\mathcal{S}}^*_\mathbb{V}[\![S]\!]\}$ ((25))

$= \{\langle \ell_i, \overline{\rho}_i \rangle \longrightarrow \langle \ell_{i+1}, \overline{\rho}_{i+1} \rangle \mid \exists n \in \mathbb{N}_*, \langle \ell_0, \overline{\rho}_0 \rangle, \dots, \langle \ell_{i-1}, \overline{\rho}_{i-1} \rangle, \langle \ell_{i+2}, \overline{\rho}_{i+2} \rangle, \dots, \langle \ell_n, \overline{\rho}_n \rangle \cdot \langle \ell_0,$
$\overline{\rho}_0 \rangle \cdots \langle \ell_n, \overline{\rho}_n \rangle \in \boldsymbol{\mathcal{S}}^*_\mathbb{V}[\![S]\!]\}$ $(\text{def. (2)—(4), (5bis), ((6)), (7), (8bis) of } \boldsymbol{\mathcal{S}}^*_\mathbb{V})$

Following the fixpoint definition of $\boldsymbol{\mathcal{S}}^*_\mathbb{V}[\![\text{while } \ell \text{ (B) } S_b]\!]$, we have to collect the transitions after 0 or one more iteration in (8bis), so the proof is on the number of fixpoint iterations of $\boldsymbol{\mathcal{F}}^*_\mathbb{I}[\![\text{while } \ell \text{ (B) } S_b]\!] X$, knowing that, by induction, the transitions of all traces in X have already been collected.

- For the basis, $\{\langle \ell, \overline{\rho} \rangle \mid \overline{\rho} \in \mathbb{Ev}_\mathbb{I}\}$ yields no transition;
- $\{\pi_2 \langle \ell', \overline{\rho} \rangle \langle \text{aft}[\![S]\!], \overline{\rho}_{\text{ff}} \rangle \mid \pi_2 \langle \ell', \overline{\rho} \rangle \in X \wedge \exists \overline{\rho}_{\text{tt}} \cdot \boldsymbol{\mathcal{B}}_\mathbb{I}[\![B]\!]\overline{\rho} = \langle \overline{\rho}_{\text{tt}}, \overline{\rho}_{\text{ff}} \rangle \wedge \ell' = \ell\}$ yields transitions $\{\langle \ell, \overline{\rho} \rangle \longrightarrow \langle \text{at}[\![S_b]\!], \overline{\rho}_{\text{ff}} \rangle \mid \exists \overline{\rho}_{\text{tt}} \cdot \boldsymbol{\mathcal{B}}_\mathbb{I}[\![B]\!]\overline{\rho} = \langle \overline{\rho}_{\text{tt}}, \overline{\rho}_{\text{ff}} \rangle\}$. The transitions of $\pi_2 \langle \ell', \overline{\rho} \rangle \in X$ have already been collected. $\overline{\rho}$ can be chosen arbitrarily for the converse inclusion;
- $\{\pi_2 \langle \ell', \overline{\rho} \rangle \langle \text{at}[\![S_b]\!], \overline{\rho}_{\text{tt}} \rangle \pi_3 \mid \pi_2 \langle \ell', \overline{\rho} \rangle \in X \wedge \exists \overline{\rho}_{\text{ff}} \cdot \boldsymbol{\mathcal{B}}_\mathbb{I}[\![B]\!]\overline{\rho} = \langle \overline{\rho}_{\text{tt}}, \overline{\rho}_{\text{ff}} \rangle \wedge \langle \text{at}[\![S_b]\!],$
$\overline{\rho}_{\text{tt}} \rangle \pi_3 \in \boldsymbol{\mathcal{S}}^*_\mathbb{V}[\![S_b]\!] \wedge \ell' = \ell\}$ yields the transitions of $\pi_2 \langle \ell', \overline{\rho} \rangle \in X$ which have already been collected by induction on the iterates, the transitions of $\langle \text{at}[\![S_b]\!],$

$\overline{\rho}_{tt}\rangle\overline{\pi}_3 \in \mathcal{S}^*_V[\![S_b]\!]$ which have already been collected in $\widehat{\mathcal{S}}^\tau_V[\![S_b]\!]$ by structural induction, plus the transitions $\{\langle \ell, \overline{\rho}\rangle \longrightarrow \langle at[\![S_b]\!], \overline{\rho}_{tt}\rangle \mid \exists \overline{\rho}_{ff} . \mathcal{B}_I[\![B]\!]\overline{\rho} = \langle \overline{\rho}_{tt}, \overline{\rho}_{ff}\rangle\}$. □

The transition semantics of a program $P ::= Sl\ \ell$, an empty statement list $Sl ::= \epsilon$, a skip statement $S ::= \ell;$, conditional statements $S ::= if\ \ell\ (B)\ S_t$ and $S ::= if\ \ell\ (B)\ S_t\ else\ S_f$, and a compound statement $S ::= \{\ Sl\ \}$. are similar.

9.4   The transition semantics generates the trace semantics

Theorem 2. *The prefix trace semantics $\mathcal{S}^*_V$ of Sections 2 and 7 is generated by the transition semantics $\widehat{\mathcal{S}}^\tau_V$ of Section 9.*

Proof (of Th. 2). The proof is by structural induction on the program components $S \in Pc$ of the language P. Let $\langle \mathbb{S}, \widehat{\mathcal{S}}^\tau_V[\![S]\!], I[\![S]\!]\rangle$ where $I[\![S]\!] \triangleq \{\langle at[\![S]\!], \rho\rangle \mid \rho \in Ev_V\}$ be the transition system of the program components S, as defined in Section 9. Let $\mathcal{S}^*(\langle \mathbb{S}, \widehat{\mathcal{S}}^\tau_V[\![S]\!], I[\![S]\!]\rangle)$ be the set of stateful prefix traces generated by this transition system, as defined in (24). We must show that $\mathcal{S}^*(\langle \mathbb{S}, \widehat{\mathcal{S}}^\tau_V[\![S]\!], I[\![S]\!]\rangle) = \mathcal{S}^*_V[\![S]\!]$ for the structural stateful prefix semantics $\mathcal{S}^*_V[\![S]\!]$ defined in Sections 2 and 7.

- We observe that traces of length 1 in $\mathcal{S}^*_V[\![S]\!]$ are all of the form $\{\langle \ell, \rho\rangle \mid \rho \in Ev_V\}$ which are exactly the same for $n = 0$ is (24). So, in the following, we just have to consider prefix traces of length strictly greater than 1.

- For the assignment statement $S ::= \ell\ x = A\ ;$, we have

$$\{\pi_0 \cdots \pi_n \mid n \in \mathbb{N} \wedge \pi_0 \in I[\![S]\!] \wedge \forall i \in [0, n[\ . \ \langle \pi_i, \pi_{i+1}\rangle \in \widehat{\mathcal{S}}^\tau_V[\![S]\!]\} \qquad \wr(24)\wr$$

$$= \{\pi_0 \cdots \pi_n \mid n \in \mathbb{N} \wedge \pi_0 \in I[\![S]\!] \wedge \forall i \in [0, n[\ . \ \langle \pi_i, \pi_{i+1}\rangle \in \{\langle \ell, \rho\rangle \longrightarrow \langle aft[\![S]\!],$$
$$\mathcal{A}[\![A]\!]\rho\rangle \mid \rho \in Ev_V\}\} \qquad \wr(26)\wr$$

$$= \{\pi_0\pi_1 \mid \langle \pi_0, \pi_1\rangle \in \{\langle \ell, \rho\rangle \longrightarrow \langle aft[\![S]\!], \mathcal{A}[\![A]\!]\rho\rangle \mid \rho \in Ev_V\}\}$$
$$\wr \text{since } \ell = at[\![S]\!] \neq aft[\![S]\!] \text{ and } \pi_0 = \langle \ell, \rho\rangle \in I[\![S]\!] \text{ by def. } I[\![S]\!]\wr$$

$$= \{\langle \ell, \rho\rangle\langle aft[\![S]\!], \mathcal{A}[\![A]\!]\rho\rangle \mid \rho \in Ev_V\} \qquad \wr \text{def. } \epsilon\wr$$

$$= \mathcal{S}^*_V[\![S]\!] \setminus \{\langle \ell, \rho\rangle \mid \rho \in Ev_V\} \qquad \wr(2)\wr$$

so we conclude that (24) generates $\mathcal{S}^*_V[\![S]\!]$ since in the proof we have left apart the trivial case of traces $\{\langle \ell, \rho\rangle \mid \rho \in Ev_V\}$ of length 1.

- For the statement list $Sl ::= Sl'\ S$, we have

$$\{\pi_0 \cdots \pi_n \mid n \in \mathbb{N} \wedge \pi_0 \in I[\![Sl]\!] \wedge \forall i \in [0, n[\ . \ \langle \pi_i, \pi_{i+1}\rangle \in \widehat{\mathcal{S}}^\tau_V[\![Sl]\!]\} \qquad \wr(24)\wr$$

$$= \{\pi_0 \cdots \pi_n \mid n \in \mathbb{N} \wedge \pi_0 \in I[\![Sl]\!] \wedge \forall i \in [0, n[\ . \ \langle \pi_i, \pi_{i+1}\rangle \in \widehat{\mathcal{S}}^\tau_V[\![Sl']\!] \cup \widehat{\mathcal{S}}^\tau_V[\![S]\!]\}$$
$$\wr(27)\wr$$

$$= \{\pi'_0 \cdots \pi'_{n'} \mid n' \in \mathbb{N} \wedge \pi'_0 \in I[\![Sl]\!] \wedge \forall i \in [0, n'[\ . \ \langle \pi'_i, \pi'_{i+1}\rangle \in \widehat{\mathcal{S}}^\tau_V[\![Sl']\!]\} \cup$$
$$\{\pi'_0 \cdots \pi'_{n'} \frown \pi''_0 \cdots \pi''_m \mid n' \in \mathbb{N} \wedge \pi'_0 \in I[\![Sl]\!] \wedge \forall i \in [0, n'[\ . \ \langle \pi'_i, \pi'_{i+1}\rangle \in$$
$$\widehat{\mathcal{S}}^\tau_V[\![Sl']\!] \wedge m \in \mathbb{N} \wedge \pi''_0 \in I[\![S]\!] \wedge \forall i \in [0, m[\ . \ \langle \pi''_i, \pi''_{i+1}\rangle \in \widehat{\mathcal{S}}^\tau_V[\![S]\!]\}$$

⦅since all states involved in $\langle \ell, \rho \rangle \in \widehat{\mathcal{S}}^{\tau}_{\mathsf{V}}[\![\mathsf{Sl}']\!]$ have $\ell \in \mathsf{labs}[\![\mathsf{Sl}']\!]$ and similarly all states involved in $\langle \ell, \rho \rangle \in \widehat{\mathcal{S}}^{\tau}_{\mathsf{V}}[\![\mathsf{S}]\!]$ have $\ell \in \mathsf{labs}[\![\mathsf{S}]\!]$ and $\pi_0 = \pi'_0 \in \mathsf{I}[\![\mathsf{Sl}]\!] = \mathsf{I}[\![\mathsf{Sl}']\!]$ so that $\mathsf{labs}[\![\mathsf{Sl}']\!] \cap \mathsf{labs}[\![\mathsf{S}]\!] = \{\mathsf{aft}[\![\mathsf{Sl}']\!]\} = \{\mathsf{at}[\![\mathsf{S}]\!]\}$ implies that the first transitions in $\pi'_0 \cdot \cdots \cdot \pi'_{n'}$ from $\pi_0 = \pi'_0$ must be transitions in $\widehat{\mathcal{S}}^{\tau}_{\mathsf{V}}[\![\mathsf{Sl}']\!]$.

Then there are two cases. The first case is when $\pi'_0 \cdots \pi'_{n'}$ never reaches a final state of $\pi'_{n'} \neq \pi''_0$ of Sl' so that $\pi'_0 \cdots \pi'_{n'} = \pi_0 \cdots \pi_n$. Otherwise, a final state $\pi'_{n'} = \pi''_0$ is reached for which $\ell = \mathsf{aft}[\![\mathsf{Sl}']\!] = \mathsf{at}[\![\mathsf{S}]\!]$ so $\pi'_0 \cdot \cdots \cdot \pi'_{n'} \frown \pi''_0 \cdot \cdots \cdot \pi''_m = \pi_0 \cdots \cdot \pi_n$ since after $\pi'_{n'} = \pi''_0$ the transitions in $\pi''_0 \cdot \cdots \cdot \pi''_m$, if any when $m > 0$, must belong to $\widehat{\mathcal{S}}^{\tau}_{\mathsf{V}}[\![\mathsf{S}]\!]$. Both cases includes the empty statement list $\mathsf{Sl}' ::= \epsilon$ for which $n' = 0$⦆

$= \mathcal{S}^*_{\mathsf{V}}[\![\mathsf{Sl}']\!] \cup \{\pi \cdot \langle \mathsf{at}[\![\mathsf{S}]\!], \rho \rangle \cdot \pi' \mid \pi \cdot \langle \mathsf{at}[\![\mathsf{S}]\!], \rho \rangle \in \mathcal{S}^*_{\mathsf{V}}[\![\mathsf{Sl}']\!] \wedge \langle \mathsf{at}[\![\mathsf{S}]\!], \rho \rangle \cdot \pi' \in \mathcal{S}^*_{\mathsf{V}}[\![\mathsf{S}]\!]\}$ ⦅ind. hyp.⦆

$= \mathcal{S}^*_{\mathsf{V}}[\![\mathsf{Sl}]\!]$ ⦅(7)⦆ $\quad\square$

— For the iteration statement $\mathsf{S} ::= \mathtt{while}\,\ell\,(\mathsf{B})\,\mathsf{S}_b$, we use the fact the prefix traces with entry label $\ell = \mathsf{at}[\![\mathsf{S}]\!] = \mathsf{aft}[\![\mathsf{S}_b]\!]$ have the form

$$\pi(n)\pi'(n) \in \widehat{\mathcal{S}}^*_{\mathsf{V}}[\![\mathsf{S}]\!] \tag{31}$$

where

— $\pi(n) \triangleq \left(\langle \ell, \rho_i \rangle \xrightarrow{\;B\;} \langle \mathsf{at}[\![\mathsf{S}_b]\!], \rho_i \rangle \pi(i) \langle \ell, \rho_{i+1} \rangle \right)_{i=1}^{n-1}$ is the trace of the first $n \geqslant 0$ iterations (reduced to $\langle \ell, \rho_0 \rangle$ for $n = 0$) such that $\forall i \in [1, n-1]$. $\left(\langle \mathsf{at}[\![\mathsf{S}_b]\!], \rho_i \rangle \pi(i) \langle \ell, \rho_{i+1} \rangle \right)_{i=1}^{n-1}$ is the maximal finite trace of the i-th iteration in the loop body S_b;

— $\ell\pi'(n)$ traces the prefix execution of the n-th iteration in the loop body S_b or a loop exit, so

$\ell\pi'(n) \in \{\langle \ell, \rho_n \rangle\} \cup \{\langle \ell, \rho_n \rangle \xrightarrow{\;B\;} \langle \mathsf{at}[\![\mathsf{S}_b]\!], \rho_n \rangle \mid \mathcal{B}[\![\mathsf{B}]\!]\rho_n = \mathsf{tt}\}$

$\cup \{\langle \ell, \rho_n \rangle \xrightarrow{\;\neg(\mathsf{B})\;} \langle \mathsf{aft}[\![\mathsf{S}]\!], \rho_n \rangle \mid \mathcal{B}[\![\mathsf{B}]\!]\rho_n = \mathsf{ff}\}$

$\cup \{\langle \ell, \rho_n \rangle \xrightarrow{\;B\;} \langle \mathsf{at}[\![\mathsf{S}_b]\!], \rho_n \rangle \pi''(n) \mid$

$\qquad \mathcal{B}[\![\mathsf{B}]\!]\rho_n = \mathsf{tt} \wedge \langle \ell, \rho_n \rangle \xrightarrow{\;B\;} \langle \mathsf{at}[\![\mathsf{S}_b]\!], \rho_n \rangle \pi''(n) \in \widehat{\mathcal{S}}^*_{\mathsf{V}}[\![\mathsf{S}_b]\!]\}$

$\cup \{\langle \ell, \rho_n \rangle \xrightarrow{\;B\;} \langle \mathsf{at}[\![\mathsf{S}_b]\!], \rho_n \rangle \pi_3 \xrightarrow{\;\mathtt{break}\;} \langle \mathsf{brk\text{-}to}[\![\mathsf{S}]\!], \rho_m \rangle \mid \mathcal{B}[\![\mathsf{B}]\!]\rho_n = \mathsf{tt} \wedge$

$\qquad \langle \mathsf{at}[\![\mathsf{S}_b]\!], \rho_n \rangle \pi_3 \xrightarrow{\;\mathtt{break}\;} \langle \mathsf{brk\text{-}to}[\![\mathsf{S}]\!], \rho_m \rangle \in \widehat{\mathcal{S}}^*_{\mathsf{V}}[\![\mathsf{S}_b]\!]\}$

Obviously the traces in (31) can be generated by the transition system.

Conversely, let $\langle \ell_0, \rho_0 \rangle \cdots \langle \ell_n, \rho_n \rangle$ be a trace generated by the transition system for an iteration S so that $\ell_0 = \mathsf{at}[\![\mathsf{S}]\!]$. By reductio ad absurdum, let $k < n$ such that $\langle \ell_0, \rho_0 \rangle \cdots \langle \ell_k, \rho_k \rangle$ is in $\mathcal{S}^*_{\mathsf{V}}[\![\mathsf{S}]\!]$ but $\langle \ell_0, \rho_0 \rangle \cdots \langle \ell_k, \rho_k \rangle \langle \ell_{k+1}, \rho_{k+1} \rangle$ is not. By recurrence, there exists $\pi_k \ell_k$ such that $\rho_k = \varrho(\pi_0\ell_0 \frown \pi_k\ell_k)$. Since we have the transition $\langle \ell_k, \rho_k \rangle \rightarrow \langle \ell_{k+1}, \rho_{k+1} \rangle$ there is one statement S' in Section 9 from which this transition comes from such that $\ell_k \in \mathsf{labs}[\![s']\!]$. The contradiction is that a similar step is possible in $\in \mathcal{S}_V^*[\![s]\!]$. We have to go on by considering all possible cases for s'. Since the reasoning is similar for all these cases, let us consider the typical cases (26) and (28).

In case (26), ℓ_k is at an assignment statement $s' ::= \ell\ \mathsf{x} = \mathsf{A}\ \mathsf{;}$. Because of unicity of the labelling, the transition $\langle \ell_k, \rho_k \rangle \longrightarrow \langle \ell_{k+1}, \rho_{k+1} \rangle$ in (26) cannot come from any other statement. The contradiction is that (2) provides a transition in $\mathcal{S}_V^*[\![s]\!]$ that abstracts to the desired transition $\langle \ell_k, \rho_k \rangle \longrightarrow \langle \ell_{k+1}, \rho_{k+1} \rangle$.

The reasoning is the same in case (28) for $\{\langle \ell, \rho \rangle \longrightarrow \langle \mathsf{aft}[\![s]\!], \rho \rangle \mid \mathcal{B}[\![\mathsf{B}]\!]\rho = \mathsf{ff}\}$ and $\{\langle \ell, \rho \rangle \longrightarrow \langle \mathsf{at}[\![s_b]\!], \rho \rangle \mid \mathcal{B}[\![\mathsf{B}]\!]\rho = \mathsf{tt}\}$. Otherwise, $\ell_k \in \mathsf{labs}[\![s_b]\!]$ and we consider recursively the contradiction within $s' = \widehat{\mathcal{S}}_V^\tau[\![s_b]\!]$. The reasoning is the same for the float interval semantics.   □

It follows from Th. 2 that we could have followed the traditional way of defining a small-step operational semantics by first postulating the transition semantics of Section 9, then deriving the stateful prefix trace semantics by (24), and finally deriving the maximal trace semantics by taking limits as in (9) and (10).

10   Conclusion

Dynamic interval analysis can be extended to ball analysis (also known as midpoint-radius interval arithmetic) [39,40].

Most applications of dynamic interval analysis involve tests (including the loop condition) on intervals but consider only the deterministic case where only one branch is taken. For example interval libraries raise an exception when more than one alternative should be taken in tests [2]. This can be understood as a trivial widening to all possible continuations after the test. When expressed as a transition system, the choice can be implemented *e.g.* by backtracking, which is natural in logic or constraint programming [35,36,38].

Our formalization of the float interval semantics as an abstraction of the real semantics uses an approximation preorder $\overset{\circ}{\sqsubseteq}{}^i$ different from the fixpoint ordering $\subseteq$ (also called computational ordering). This is a rare example in abstract interpretation with [9,34].

Dynamic interval analysis is different from other instrumented dynamic analyses for runtime verification [1,12,21,22] in that it does collect interval information upon executions, but does not check the collected information against a specification. Instead it replaces that execution (on reals or floats) by another one (on float intervals).

More generally, runtime verification of single executions collects information on the execution to check the execution against a formal specification, or to protect against errors [23]. Since only safety properties can be checked at runtime, this instrumented semantics can be formalized by abstract interpretation of the program prefix trace semantics $\mathcal{S}_V^*[\![s]\!]$.

- The abstraction $\alpha_h(\pi_0 \cdots \pi_n) \in \mathbb{D}$ instruments the prefix $\pi_0 \cdots \pi_n$ of a trace π in a domain $\mathbb{D}$;

- The instrumented trace $\alpha_h(\pi) \triangleq \langle \pi_0, \alpha_h(\pi_0) \rangle \langle \pi_1, \alpha_h(\pi_0 \pi_1) \rangle \langle \pi_2, \alpha_h(\pi_0 \pi_1 \pi_2) \rangle \cdots$ $\langle \pi_n, \alpha_h(\pi_0 \pi_1 \cdots \pi_n) \rangle \cdots$ on states $\mathbb{S}^h \triangleq \mathbb{S}_\mathbb{V} \times \mathbb{D}$ collects this information during execution;

- The instrumented semantics is $\mathcal{S}^h[\![s]\!] \triangleq \alpha_h(\mathcal{S}^*_\mathbb{V}[\![s]\!]) \in \wp(\mathbb{S}^{h^+})$ where $\alpha_h(\Pi) \triangleq \{\alpha_h(\pi) \mid \pi \in \Pi\}$ is the set of instrumented traces of the semantics $\mathcal{S}^*_\mathbb{V}[\![s]\!] \in \wp(\mathbb{S}^+)$. It follows that $\langle \wp(\mathbb{S}^+), \subseteq \rangle \xrightleftharpoons[\alpha_h]{\gamma_h} \langle \wp(\mathbb{S}^{h^+}), \subseteq \rangle$.

We have provided the example of interval arithmetics. Another example would compute with float and collect rounding errors to guard against meaningless computations. An execution involving integers would collect their minimum and maximum values.

Moreover, the instrumented semantics must be checked by providing

- a specification S (such as an invariant, temporal logic, etc.);
- A specification abstraction $\langle \wp(\mathbb{S}^{h^+}), \subseteq \rangle \xrightleftharpoons[\alpha_S]{\gamma_S} \langle \mathbb{B}, \Leftarrow \rangle$ into Booleans checking that the specification is satisfied at runtime. In practice abstraction providing more information than a binary decision would be preferable.

The best dynamic analysis semantics $\mathcal{S}^d[\![s]\!]$ is then $\mathcal{S}^d[\![s]\!] \triangleq \alpha_S(\alpha_h(\mathcal{S}[\![s]\!]))$. An instrumented dynamic analysis can be directly derived from the instrumented semantics by considering a single execution at a time.

An example would be the specification of bounds for integer variables in a language like Pascal. The best dynamic analysis semantics $\mathcal{S}^d[\![s]\!]$ is implemented by runtime checks.

It might be that $\alpha_S(\alpha_h(\mathcal{S}[\![s]\!]))$ is not computable or too expensive to compute. An example is regular model checking [5] where executions are monitored by a regular expression specifying sequences of invariants (and more generally any temporal logic specification can be handled as in [5]).

In that case, what can define an approximation preorder $\overset{\circ}{\sqsubseteq}^i$ (allowing for approximate instrumentation and check) and soundness would then be $\alpha_S(\alpha_h(\mathcal{S}[\![s]\!]))$ $\overset{\circ}{\sqsubseteq}^i \mathcal{S}^d[\![s]\!]$. For example, verification by regular model checking [5] would become debugging by bounding executions or ignoring some checks.

By deriving the transition system from the instrumented checking semantics $\mathcal{S}^d[\![s]\!]$, we have a formal specification of the code to be generated for the runtime analysis, thus paving the way for certified runtime analysis (similar to certified compilation [27] or certified static analysis [26]). Notice that trace abstractions are more general than simulations [28]. Notice that trace abstractions are more general than simulations [28] for such correctness proofs.

A static analysis would be derived by a further finitary abstraction of all executions defined by the instrumented semantics $\alpha_h(\mathcal{S}[\![s]\!])$ (e.g. using extrapolators and interpolators [4] or abstraction into Noetherian abstract domains).

The reduced product of the static and dynamic semantics would formalize the idea that the dynamic semantics can be simplified thanks to a preliminary static analysis. A single execution of this reduced product would certainly be more efficient since some runtime tests would have been eliminated in the reduced product. For the integer interval example, this would definitely reduce the number of runtime checks.

Acknowledgement. This work was supported in part by NSF Grant CNS-1446511. Any opinions, findings, and conclusions or recommendations expressed in this material are those of the author and do not necessarily reflect the views of the National Science Foundation.

References

1. Bartocci, E., Falcone, Y., Francalanza, A., Reger, G.: Introduction to runtime verification. In: Lectures on Runtime Verification. Lecture Notes in Computer Science, vol. 10457, pp. 1–33. Springer (2018)
2. Brönnimann, H., Melquiond, G., Pion, S.: The design of the Boost interval arithmetic library. Theor. Comput. Sci. **351**(1), 111–118 (2006)
3. Cousot, P.: The calculational design of a generic abstract interpreter. In: Broy, M., Steinbrüggen, R. (eds.) Calculational System Design. NATO ASI Series F. IOS Press (1999)
4. Cousot, P.: Abstracting induction by extrapolation and interpolation. In: VMCAI. Lecture Notes in Computer Science, vol. 8931, pp. 19–42. Springer (2015)
5. Cousot, P.: Calculational design of a regular model checker by abstract interpretation. In: ICTAC 2019. Lecture Notes in Computer Science, vol. 11884, pp. 3–21. Springer (2019)
6. Cousot, P., Cousot, R.: Abstract interpretation: A unified lattice model for static analysis of programs by construction or approximation of fixpoints. In: POPL. pp. 238–252. ACM (1977)
7. Cousot, P., Cousot, R.: Constructive versions of Tarski's fixed point theorems. Pacific Journal of Mathematics **82**(1), 43–57 (1979)
8. Cousot, P., Cousot, R.: Systematic design of program analysis frameworks. In: POPL. pp. 269–282. ACM Press (1979)
9. Cousot, P., Cousot, R.: Galois connection based abstract interpretations for strictness analysis (invited paper). In: Formal Methods in Programming and Their Applications. Lecture Notes in Computer Science, vol. 735, pp. 98–127. Springer (1993)
10. Damouche, N., Martel, M., Chapoutot, A.: Numerical program optimisation by automatic improvement of the accuracy of computations. IJIEI **6**(1/2), 115–145 (2018)
11. Delmas, D., Éric Goubault, Putot, S., Souyris, J., Tekkal, K., Védrine, F.: Towards an industrial use of FLUCTUAT on safety–critical avionics software. In: FMICS. Lecture Notes in Computer Science, vol. 5825, pp. 53–69. Springer (2009)
12. Falcone, Y., Havelund, K., Reger, G.: A tutorial on runtime verification. In: Broy, M., Peled, D., Kalus, G. (eds.) Engineering Dependable Software Systems, NATO Science for Peace and Security Series, D: Information and Communication Security, vol. 34, pp. 141–175. IOS Press (2013)
13. Ghorbal, K., Éric Goubault, Putot, S.: The zonotope abstract domain Taylor1+. In: CAV. Lecture Notes in Computer Science, vol. 5643, pp. 627–633. Springer (2009)
14. Goldberg, D.: What every computer scientist should know about floating–point arithmetic. ACM Comput. Surv. **23**(1), 5–48 (1991)
15. Éric Goubault, Putot, S.: Static analysis of numerical algorithms. In: SAS. Lecture Notes in Computer Science, vol. 4134, pp. 18–34. Springer (2006)

16. Éric Goubault, Putot, S.: A zonotopic framework for functional abstractions. Formal Methods in System Design **47**(3), 302–360 (2015)
17. Éric Goubault, Putot, S.: Inner and outer reachability for the verification of control systems. In: HSCC. pp. 11–22. ACM (2019)
18. Éric Goubault, Putot, S., Baufreton, P., Gassino, J.: Static analysis of the accuracy in control systems: Principles and experiments. In: FMICS. Lecture Notes in Computer Science, vol. 4916, pp. 3–20. Springer (2007)
19. Éric Goubault, Putot, S., Sahlmann, L.: Inner and outer approximating flowpipes for delay differential equations. In: CAV (2). Lecture Notes in Computer Science, vol. 10982, pp. 523–541. Springer (2018)
20. Éric Goubault, Putot, S., Védrine, F.: Modular static analysis with zonotopes. In: SAS. Lecture Notes in Computer Science, vol. 7460, pp. 24–40. Springer (2012)
21. Havelund, K., Goldberg, A.: Verify your runs. In: VSTTE. Lecture Notes in Computer Science, vol. 4171, pp. 374–383. Springer (2005)
22. Havelund, K., Reger, G., Rosu, G.: Runtime verification past experiences and future projections. In: Computing and Software Science. Lecture Notes in Computer Science, vol. 10000, pp. 532–562. Springer (2019)
23. Havelund, K., Rosu, G.: Runtime verification - 17 years later. In: RV. Lecture Notes in Computer Science, vol. 11237, pp. 3–17. Springer (2018)
24. IEEE: IEEE Standard for Binary Floating–Point Arithmetic. American National Standards Institute and Institute of Electrical and Electronic Engineers, ANSI/IEEE Standard 754-1985 (1985)
25. Isaacson, E., Keller, H.B.: Analysis of Numerical Methods. Dover Books on Mathematics (1994)
26. Jourdan, J.H., Laporte, V., Blazy, S., Leroy, X., Pichardie, D.: A formally–verified C static analyzer. In: POPL. pp. 247–259. ACM (2015)
27. Leroy, X.: Formal verification of a realistic compiler. Commun. ACM **52**(7), 107–115 (2009)
28. Leroy, X.: Formally verifying a compiler: What does it mean, exactly? In: ICALP. LIPIcs, vol. 55, pp. 2:1–2:1. Schloss Dagstuhl – Leibniz–Zentrum für Informatik (2016), (Slides at `https://xavierleroy.org/talks/ICALP2016.pdf`)
29. Martel, M.: Rangelab: A static–analyzer to bound the accuracy of finite–precision computations. In: SYNASC. pp. 118–122. IEEE Computer Society (2011)
30. Monniaux, D.: The pitfalls of verifying floating–point computations. ACM Trans. Program. Lang. Syst. **30**(3), 12:1–12:41 (2008)
31. Moore, R.E.: Interval Analysis. Prentice Hall (1966)
32. Moore, R.E.: Methods and Applications of Interval Analysis. SIAM Studies in Applied Mathematics, SIAM (1995)
33. Moore, R.E., Kearfott, R.B., Cloud, M.J.: Introduction to Interval Analysis. Society for Industrial and Applied Mathematics (Mar 2009)
34. Mycroft, A.: The theory and practice of transforming call–by–need into call–by–value. In: Symposium on Programming. Lecture Notes in Computer Science, vol. 83, pp. 269–281. Springer (1980)
35. Older, W.J.: CLP (intervals). ACM Comput. Surv. **28**(4es), 71 (1996)
36. Older, W.J., Vellino, A.: Constraint arithmetic on real intervals. In: WCLP. pp. 175–195. MIT Press (1991)
37. Overton, M.L.: Numerical Computing with IEEE Floating Point Arithmetic – Including One Theorem, One Rule of Thumb, and One Hundred and One Exercices. SIAM (2001)

38. Truchet, C., Christie, M., Normand, J.M.: A tabu search method for interval constraints. In: CPAIOR. Lecture Notes in Computer Science, vol. 5015, pp. 372–376. Springer (2008)
39. Van Der Hoeven, J.: Ball arithmetic. In: Beckmann, A., Gaßner, C., Löwe, B. (eds.) International Workshop on Logical Approaches to Barriers in Computing and Complexity, pp. 179—208. No. 6 in Preprint–Reihe Mathematik, Ernst–Moritz–Arndt–Universität Greifswald (2010)
40. Van Der Hoeven, J., Lecerf, G.: Evaluating straight–line programs over balls. In: ARITH. pp. 142–149. IEEE Computer Society (2016)
41. Winskel, G.: A note on powerdomains and modality. In: FCT. Lecture Notes in Computer Science, vol. 158, pp. 505–514. Springer (1983)

Runtime Verification

Runtime Verification: Passing on the Baton

Christian Colombo[1]([✉]) [iD], Gordon J. Pace[1]([✉]), and Gerardo Schneider[2]([✉]) [iD]

[1] University of Malta, Msida, Malta
christian.colombo@um.edu.mt, gordon.pace@um.edu.mt
[2] University of Gothenburg, Gothenburg, Sweden
gersch@chalmers.se

Abstract. Twenty years have passed since the first workshop on runtime verification—the area has grown and evolved with hundreds of papers published and a sizeable number of mature tools developed. In a special occasion like this it is good to look back, but it is also good to look forward to the future. In this paper, we outline a very brief history of runtime verification, and propose a way of passing the knowledge down to future generations of academics and industry practitioners in the form of a roadmap for teaching runtime verification. The proposal, based on our experience, not only equips students with the fundamental theory underpinning runtime verification, but also ensures they have the required skills to engineer it into industrial systems. Our hope is that this would increase uptake and eventually give rise to the establishment of industry-grade tools.

1 Introduction

The field of *runtime verification* (RV) is a relatively new research area within formal methods that complements classical static (and usually exhaustive) verification techniques such as static analysis, model checking and theorem proving, as well as dynamic techniques like testing. Runtime verification is a *dynamic* technique, i.e., it is used while running the system or to analyse real executions of the system. Runtime verification has a more practical approach than static techniques in the sense that analysing a *single* (as opposed to all) execution trace of a system (usually the current execution) is significantly more manageable.

Researchers in the area have taken different takes on the exact definition of runtime verification: sometimes it is also referred to as runtime monitoring, trace analysis, dynamic analysis, etc. That said, the idea of using *verification* in its name implies a notion of correctness with respect to some predefined property.

Despite the variations in the runtime verification community regarding terminology and scope, there are at least two things researchers in the area agree on. First, the runtime verification field (as a community) grew out of the mainstream formal verification one starting from the RV workshop established in

2001[1] which was organised by Klaus Havelund and Grigore Rosu.[2] In fact, the term *runtime verification* was first introduced as the name of that workshop. Second, a key person responsible for making the area what it is today was Klaus Havelund[3] and indeed, Havelund presented a number of papers (co-authored with Rosu and Giannakopoulou) in 2001 on the new, and still unnamed, area of runtime verification [HR01a, HR01b, GH01].

In this paper, written for Klaus Havelund's 65-year *Festschrift*, we focus on how the *RV baton* has been passed since the beginning of the area, via successive scientific results, and how we can pass it on to future generations via teaching. We provide a very brief overview of some historical facts on RV, and present a roadmap for teaching runtime verification. One of the main reasons for choosing this as a topic for such an occasion is that Havelund has, since the very beginning of his research in runtime verification, been interested in promoting the area via numerous talks at conferences and tutorials in summer and winter schools.

Despite the fact that runtime verification has frequently been touted as being industry-friendly, and to have a low barrier to entry, uptake in industrial projects is surprisingly rare. And although one finds many features of runtime verification used in the industry, whether it is in the form of assertions or that of behavioural sanity checks, what is rare is the adoption of the whole philosophy of separation-of-concerns between specification and implementation. From our experience, the more sophisticated specification techniques, e.g., state transition models, are mostly used as ex ante *drivers* for design and development, and not as ex post *oracles* for ensuring correctness. One of the most positive outcomes of projects with industry partners we have had was that aspects of the notion of monitoring of complex properties and specifications spilled over into in-house tools and internal procedures—either in the form of sanity checking executed on data collected in log files, or in the form of internal logic to ensure the well-formedness of runtime behaviour of objects.

There are different paths which can be taken when designing a course on runtime verification. One can go for a primary focus on the theoretical foundations of the discipline or one can take a more pragmatic, hands-on approach and dedicate a substantial part of the course on exposing tools and their design to the students. In an ideal world, one would cover both bases, however, with limited time one has to determine a primary (if not sole) focus. With the discipline being rooted in formal methods and elements of theoretical computer science, we have noted that often the focus many take when lecturing runtime verification is primarily a theoretical one, with a practical element using a (usually in-house) runtime verification tool to illustrate the concepts. Alas, given that there are no standard runtime verification tools yet which the industry has adopted, and given that academic tools are, by their very nature, typically not sufficiently dependable to be used in the real-world, we found that the content

---

[1] http://www.runtime-verification.org/rv2001.

[2] The workshop was held for many years till it became a conference in 2010 [BFF+10]; the conference has held every year since then.

[3] https://www.havelund.com/.

of the course rarely spilled into the students' working life after completing their degree programme.

In this context, going beyond the use of an existing tool and providing the students with deeper understanding of design issues arising when building a runtime verification tool, has the foreseen advantage that ideas and principles from the field of runtime verification can slowly permeate into industrial projects through the development of in-house libraries and tools. This is the approach we advocate in this paper.

This paper is organised as follows: We first provide a high-level introduction to RV including a brief history of the area in Sect. 2. Next, in Sect. 3, we outline the main topics of a proposed hands-on course on runtime verification. This is followed by an account on our experience of teaching various instances of the course in Sect. 4 and we conclude in Sect. 5.

2 Runtime Verification: A Very Brief Introduction and History

This section is divided in three subsections. We first discuss what is runtime verification and its connection with monitoring. The second part is concerned with the concept of monitorability from a historical perspective. We finally give a very brief historical overview of the development of the area.

2.1 On Runtime Verification and Monitoring

The term *runtime verification* appears to have been used for the first time in 2001 as the name of a workshop, *RV'01—First Workshop on Runtime Verification*, organised by Klaus Havelund and Grigore Rosu. According to Havelund et al. [HRR19]: *"[our] initial interest in RV started around 2000 [...] Our initial efforts were inspired by Doron Drusinky's Temporal Rover system [30] for monitoring temporal logic properties, and by the company Compaq's work on predictive data race and deadlock detection algorithms [36]."*[4]

But what is runtime verification? There are many slightly different definitions in the literature and researchers use one or the other depending on their own personal views or on the aspect they want to emphasise. For our purposes we take here the definition given by Leucker [Leu11]:

> *Runtime verification* is the discipline of computer science that deals with the study, development, and application of those verification techniques that allow checking whether a run of a system under scrutiny (SUS) satisfies or violates a given correctness property. Its distinguishing research effort lies in synthesising monitors from high level specifications.

Given a crucial component in runtime verification is the concept of *monitoring*, one may wonder what the big deal is about this new area; after all

---

[4] In this paper, reference [30] appears as [Dru00], and reference [36] as [Har00].

monitoring techniques have been around for a very long time and used before 2000—if not by the formal methods community, then by computer scientists in other research communities and by practitioners. Indeed, we are all familiar with *monitoring programs* we execute in our computers to let us know which processes are running and how much CPU they are using, etc.

Even though monitoring is indeed a very central element in runtime verification, we may say that runtime verification goes beyond simply observing a system's behaviour. Is thus "monitoring" a part of runtime verification, or *vice versa*? You can see it in both ways depending on your own choice of use of terms. If monitoring is seen as a generic term for having a program that interacts (runs in parallel) with the SUS, then runtime verification could be considered a particular case where such "interaction" is determined by observing events and flagging whether a property (encapsulated in the monitor) is satisfied or violated. On the other hand, runtime verification may be seen as a general area of which monitoring is a specific subarea (a particular case where the monitor just observes and accepts all executions of the SUS).

Different runtime verification researchers have (historically) used different terms for different things in different ways, and although taxonomies have been proposed e.g. [FKRT18], one still does not find uniform use in the literature. For the sake of this paper, we distinguish between the following different kinds of monitoring activity:

Observers are monitors that collect information from the SUS. This collection (logging events) might be done for different purposes, most of the time for *a posteriori* analysis to: perform statistics, identify faults, identify security breaches, assign blame (e.g., for legal reasons), etc.

Verifiers are monitors that encapsulate a verification property. Verifiers may be written to detect satisfaction or violations of the given property.

Reaction injectors handle the introduction of additional logic into the SUS at points when the verifier matches a specification. This has been used in a variety of ways in the literature, which can be categorised broadly as follows:

> **Enforcers** are reactions intended to enforce a given property. They usually act by intercepting events observed, identifying when a violation might occur, and modifying them (or more rarely modifying the system state) so the property is not violated.

> **Controllers** are reactions directly affecting the SUS meant to introduce new behaviour. Depending on observed events, the reaction logic would ensure that the SUS behaves in specific ways.[5] This approach includes monitoring-oriented programming in which the controller may introduce completely new features to the SUS.

> **Reparators** are reactions used for when the system has already violated a given property so, for instance, noting unexpected behaviour by a user,

---

[5] One may prefer the term *actuators* instead in order to not confuse it with the controllers as used in the controller synthesis research area (they have similar purpose but we are not here concerned with synthesising controllers that are correct for *all* executions of the SUS).

the reparators may disable that user in order to allow for further investigation before proceeding. In a way, reparations can be seen as enforcers running late (or enforcers as reparations running early), but there still lies a difference in that the former tries to fix what already went wrong, while the latter redirects behaviour to avoid what is still to happen.

Compensators are a specific form of reparation in which the additional logic will keep track of recent behaviour of the SUS so that, if a violation occurs, recent behaviour can be undone in order to restore the SUS to a sane state. For instance, if a financial transaction is decomposed into smaller sub-transactions, if a later one fails, violating the property, the effect of the earlier ones is undone.

The prevalent view in the runtime verification community is that monitors and verification logic should not be programmed directly, but should rather be extracted from (semi-) formal descriptions. This is even the case for observers, as we might be interested in events in a particular context, or ones which happen when a particular property is satisfied.[6]

So, in runtime verification we usually follow the steps below:

1. Choosing a suitable (formal) specification language;
2. Specifying (un)desired system behaviour;
3. Generating an event-listening monitor from the specification;
4. Synthesising the event verification algorithm;
5. Connecting a monitor to the SUS;
6. Analysing the verdict of the monitor, if suitable;
7. Triggering a reaction of a fitting kind, if applicable.

2.2   On the Concept of Monitorability

Another, related but somehow orthogonal aspect, is the question: What can(not) be monitored? This plays the same role as *decidability* in more standard formal verification. In the runtime verification community, this is called *monitorability*.

The first definition of monitorability was given by Kim et al. [KKL+02], where the objective of monitoring was set only to detect violations of safety properties over infinite executions.

Pnueli and Zaks [PZ06] generalised the notion of monitorability, for both acceptance and violations of LTL formulae. The idea is that the purpose of a monitor is to determine whether every (possibly infinite) continuation of the current execution is a model or a counter-example of the monitored property: A monitor should thus give a definite verdict as soon as one is possible.

Additional results concerning monitorability were later presented by Bauer et al. [BLS07,BLS11], where it was shown that the set of monitorable LTL properties is a superset of the union of safety and co-safety properties, and

---

[6] There are exceptions though. For instance, if the observer monitor just logs *all* events in the execution trace, there is no need to write any formal specification.

Falcone et al. showed that it is a superset of the set of obligation properties [FFM09,FFM12].

More recently, Havelund and Peled [HP18] introduced a finer-grained taxonomy of monitorable properties, among other things distinguishing between *always* finitely satisfiable (or refutable), and *sometimes* finitely satisfiable where only some prefixes are required to be monitorable (for satisfaction). They also presented a connection between monitorability and classical safety properties.

Monitorability for hyperproperties, i.e., properties over sets of sets of traces, in particular for HyperLTL [CFK+14], was first studied in [AB16]. This was later generalised to the full fragment of alternation-free formulas using formula rewriting [BSB17], which can also monitor alternating formulas but only with respect to a fixed finite set of finite traces.

In more recent work, Stucki et al. [SSSB19] presented richer definitions of monitorability for both trace- and hyper-properties, including the possibility of making use of information from the system being monitored (an approach they call *grey-box monitoring*). Gray-box monitoring combines static analysis/verification and runtime verification, enabling the monitoring of properties that are non-monitorable in a black-box manner. This new taxonomy of monitorability generalises over previous definitions given in the literature, including that of Havelund and Peled mentioned above, and it also covers the computability limitations of monitors as programs, not expressed in previous definitions.

2.3   A Very Brief History of Runtime Verification

Now that we have given some definitions (and intuition) about runtime verification and discussed the notions of monitorability, we give a very brief (non-exhaustive and without much detail) synthetic account on some historical developments in runtime verification.

What can be considered to be the first runtime verification paper appeared in the RV'01 workshop as mentioned above. Havelund and Rosu [HR01a] presented a general framework for analysing execution traces based on LTL specifications (only with future operators first, extended with past later), embodied in the Java PathExplorer, JPaX. The limitations of the framework, most notably the lack of data handling, were addressed by Havelund and other colleagues in the years that followed. Two such extensions appeared in 2003–2004: MOP [CR03] and EAGLE [BGHS04], supporting the monitoring of events with data, and allowing user-defined temporal operators (using a logic similar to linear time μ-calculus). One year later, the HAWK system was developed, described by the authors as *"an attempt to tie EAGLE to the monitoring of Java programs with automated code instrumentation using aspect-oriented programming, specifically AspectJ"*.

The idea of using four-valued semantics (introduced in [Dru00]) was used by Leucker and colleagues in the context of runtime verification in 2007 [BLS07]. The main motivation was that models of classical temporal logic formulae are usually infinite streams of events, whereas at runtime, we are mostly concerned with finite (prefixes of) traces, and the partial observation needs to give inconclusive verdicts. That paper introduced a four-valued semantics for LTL over finite traces extending the classical LTL semantics.

In 2008, Havelund et al. investigated the use of monitors *as* aspects [HRR19]: *"In previous solutions (such as HAWK and MOP) we have seen monitors translated to aspects. A more radical approach is to take the view that monitors are aspects. [...] An (unfinished) attempt in this direction was XspeC [50], designed to be an extension of ACC (an aspect-oriented programming framework for C) with data parameterised monitoring using state machines."*[7] This idea is echoed in the proposition of an AspectJ extension enabling the detection of race conditions at runtime [BH10].

The same year, Chen et al. [CSR08] developed a *predictive* runtime analysis technique to "predict" concurrency errors that did not happen in the observed execution but which could have happened under a different thread scheduling. The approach was implemented in the tool jPredictor for Java.

In two subsequent articles published in 2008 and 2009 Colombo et al. proposed an automata-based approach to runtime verification, based on symbolic automata with stopwatches (the specification language was called DATE: Dynamic Automata with Timers and Events) [CPS08, CPS09a]. The approach was implemented into the LARVA tool [CPS09b] targeting Java programs (using AspectJ for the instrumentation).

In 2012 Zhang et al. provided a predictive semantics for runtime verification monitors [ZLD12], which was used later in 2016 by Pinisetty et al. to produce a predictive enforcement mechanism: by using *a priori* knowledge of the system some events could be produced faster in order to allow for earlier verdicts [PPT+16].

Another automaton-based runtime verification approach was proposed in 2012 by Barringer et al. [BFH+12]: Quantified Event Automata (QEA) are automata supporting quantification over data.

Runtime verification has been applied to one of the recent trends in verification and security: Hyperproperties. In 2017 Finkbeiner et al. [FHST17] proposed an automaton-based algorithm for monitoring HyperLTL, also for formulas with quantifier alternation, but for a fixed trace set. The complexity of monitoring different fragments of HyperLTL was studied in detail in [BF18].

One of the areas still in development is the combination of runtime verification with other validation and verification techniques. Bodden et al.'s pioneering work in the combination of static and dynamic analysis was embodied in their tool Clara [BL10], followed up by other such as Chimento et al.'s approach to combine control- and data-oriented properties for deductive analysis and runtime verification [CAPS15, ACPS17] and Azzopardi et al.'s work to address static analysis with symbolic state [ACP17].

In recent years, runtime verification has also been combined with testing in different ways e.g. [CAS18, CCF+16, DLT13]. For other (later) developments (log analysis, DSLs, etc.), see the accounts in [HR18, HRR19], and for the use of runtime verification beyond software see [SSA+19].

---

[7] Reference [50] in the quote appears as [HW08] here.

Since 2014, besides continuing with the RV yearly conference, the community has also been coordinating an International Competition on Runtime Verification (CRV) [BFB+19], with the aim to compare and evaluate runtime verification tools. During the period December 2014 till December 2018, the European scientific network for the COoperation in Science and Technology (COST) on Runtime Verification beyond Monitoring (ARVI) was approved, funded within the European Horizon 2020 framework programme.[8] ARVI included scientists from 26 European countries and Australia. Besides workshops and meetings, the ARVI COST Action organised a series of Graduate Schools on runtime verification, where top researchers in runtime verification, including Klaus Havelund, have given lectures and tutorials.

See Havelund's two retrospective papers [HR18,HRR19] on his own (and his co-authors') account on the historical context and research development based on his own contributions to runtime verification. For a taxonomy of runtime verification see, for instance [Leu11,FKRT18].

In the rest of the paper we present a roadmap to instruct new (under)graduate students in computer science in this exciting and still growing research area, which starts to be noticed by industry as an alternative and complement to testing, and other formal verification techniques.

3   A Hands-On Runtime Verification Course

In this section we outline the narrative of a course on runtime verification, focusing on ensuring that the students are exposed to relevant practical issues going beyond the use of existing tools to the actual development of one. Through the chain of concepts presented, we mention how salient issues in runtime verification can be communicated to the students as they build their tools.

3.1   Introduction to Runtime Verification

The course is proposed to start with an introduction to runtime verification, including the theoretical justification and terminology. The course can be motivated through the need for verification of systems, and a runtime approach justified by highlighting to the students the difference in complexity between the language inclusion and the word inclusion problems. The choice of a three-valued representation of verification outcome can be thus justified and explained.

Furthermore, students are exposed to the complexity of runtime checking of different types of properties e.g. showing how a property such as *"Function recordTemperature() should never be called with a value greater than 50"* requires no additional monitoring memory, whilst a property such as *"Function recordTemperature() can only be called if initialiseThermometer() was called earlier"* requires one bit of memory (recording whether the initialisation function was called), and a property such as *"The difference between the two most*

---

[8] https://www.cost.eu/actions/IC1402.

common parameter values passed to function recordTemperature() *will never exceed 20"* requires keeping a histogram of parameters passed to the function, which may grow linearly with respect to the length of the history, thus effectively resulting in a memory leak.

On the basis of this view of runtime verification, one can then look at the architecture of the runtime verified system, highlighting how the event observers, verification algorithms and reaction code interact with the underlying SUS. Students can thus be exposed to different instrumentation approaches, from inlined to separation of specification and implementation concerns. Finally, drawing from the discussion of complexity which came earlier, one can motivate different verification architectures—online vs. offline, synchronous vs. asynchronous, etc.

After such an introduction, students will be ready to be exposed to the practical considerations of runtime verification.

3.2 Introduction to Monitoring Through Assertions

Throughout the unit, we propose the adoption of a single SUS—one which is not trivial, yet tractable to understand by the students. The choice and design of such a system should ensure that it contains sufficient complexity to justify the verification techniques and specification languages presented in the course. Students would find the use of a logic such as LTL to be overkill (thus perceived as impractical) if applied to a simple input-output use case, so a more sophisticated business case is required in order to motivate the need of certain sophisticated techniques used in runtime verification.

In this paper, we will illustrate our proposed approach by using examples from a financial transaction system, based on one which two of the authors have used (see Sect. 4). However, this is done to illustrate our proposed approach and, needless to say, other real-world examples serve equally well.

To make it easy for students to latch on to runtime verification, we are proposing to start with its simplest form of monitoring and sanity checking of a systems—the use of assertions, a technique with which students but also software developers and testers are already familiar. Such an assertion is useful to check a particular condition and raise a labelled flag if found to be false.

A simple assertion might involve checking that a user is not from a particular country or region before being granted *Gold User* status. This is an example of a point property[9] which does not involve any references to other states of the system's timeline. By having the students analyse the code and identify the place where a user's status is being lifted to *Gold*, and adding an assertion to check for the user's country, exposes them to the use of assertions in runtime sanity checking of the system state.

The aim of such simple examples is to highlight the ease-of-use of assertions. However, through the introduction of more complex properties, the students quickly realise that the additional code to store information about the context

---

[9] *Point* as in being possible to verify by checking for a particular condition at a particular point in the control logic of the system.

(e.g. execution history) becomes an additional burden on the SUS. Properties involving sequences of events e.g. *"No user should log into the system before it is initialised"* highlights the difference arising from the fact that checking such a property requires linking two points in the code—the initialisation point (where one would have to set a flag), and the login point (where one would have to check for the status of the flag). With even more complex properties such as *"The administrator must reconcile accounts every 1000 attempted external money transfers or whenever an aggregate total of one million dollars in attempted external transfers is reached"*, students are exposed to the limitations of such a manual approach to monitoring, and that it is far from the ideal way of runtime checking a system due to:

Non-modular code: Students need to locate several points in the code and add variable declarations which are accessible from such points. This brings with it all the disadvantages of poor modularity, including a maintenance nightmare.

Error-prone code: It is easy to make mistakes in the code which is meant to check the system, hence defeating the whole purpose. A substantial part of this issue is due to the non-modularity mentioned in the previous point. However, it is also because the monitor is expressed at the same level of abstraction as the system itself.

3.3   Instrumenting Monitors

In order to address the issue of non-modularity of runtime verification code, students are then introduced to aspect-oriented programming (AOP).[10] This provides a modular way of programming cross-cutting concerns, i.e., aspects of a system which span other modules. Similar to event logging (another main application of AOP), runtime verification interacts with virtually all the modules of a system—making it an ideal application of AOP. At the same time, having been exposed to the spaghetti code resulting from merging the monitoring and verification code in the SUS, the students understand the need for tool support.

After providing basic AOP syntax, students can modify all their monitoring checks and verification code (including variable declarations for additional monitoring state) into a single aspect file independent of the SUS, but which can be compiled in order to automatically combine the two together. In this manner, students are exposed to the double benefit of (i) having all runtime verification-related code in one place, while also (ii) avoiding mistakes resulting from manual instrumentation.

At this point in the course, the students will have been exposed to tools to separate the SUS from the event monitoring, verification and reaction code. However, the latter part remains a combination of the three concerns mentioned, which we will now seek to separate.

---

[10] In a course using Java one can adopt a tool such as AspectJ.

3.4 Verification Algorithms

With the modularity attained through the use of AOP tools, the focus can now be turned to the separation between the monitoring, verification and reaction code. Students will be guided to start building *ad hoc* verification code for particular properties with increasing complexity, mostly to highlight how this results in an increase in monitoring state and complexity of the monitoring code not resolved through the use of AOP. Starting with a simple point property e.g. *"Only approved users may be given gold status"*, we proceed to simple temporal properties e.g. *"The approval of a user will always fail unless their profile was previously verified"* and more complex ones e.g. *"The user cannot be reported for more than three times without being disabled"*. Finally, we add more complex elements including real-time constraints e.g. *"If a user performs transactions of more than €5000 in total in any 24 h window without having undergone due diligence checks in the previous month, he or she must be blacklisted within 2 h"*.

It quickly becomes evident that the level of complexity of the verification code reaches a stage where bugs could easily arise, subverting the advantages of verification in the first place. This leads to the use of specification languages and automated compilation of verification algorithms for them, thus abstracting the verification code up to a logic specification.

In order to build the complexity of verification code in a stepwise manner, we present the student with a sequence of abstraction levels, each of which simplifies the expression of the specification at the cost of the use of a more sophisticated and complex specification language:

1. We propose to start with a simple rule based language e.g. a guarded command language with rules of the form *event | condition ↦ action* which provides only a thin layer above the AOP code—events correspond to pointcuts, while the condition and action simply correspond to a standard conditional in the underlying programming language. In this manner, we start to abstract away from the AOP tool syntax, specialising to a specification language. However, clearly this can be shown to yield little gain in terms of specification abstraction.

2. We then move on to the runtime verification of safety properties on finite traces [HR02]. One way of expressing sequentiality properties is to use a graph-based formalism, an approach that students would typically already be familiar with from formal languages and automata courses. We propose to start with deterministic automata with transitions labelled by guarded commands, and show how they can be used to express properties which use a notion of temporal sequentiality. The students are given the task of building a translator from such automata into the underlying guarded command language. The exercise highlights the fact that new state is introduced at the lower level (keeping track of the state of the automaton), which is implicit in the abstract specification. This brings across the message that most abstract specification languages allow implicit encoding of states.
   Furthermore, the students are asked to consider adding non-determinism, and quickly run into a myriad of dead ends as they solve one problem only to

encounter another. Results they would already be familiar with, showing the equivalence of the expressive power of deterministic and non-deterministic automata lulls them into a fake sense of ease, only to discover they cannot simply perform the transformation they are familiar with due to the actions resulting in transitions having a side effect and that multiple runs of the SUS cannot be kept simultaneously. We feel that such an exercise gives the students a better understanding for the need of determinism (or at least not having the monitor interfere with the SUS) than any theoretical results would. In addition, the power of the symbolic state of the automata (any monitoring information maintained by the actions) is highlighted.

3. Moving away from graph-based formalisms we propose another formalism with which the students are familiar—regular expressions. Using regular expressions to write properties [SELS05], students can also be exposed to different interpretations of a single specification language—do we write a regular expression to express bad behaviour e.g. writing $(login \cdot \overline{logout}^* \cdot logout)^* \cdot \overline{login}^* \cdot read$ to express the property that no reads should be done outside of a login session[11] or to express the good (expected behaviour) e.g. $(login \cdot (read + write)^* \cdot logout)^*$ to express the same property as above.

   Students start by programming a translation from regular expressions to finite state automata to understand better the complexity of coding the translation, the blowup in states and difficulty in handling non-determinism in regular expressions. This is used to motivate the use of Brzozowski's derivatives [Brz64], which results in a much simpler implementation. In this manner, students will be exposed to the notions of derivatives on a formalism they are already familiar with, and get to program it themselves.

4. Finally, we move on to the use of Linear Temporal Logic (LTL) and present Havelund et al.'s derivative-based approach [HR01b] which is now readily accessible to the students. In order to tie the knot back to where we started off from, we also present Leucker et al.'s automaton-based approach to LTL monitoring [BLS11].

The bulk of the course, in fact lies in this part of the course. In programming the different solutions themselves, the students get to explore different possibilities and understand better the pros and cons of different approaches.

3.5   Real-Time Properties

Given the ubiquity of real-time concerns in systems which are worth monitoring, if time permits, a course on runtime verification should ideally touch upon the monitoring of real-time properties. Students should appreciate the challenges that this brings about, particularly due to the fact that monitoring itself modifies the timing of the underlying system [CPS09b]. We note that this issue is not

---

[11] We use standard regular expression syntax here, with a indicating the occurrence of that event, $\overline{a}$ to indicate the occurrence of any event other than a, $e \cdot e'$ to indicate sequential composition of two sub-expressions, $e + e'$ to indicate the choice and e^* to indicate any number of repetitions.

limited to timing, but to any element of the system which is self-reflective, e.g., if the SUS considers its own level of memory consumption.

When dealing with real-time issues, there are two main kinds of properties: those which can be monitored through system events and those which require additional timer-events to wake the monitor up at crucial points in time. The former are lower-bound properties, e.g., there should not be more than five login attempts in a five minute period, while the latter are upper-bound, e.g., for the account to remain active, there should at least be one successful login each month. Students learn that it suffices to hook existing system events, e.g., login attempts, to monitor lower-bound properties, but a timer would be required for upper-bound ones, e.g., reset after each successful login and going off when a month elapses. At this point, it is useful to introduce the notion of detecting bugs "as soon as possible". Technically, upper-bound properties can also be detected through system events, albeit much later than their occurrence: e.g., a flag is raised when the user attempts to login in six months after their last interaction.

3.6 Offline Monitoring

Several works applying runtime verification to industry (see, for example, reports on work on real-world systems such as [BGHS09, CPA12, Hav15, CP18a, CP18b]) have resorted to offline monitoring for minimal intrusion—effectively rendering it equivalent to event logging. This reality suggests that a course on runtime verification including offline monitoring, would provide the students with useful, applicable, practical knowledge.

Students are made aware that unlike the online version, where the system method call can be used to obtain system state on demand, in the offline case, anything which is not stored is not available. Similarly, another limitation is that reparation actions cannot be taken by the monitor when it is completely detached from the system.

Switching from online to offline monitoring requires that traces are stored in monitor-consumable format. Usually this involves keeping track of the method calls, the arguments passed, and possibly return values. Any system state which is required by the monitor also needs to be stored, e.g., globally accessible values which are never passed as parameters. Next, one would have to choose how to store the trace, with the most universal approach being a text file. While this is highly convenient, when dealing with complex objects appropriate toString and parse methods might need to be added.

Once students are made aware of the repercussions of switching to offline monitoring, the aspect-oriented mechanism previously used for monitoring, is reduced to just event logging in a text file. Next comes the task of reconfiguring the monitor to consume events from the file rather than directly through AOP. With little modifications to the code, students are guided to appreciate how existing monitors can be connected to a log file parser (instead of the original system) through AOP: Each time the parser consumes a line from the log file, a dummy method is called which triggers the monitor.

3.7 Advanced Topics

We can never expect that a runtime verification course is exhaustive; several aspects would naturally be left out. However, to help students see the relevance of the topic and connect it to their work, the instructor can try to latch on to what they are already working on and discuss advanced topics. For example, for a student working on the analysis of security and privacy properties, studying runtime verification for hyperproperties becomes an imperative. Students with a background in statistics can perhaps appreciate more the need for on-the-fly calculation when dealing with stream processing. Those focusing on concurrent and distributed systems can be helped to appreciate the different questions and new challenges not present when analysing sequential and monolithic programs. For students with a more formal background, one can discuss questions such as what is monitorability and its limits, how specifications can be inferred from execution traces, how static analysis can alleviate dynamic analysis, etc. Similar connections can be found with other areas such as smart contracts, testing, embedded devices, etc.

As a means of wrapping up the unit, having a session on current challenges in runtime verification exposes the students to the frontiers of the research area. In the past we have discussed selected topics on the lines of those appearing in [SSA+19], including transactional information systems, contracts and policies, security and sampling-based runtime verification.

4   Lecturing Experience

One of the main drivers behind the setting up of a heavily hands-on unit offered to computer science students was that of ensuring that the students can see the practical relevance of runtime verification techniques. By exposing them to the theory but also putting a big emphasis on the practical side of how runtime verification tools can be built, we hoped to see, after the students graduate and integrate in development teams, an increase in awareness and adoption in the industry opening new opportunities for research collaboration.

It is worth mentioning also other biases in our lecturing approach. At the time we started working on runtime verification, in 2005, most of the work focused on verifying system-wide properties and (slightly later) per-object specifications.[12] When we sought out industry partners with whom to work, in order to ensure the practical relevance of our results, we repeatedly encountered properties which were neither system nor object-based, but rather transaction-based. In fact, a single transaction could transcend multiple objects.[13] This led to our own specification language and tool Larva [CPS08] which allows the verification engineer

---

[12] It is worth highlighting that the authors initial work in runtime verification was done jointly. However, some of the discussion which follows, regarding ongoing collaborative projects and lecturing is specific to the University of Malta, although much of what we describe was discussed between all three authors at the time.

[13] The transaction object before serialisation and the object after serialisation should be treated as the same object based on a logical identifier.

to adjust the notion of verification unit identity for the specification at hand. Another major departure from the *status quo* at the time, was to adopt the use of symbolic automata for specifications. This was also partially motivated by our experience in the projects we had with industry partners: (i) the graphical representation of the properties were digestible for the software engineers (justifying the use of automata); and (ii) the fact that variable declaration, querying, and manipulation was supported, not only made the notation more expressive, but also felt familiar for the same engineers (hence the choice of making them symbolic).[14]

Based on our research and collaboration at that time, we thus designed and delivered units on runtime verification both at undergraduate and graduate level. Although, over the years, much changed in terms of content and organisation, the philosophy behind the approach and the general content remained largely unchanged. At the undergraduate level, runtime verification was covered as part of a verification techniques course which introduced students to the ideas of formal specifications and formal verification techniques with particular focus on runtime verification, model checking, and model-based testing. At a Masters level, however, our aim was to go deeper and train students to be runtime verification engineers, i.e., by the end of the unit, they are able to build their own tools. We do this by incrementally providing skeleton code of a basic runtime verification tool, until by the end of the unit, the tool supports a number of specification languages (as discussed in this paper) for which it generates AspectJ and Java code which readily monitors a Java system. This material[15] was covered in a unit consisting of 28 student contact hours including practical hands-on sessions.

The practicality of the course, as well as the empowerment the students feel by building their own tool, has led to positive feedback from the students. A cut-down version of the course has also been given in a number of other contexts: ECI Winter School in Computer Science in Buenos Aires[16] (2013), the RV summer school in Madrid[17] (2016), and the RV winter school in Pratz sur Arly[18] (2018).

When we designed the course, it was envisaged as a means for the ideas and principles from the field of runtime verification to slowly permeate into the industry through the development of in-house libraries and tools. Anecdotally, based on newer collaborative projects and interaction with former students, we believe that this has happened. Obviously, it is unclear how much of this was due to the infusion of students aware of runtime verification theory and techniques into the industry, and how much of it is due to changing industry practice.

---

[14] There were other advantages for these choices, such as the possibility of also manipulating the monitored system state (as a reaction to observations), and the seamless introduction of a stopwatch API. However, these aspects fall outside the scope of this paper.

[15] Anyone interested in using the material may get in touch with the authors.

[16] https://meals-project.eu/node/67.

[17] https://rv2016.imag.fr/?page_id=128.

[18] https://www.youtube.com/watch?v=Vyz6kte4PVk.

5   Conclusions

On this special occasion of Klaus Havelund's 65-year *Festschrift*, we take the opportunity to look back to the inception of the area of runtime verification and also to the future—the history is logged in the workshop and conference proceedings, and yet like a monitor ourselves, it is good to reflect on the past and react to influence the future.

It is in this spirit that we provide a brief overview of how runtime verification evolved in the past 20 years, leading up to a substantial number of academically-mature tools by a wide community of researchers. At the current juncture of the story, we feel that the time is ripe to push for more practical use of the techniques, particularly in industrial settings. Thus, we propose a roadmap for teaching runtime verification to upcoming generations, leading them to become hands-on runtime verification engineers. Several instances of this roadmap have been delivered over the past years and the outcome and feedback have been encouraging.

For the future, as software continues to increasingly play a crucial part in the global life of humanity and runtime verification becomes ever more relevant in its promise of safety, dynamism, and immediacy, we hope that as a community we rise up to the occasion and make better known the theories and techniques which have been developed and honed in through years of hard work.

Acknowledgements. This research has been partially supported by the Swedish Research Council (*Vetenskapsrådet*) under Grant 2015-04154 "PolUser".

References

[AB16]   Agrawal, S., Bonakdarpour, B.: Runtime verification of k-safety hyperproperties in HyperLTL. In: CSF 2016, pp. 239–252. IEEE CS Press (2016)

[ACP17] Azzopardi, S., Colombo, C., Pace, G.J.: Control-flow residual analysis for symbolic automata. In: PrePost@iFM 2017, Volume 254 of EPTCS, pp. 29–43 (2017)

[ACPS17] Ahrendt, W., Chimento, J.M., Pace, G.J., Schneider, G.: Verifying data- and control-oriented properties combining static and runtime verification: theory and tools. Formal Methods Syst. Des. **51**(1), 200–265 (2017). https://doi.org/10.1007/s10703-017-0274-y

[BF18]   Bonakdarpour, B., Finkbeiner, B.: The complexity of monitoring hyperproperties. In: CSF 2018, pp. 162–174. IEEE CS Press (2018)

[BFB+19] Bartocci, E., et al.: First international competition on runtime verification: rules, benchmarks, tools, and final results of CRV 2014. Int. J. Softw. Tools Technol. Transf. **21**(1), 31–70 (2019). https://doi.org/10.1007/s10009-017-0454-5

[BFF+10] Barringer, H., et al. (eds.): RV 2010. LNCS, vol. 6418. Springer, Heidelberg (2010). https://doi.org/10.1007/978-3-642-16612-9

[BFH+12] Barringer, H., Falcone, Y., Havelund, K., Reger, G., Rydeheard, D.: Quantified event automata: towards expressive and efficient runtime monitors. In: Giannakopoulou, D., Méry, D. (eds.) FM 2012. LNCS, vol. 7436, pp. 68–84. Springer, Heidelberg (2012). https://doi.org/10.1007/978-3-642-32759-9_9

[BGHS04] Barringer, H., Goldberg, A., Havelund, K., Sen, K.: Rule-based runtime
verification. In: Steffen, B., Levi, G. (eds.) VMCAI 2004. LNCS, vol. 2937,
pp. 44–57. Springer, Heidelberg (2004). https://doi.org/10.1007/978-3-540-
24622-0_5

[BGHS09] Barringer, H., Groce, A., Havelund, K., Smith, M.H.: An entry point for
formal methods: specification and analysis of event logs. In: FMA 2009,
Volume 20 of EPTCS, pp. 16–21 (2009)

[BH10] Bodden, E., Havelund, K.: Aspect-oriented race detection in Java. IEEE
Trans. Softw. Eng. **36**(4), 509–527 (2010)

[BL10] Bodden, E., Lam, P.: Clara: partially evaluating runtime monitors at compile
time. In: Barringer, H., et al. (eds.) RV 2010. LNCS, vol. 6418, pp. 74–88.
Springer, Heidelberg (2010). https://doi.org/10.1007/978-3-642-16612-9_8

[BLS07] Bauer, A., Leucker, M., Schallhart, C.: The good, the bad, and the ugly, but
how ugly is ugly? In: Sokolsky, O., Taşıran, S. (eds.) RV 2007. LNCS, vol.
4839, pp. 126–138. Springer, Heidelberg (2007). https://doi.org/10.1007/
978-3-540-77395-5_11

[BLS11] Bauer, A., Leucker, M., Schallhart, C.: Runtime verification for LTL and
TLTL. ACM Trans. Softw. Eng. Methodol. **20**(4), 14 (2011)

[Brz64] Brzozowski, J.A.: Derivatives of regular expressions. J. ACM **11**(4), 481–494
(1964)

[BSB17] Brett, N., Siddique, U., Bonakdarpour, B.: Rewriting-based runtime verification for alternation-free HyperLTL. In: Legay, A., Margaria, T. (eds.)
TACAS 2017. LNCS, vol. 10206, pp. 77–93. Springer, Heidelberg (2017).
https://doi.org/10.1007/978-3-662-54580-5_5

[CAPS15] Chimento, J.M., Ahrendt, W., Pace, G.J., Schneider, G.: STARVOORS?:
a tool for combined static and runtime verification of Java. In: Bartocci,
E., Majumdar, R. (eds.) RV 2015. LNCS, vol. 9333, pp. 297–305. Springer,
Cham (2015). https://doi.org/10.1007/978-3-319-23820-3_21

[CAS18] Chimento, J.M., Ahrendt, W., Schneider, G.: Testing meets static and runtime verification. In: FormaliSE 2018, pp. 30–39. ACM (2018)

[CCF+16] Cauchi, A., Colombo, C., Francalanza, A., Micallef, M., Pace, G.J.: Using
gherkin to extract tests and monitors for safer medical device interaction
design. In: ACM SIGCHI EICS 2016, pp. 275–280. ACM (2016)

[CFK+14] Clarkson, M.R., Finkbeiner, B., Koleini, M., Micinski, K.K., Rabe, M.N.,
Sánchez, C.: Temporal logics for hyperproperties. In: Abadi, M., Kremer,
S. (eds.) POST 2014. LNCS, vol. 8414, pp. 265–284. Springer, Heidelberg
(2014). https://doi.org/10.1007/978-3-642-54792-8_15

[CP18a] Colombo, C., Pace, G.J.: Considering academia-industry projects meta-
characteristics in runtime verification design. In: Margaria, T., Steffen, B.
(eds.) ISoLA 2018. LNCS, vol. 11247, pp. 32–41. Springer, Cham (2018).
https://doi.org/10.1007/978-3-030-03427-6_5

[CP18b] Colombo, C., Pace, G.J.: Industrial experiences with runtime verification
of financial transaction systems: lessons learnt and standing challenges. In:
Bartocci, E., Falcone, Y. (eds.) Lectures on Runtime Verification. LNCS, vol.
10457, pp. 211–232. Springer, Cham (2018). https://doi.org/10.1007/978-3-
319-75632-5_7

[CPA12] Colombo, C., Pace, G.J., Abela, P.: Safer asynchronous runtime monitoring
using compensations. Formal Methods Syst. Des. **41**(3), 269–294 (2012).
https://doi.org/10.1007/s10703-012-0142-8

[CPS08]   Colombo, C., Pace, G.J., Schneider, G.: Dynamic event-based runtime monitoring of real-time and contextual properties. In: Cofer, D., Fantechi, A. (eds.) FMICS 2008. LNCS, vol. 5596, pp. 135–149. Springer, Heidelberg (2009). https://doi.org/10.1007/978-3-642-03240-0_13

[CPS09a]   Colombo, C., Pace, G.J., Schneider, G.: LARVA – safer monitoring of real-time Java programs (tool paper). In: SEFM 2009, pp. 33–37. IEEE Computer Society (2009)

[CPS09b]   Colombo, C., Pace, G.J., Schneider, G.: Safe runtime verification of real-time properties. In: Ouaknine, J., Vaandrager, F.W. (eds.) FORMATS 2009. LNCS, vol. 5813, pp. 103–117. Springer, Heidelberg (2009). https://doi.org/10.1007/978-3-642-04368-0_10

[CR03]   Chen, F., Rosu, G.: Towards monitoring-oriented programming: a paradigm combining specification and implementation. In: RV 2003, vol. 89, pp. 108–127. ENTCS (2003)

[CSR08]   Chen, F., Serbanuta, T.-F., Rosu, G.: jPredictor: a predictive runtime analysis tool for Gava. In: ICSE 2008, pp. 221–230. ACM (2008)

[DLT13]   Decker, N., Leucker, M., Thoma, D.: jUnit^{RV}–adding runtime verification to jUnit. In: Brat, G., Rungta, N., Venet, A. (eds.) NFM 2013. LNCS, vol. 7871, pp. 459–464. Springer, Heidelberg (2013). https://doi.org/10.1007/978-3-642-38088-4_34

[Dru00]   Drusinsky, D.: The temporal rover and the ATG rover. In: Havelund, K., Penix, J., Visser, W. (eds.) SPIN 2000. LNCS, vol. 1885, pp. 323–330. Springer, Heidelberg (2000). https://doi.org/10.1007/10722468_19

[FFM09]   Falcone, Y., Fernandez, J.-C., Mounier, L.: Runtime verification of safety-progress properties. In: Bensalem, S., Peled, D.A. (eds.) RV 2009. LNCS, vol. 5779, pp. 40–59. Springer, Heidelberg (2009). https://doi.org/10.1007/978-3-642-04694-0_4

[FFM12]   Falcone, Y., Fernandez, J.-C., Mounier, L.: What can you verify and enforce at runtime? Int. J. Softw. Tools Technol. Transf. (STTT) **14**(3), 349–382 (2012). https://doi.org/10.1007/s10009-011-0196-8

[FHST17]   Finkbeiner, B., Hahn, C., Stenger, M., Tentrup, L.: Monitoring hyperproperties. In: Lahiri, S., Reger, G. (eds.) RV 2017. LNCS, vol. 10548, pp. 190–207. Springer, Cham (2017). https://doi.org/10.1007/978-3-319-67531-2_12

[FKRT18]   Falcone, Y., Krstić, S., Reger, G., Traytel, D.: A taxonomy for classifying runtime verification tools. In: Colombo, C., Leucker, M. (eds.) RV 2018. LNCS, vol. 11237, pp. 241–262. Springer, Cham (2018). https://doi.org/10.1007/978-3-030-03769-7_14

[GH01]   Giannakopoulou, D., Havelund, K.: Automata-based verification of temporal properties on running programs. In: ASE 2001, pp. 412–416. IEEE Computer Society (2001)

[Har00]   Harrow, J.J.: Runtime checking of multithreaded applications with visual threads. In: Havelund, K., Penix, J., Visser, W. (eds.) SPIN 2000. LNCS, vol. 1885, pp. 331–342. Springer, Heidelberg (2000). https://doi.org/10.1007/10722468_20

[Hav15]   Havelund, K.: Rule-based runtime verification revisited. Int. J. Softw. Tools Technol. Transf. **17**(2), 143–170 (2015). https://doi.org/10.1007/s10009-014-0309-2

[HP18]   Havelund, K., Peled, D.: Runtime verification: from propositional to first-order temporal logic. In: Colombo, C., Leucker, M. (eds.) RV 2018. LNCS, vol. 11237, pp. 90–112. Springer, Cham (2018). https://doi.org/10.1007/978-3-030-03769-7_7

[HR01a] Havelund, K., Rosu, G.: Monitoring Java programs with Java PathExplorer. ENTCS **55**(2), 200–217 (2001)

[HR01b] Havelund, K., Rosu, G.: Monitoring programs using rewriting. In: ASE 2001, pp. 135–143 (2001)

[HR02] Havelund, K., Roşu, G.: Synthesizing monitors for safety properties. In: Katoen, J.-P., Stevens, P. (eds.) TACAS 2002. LNCS, vol. 2280, pp. 342–356. Springer, Heidelberg (2002). https://doi.org/10.1007/3-540-46002-0_24

[HR18] Havelund, K., Roşu, G.: Runtime verification - 17 years later. In: Colombo, C., Leucker, M. (eds.) RV 2018. LNCS, vol. 11237, pp. 3–17. Springer, Cham (2018). https://doi.org/10.1007/978-3-030-03769-7_1

[HRR19] Havelund, K., Reger, G., Roşu, G.: Runtime verification past experiences and future projections. In: Steffen, B., Woeginger, G. (eds.) Computing and Software Science. LNCS, vol. 10000, pp. 532–562. Springer, Cham (2019). https://doi.org/10.1007/978-3-319-91908-9_25

[HW08] Havelund, K., Van Wyk, E.: Aspect-oriented monitoring of C programs. In: IARP-IEEE/RAS-EURON 2008 (2008)

[KKL+02] Kim, M., Kannan, S., Lee, I., Sokolsky, O., Viswanathan, M.: Computational analysis of run-time monitoring - fundamentals of Java-MaC. In: RV 2002, Volume 70 of ENTCS, pp. 80–94 (2002)

[Leu11] Leucker, M.: Teaching runtime verification. In: Khurshid, S., Sen, K. (eds.) RV 2011. LNCS, vol. 7186, pp. 34–48. Springer, Heidelberg (2012). https://doi.org/10.1007/978-3-642-29860-8_4

[PPT+16] Pinisetty, S., Preoteasa, V., Tripakis, S., Jéron, T., Falcone, Y., Marchand, H.: Predictive runtime enforcement. In: ACM SAC 2016, pp. 1628–1633. ACM (2016)

[PZ06] Pnueli, A., Zaks, A.: PSL model checking and run-time verification via testers. In: Misra, J., Nipkow, T., Sekerinski, E. (eds.) FM 2006. LNCS, vol. 4085, pp. 573–586. Springer, Heidelberg (2006). https://doi.org/10.1007/11813040_38

[SELS05] Sammapun, U., Easwaran, A., Lee, I., Sokolsky, O.: Simulation of simultaneous events in regular expressions for run-time verification. In: RV 2004, Volume 113 of ENTCS, pp. 123–143 (2005)

[SSA+19] Sánchez, C., et al.: A survey of challenges for runtime verification from advanced application domains (beyond software). Formal Methods Syst. Des. **54**(3), 279–335 (2019). https://doi.org/10.1007/s10703-019-00337-w

[SSSB19] Stucki, S., Sánchez, C., Schneider, G., Bonakdarpour, B.: Gray-box monitoring of hyperproperties. In: ter Beek, M.H., McIver, A., Oliveira, J.N. (eds.) FM 2019. LNCS, vol. 11800, pp. 406–424. Springer, Cham (2019). https://doi.org/10.1007/978-3-030-30942-8_25

[ZLD12] Zhang, X., Leucker, M., Dong, W.: Runtime verification with predictive semantics. In: Goodloe, A.E., Person, S. (eds.) NFM 2012. LNCS, vol. 7226, pp. 418–432. Springer, Heidelberg (2012). https://doi.org/10.1007/978-3-642-28891-3_37

Hardware-Assisted Online Data Race Detection

Faustin Ahishakiye[1], José Ignacio Requeno Jarabo[1,2], Violet Ka I Pun[1(✉)], and Volker Stolz[1(✉)]

[1] Western Norway University of Applied Sciences, Bergen, Norway
{fahi,jirj,vpu,vsto}@hvl.no
[2] Complutense University of Madrid, Madrid, Spain
jrequeno@ucm.es

Abstract. Dynamic data race detection techniques usually involve invasive instrumentation that makes it impossible to deploy an executable with such checking in the field, hence making errors difficult to debug and reproduce. This paper shows how to detect data races using the COEMS technology through continuous online monitoring with low-impact instrumentation on a novel FPGA-based external platform for embedded multicore systems. It is used in combination with formal specifications in the high-level stream-based temporal specification language TeSSLa, in which we encode a lockset-based algorithm to indicate potential race conditions. We show how to instantiate a TeSSLa template that is based on the Eraser algorithm, and present a corresponding light-weight instrumentation mechanism that emits necessary observations to the FPGA with low overhead. We illustrate the feasibility of our approach with experimental results on detection of data races on a sample application.

Keywords: Runtime verification · Data race detection · FPGA · Lockset algorithm

1 Introduction

Data races occur in multi-threaded programs when two or more threads access the same memory location concurrently, with at least one write access, and the threads are not using any exclusive locks to control their accesses to that location. They are usually difficult to detect using tests as they depend on the interleaving and scheduling of tasks at runtime. Static analysis techniques frequently suffer from false positives due to over-abstraction, although precise results for source code written in a particular style is certainly feasible. We do not want to discount this field and recent advances, but focus on dynamic techniques for the present occasion.

Races and other concurrency issues have featured prominently in area of Runtime Verification (RV), where precise formal specifications are used at runtime to monitor, and possibly influence, a running system (as opposed to static verification). Our guest of honor (see [12] for an extensive account of his work)

E. Bartocci et al. (Eds.): Havelund Festschrift, LNCS 13065, pp. 108–126, 2021.
https://doi.org/10.1007/978-3-030-87348-6_6

has been one of the founders of the RV workshop- and conference series, and has indeed contributed to the study of the dynamic nature of races with a contribution to the very first workshops [13,14], which has since withstood the test of time [15]. His exploits—which indicate that he is rather aiming for a marathon than a sprint in the race to formal verification—did not stop there: Together with Artho and Biere, he lifted the abstract formal concepts into a practical software engineering setting, where, although race-free in the original sense of the definition, they captured patterns that indicate flawed access to data structures [3]. Source-code instrumentation is one of the go-to solutions to inject RV mechanisms into existing software [10]. His further research with Bodden in a similar direction resulted in the suggestion of a new feature for aspect-orientated programming, a technique for manipulating programs on a higher level, that would facilitate better addressing of concurrency concerns [6].

Although runtime checking only give a limited view on the behaviour of the concretely executed code, it allows precise reporting of actual occurrences, which can be used to predict potential erroneous behaviour across different runs [16]. However, this runtime analysis is not enabled in the final product: inline dynamic data race detection techniques come with invasive instrumentation for each memory access that makes it prohibitive to deploy an executable with such checking in the field [22]. This also makes reproducing errors challenging.

In this article, we take earlier RV attempts for race analysis further and present a *non-intrusive* approach to monitoring applications on embedded system-on-chips (SoCs) for data races using the COEMS platform [8] which aims to eliminate the overhead of dynamic checking by offloading it to external hardware.[1] The platform offers control-flow reconstruction from processor-traces (here: the Arm CoreSight control-flow trace), and data-traces through explicit instrumentation [26]. Race checking is executed on an FPGA on a separate hardware-platform to minimize impact on the system under observation. Our experimental results show that the necessary instrumentation in the target application incurs the expected *fixed, predictable* overhead, and is not affected by the time required for race checking. Our use of the high-level stream-based temporal specification language, TeSSLa [21], means that the reconfiguration of the monitor is substantially faster than synthesising VHDL (few seconds vs. dozens of minutes), and allows end-users to customize the race checker specification to their needs without being FPGA-experts.

This is not possible with other specification-based approaches that directly aim to use the integrated FPGA of a SoC. These approaches do not offer the quick reconfiguration possible with the COEMS platform but require full time-consuming reconfiguration, and do not support the use of control-flow tracing due to the limited capacity of the SoC.

The approach proposed in this paper is more flexible than a dedicated race checker implemented on the FPGA: to the best of our knowledge, such a general solution does not exist, though it is of course in principle possible. It would

---

[1] The EU Horizon 2020 project "COEMS–Continuous Observation of Embedded Multicore Systems", https://www.coems.eu.

not offer the end-user flexibility in terms of fast reconfiguration that we gain through TeSSLa, and, again due to the space restrictions on SoCs, would not be able to benefit from control-flow tracing features that are important for future optimisations and integration with our analyses.

Our *hardware*-based approach can be used in safety-critical systems such as the aerospace and railway-domains where certification is necessary. In these domains, using a software inline race-checker such as ThreadSanitizer [28] is not possible as the tooling for instrumentation and online race-checking is not certified for those systems, if it even exists. For example, ThreadSanitizer support for Arm32 SoCs is not part of the LLVM toolchain [23]. In contrast to software-based approaches, our instrumentation for the application under test has straightforward complexity and gives predictable performance overhead independent from whether or not race checking is enabled. This is especially important for software development in these safety-critical domains, as again for certification purposes, it is not permissible to, e.g., deploy a separate version for debugging or troubleshooting on demand in the field. Any debugging and trace support must be already integrated in the final product.

The COEMS FPGA requires a compiled monitor-configuration. As this configuration needs to be generated for a specific binary under test, we present in this paper our approach where we instantiate a template that monitors a fixed number of memory locations for consistent access through a fixed number of locks. Although these numbers need to be determined before starting the monitoring, the flexibility of TeSSLa allows us to also deal with an unbounded number of threads, and limited monitoring of dynamically allocated memory and locks. Additionally, our instrumentation supports recording traces in files, and offline analysis of execution traces with the TeSSLa interpreter only. This aids in quick prototyping of new specifications on vanilla developer machines without replicating a full setup of SoC and COEMS hardware.

The paper is structured as follows. After this introduction, Sect. 2 explains the related work. Section 3 details the data race detection in the COEMS framework. Section 4 illustrates the feasibility of our approach and presents performance data on detecting data race errors in a Linux `pthreads`-based case study. Experimental results and software are published in public repositories. Finally, Sect. 5 gathers the conclusions and future work.

2   Our Approach and Related Work

Traditionally, data races have been approached from two sides: *static analyses* check the source code and report potential errors. To that end, over-approximations of program behaviours are used (e.g., in terms of variable accesses and lock operations), which may lead to uncertainties on whether a particular behaviour will actually occur during runtime due to general issues on decidability. This frequently generates too many warnings of potential problems for developers to be useful. These uncertainties can be minimised if decisions such as the number of threads to spawn are fixed at compile time. Static analysers may also have limited support for particular language features.

In contrast to checking the code before it runs, *dynamic analyses* look at individual executions of a program. Although this can only analyse the behaviour of the concretely executed code, it can accurately identify the actual occurrences of defects. These can then be traced back to the buggy code that resulted in the potentially erroneous behaviour. Both techniques in general rely on the availability of the source code, and, in the case of dynamic analyses, the possibility of recompilation with additional instrumentation.

As dynamic analyses for data race detection need to record historic behaviour during execution, they often interfere in terms of computation time and memory consumption. For example, the popular dynamic ThreadSanitizer integrated with the LLVM compiler toolchain slows down executions by a factor of 10 to 100, depending on the workload [28,30]. This is one reason why dynamic analysers are traditionally only employed during development and testing, but not included on the production system [29].

The COEMS project developed a hardware-based solution, in which a *field-programmable gate array* (*FPGA*) checks the execution trace in parallel to the running system with minimal interference. The hardware is adapted for analysing events described in the stream-based specification language TeSSLa [21]. Using an intermediate specification language that is executable on the FPGA can avoid the time-consuming re-synthesisation of the FPGA when changing specifications.

We have ported the gist of the Eraser algorithm [27] to the subset of the TeSSLa language that is supported on the hardware. An alternative approach already used the TeSSLa-interpreter, but was not suitable for compilation onto an FPGA due to the dynamic data structures (sets and maps) that only the interpreter offers [19].

Firstly, we adapt the software-based analysis, which relied on dynamic data structures such as sets and maps in the TeSSLa interpreter, to the hardware-specific implementation of the COEMS trace box (see Sect. 3 for details). As the complete specification does not fit onto the FPGA, we then split the specification into two parts: the performance-relevant portion of the TeSSLa specification is processed on the FPGA (filtering accesses), and the final tracking of which lock protects which memory is done in the interpreter which receives the intermediate output from the FPGA. Additionally, we also allow monitoring of dynamically allocated memory and locks.

The Eraser algorithm is certainly no longer the state of the art in dynamic race detection (or rather, checking locking discipline), but has the advantage that it can be captured in a state machine that is instantiated per memory location and set of locks. Even though it conceptually uses sets, assuming that the number of used memory locations and locks is statically known, we can statically derive the necessary streams.

Such a static encoding should be possible also for the more modern FastTrack-algorithm by Flanagan and Freund [11], which uses lightweight vector clocks and the happens-before relation to avoid false positives. Their article includes a detailed description of the necessary data structures, and uses thread-ids as offset into arrays. Our approach here requires focusing on a fixed number of memory locations and locks, but can deal with an arbitrary number of threads. We leave an encoding into TeSSLa of FastTrack to future work—for a statically decidable set of threads it should certainly be possible, with the necessary vector-clocks also being maintained on the FPGA-side.

An observation-based race checker that tracks memory accesses and lock operations can also be implemented through the help of virtualisation. Gem5 [5, 17] is such a framework. Virtualisation means on the one hand that observation cannot be done on a deployed system in the field but only in the lab and with a limited number of supported peripherals. On the other hand, control-flow events can easily be explicitly generated, no expensive reconstruction is necessary: in full virtualisation, we can directly match on any assembly instruction, and not only branches like with the COEMS hardware. In fact, in such a scenario, it would be straightforward to use Gem5 as event source, where the virtualisation sends events on to a TeSSLa interpreter checking the trace against our specification. Gem5 does not directly offer a high-level specification language for monitoring. Given the high event rate of observations on memory accesses, we expect a similar performance impact like the one reported for ThreadSanitizer.

Another prominent example where a high-level specification is synthesised into an FPGA is RTLola [4]. This differs from our approach in the following: the specification language puts a stronger emphasis on periodic data than we do with our discrete TeSSLa events. Furthermore, RTLola is synthesized via VHDL onto the FPGA, and hence has a high turn-around time for reconfiguration. Communication between the system-under-test and the verification logic is left open to the user and requires knowledge of VHDL, though of course in principle data events can then be emitted through instrumentation. In contrast to our solution, an RTLola specification cannot benefit from control-flow tracing, since control-flow reconstruction is not available as specification and hence cannot be compiled onto the FPGA, and furthermore would exceed the capacity of current SoCs both in terms of space and execution speed [26]. We leave performance evaluation of RTLola execution for race checking purposes on the FPGA to future work, but note that providing an API for the instrumentation to the monitor requires VHLD-knowledge.

A similar direct approach via hardware-synthesis has been taken for Signal Temporal Logic (STL) [18]. It would certainly be feasible to encode a race checker in STL, but that would not be playing to STL's strength in terms of timing properties (which are not relevant for race checking) and observing signals on a wire (as opposed to a programmable interface to send values from the instrumented code to the monitor).

The R2U2 [25] monitoring system for unmanned aerial vehicles provides a generic observation component on an SoC. Again, events must be explicitly emitted, and no control-flow reconstruction is available. Similar to our approach, and unlike in RTLola, this component is generic and is parametrised by compiled specifications. R2U2 uses Metric Temporal Logic specifications (MTL), which are very suitable to describe, e.g. timing properties. While it is certainly possible to specify our race checker in MTL, we leave it to future experimental evaluation

Fig. 1. COEMS trace box containing FPGA (left) and SoC (right)

how many instances of the race pattern (in terms of memory location/protecting lock) would be feasible, and how the communication bus would uphold under varying event rates.

3 Data Race Detection with COEMS

In the following, we first briefly introduce COEMS infrastructure. Then, we describe the workflow of data race detection with the COEMS tools. After that, we explain the idea of the lockset-based Eraser algorithm and our translation into TeSSLa.

3.1 COEMS Infrastructure

The COEMS project provides a novel observer platform for online monitoring of multicore systems. It offers a non-intrusive way to gain insights of the system behaviour, which are crucial for detecting non-deterministic failures caused by, for example, accessing inconsistent data as a result of race conditions.

To observe SoCs, the platform uses the tracing capabilities that are available on many modern multicore processors. Such capabilities provide highly com-pressed tracing information over a separate tracing port. This information allows the COEMS system to reconstruct the sequence of instructions executed by the processor [26]. The instruction sequence- and data trace can then be analysed online by a reconfigurable monitoring unit. Figure 1 shows the COEMS FPGA enclosure, the Arm-based Enclustra SoC that serves as system under test, and the AURORA interface connecting both.

As soon as the program starts running on the Enclustra board, control flow messages are generated via the Arm CoreSight module and transmitted, together with user-specified data trace messages from any instrumentation, through the AURORA interface to the COEMS trace box. Internally, the Instruction

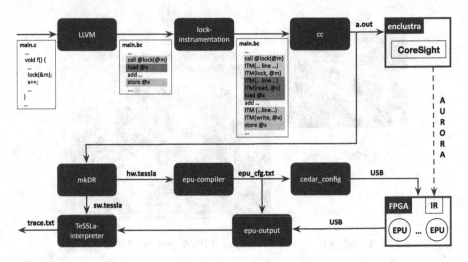

Fig. 2. Lock instrumentation and race monitoring using the COEMS technology

Reconstruction (IR) module reconstructs an accurate execution trace of both cores from the platform-specific compressed format into a stream-based format suitable for analysing properties defined in the TeSSLa language. The flexibility of the TeSSLa language allows expressing different kinds of analyses for functional or timing properties in terms of stream events. A TeSSLa specification is then compiled to a configuration of the Event Processing Units (EPUs) [7] of the monitoring unit, which are specialised units on the FPGA implementing low-level TeSSLa stream operations. The events of the TeSSLa streams are efficiently processed by the EPUs in the trace box. To cope with the potentially massive amount of tracing data generated by the processors, the COEMS system is implemented in hardware using an FPGA-based event processing system. The current COEMS prototype implements eight parallel EPUs.

Compared to existing monitoring approaches, COEMS provides several advantages, most notably is its non-intrusive method to observe and verify the actual behaviour of the observed system, i.e., the system behaviour will not be affected by the monitoring. As no trace data has to be stored, systems can be monitored autonomously for extended periods of time. Furthermore, the trace box reports results of a TeSSLa analysis almost immediately as the processing delay introduced by the trace box is negligible. In contrast to other hardware-based runtime verification techniques [9, 29], changing the specification does not require circuit synthesis, but only a TeSSLa compilation. Hence, the focus of observation can be changed during runtime by reconfiguring the EPUs quickly.

3.2   Instrumentation and Data Race Monitoring

The current COEMS framework supports data race detection for `pthread` programs that can be recompiled using LLVM. We illustrate the workflow of instrumentation and data race monitoring in Fig. 2.

We first instrument the application under test during compilation, so that the executable emits information to the COEMS trace box at runtime. We insert calls to instrumentation (i) after taking a lock, (ii) before releasing a lock, and (iii) on shared memory accesses with the help of LLVM, which will send the thread-id and observed action. As an optimisation, we use the LLVM analysis framework to only instrument memory accesses to potentially shared memory: through escape-analysis, this can already eliminate instrumentation e.g. on iteration variables of tight loops. Then, we compile and link the instrumented LLVM intermediate code (.bc) into a binary file (a.out). The instrumentation should hence be easy to integrate into existing build-setups.

Secondly, we copy the binary to the system under observation (enclustra) where we will later run it. The mkDR-script instantiates a TeSSLa specification template with the memory addresses and mutexes to be observed, based on the names of global variables. Expert users have the option of more fine-grained control on the instantiation, e.g., to monitor dynamically allocated memory. The specification is tailored to each program; thus, it should be regenerated from the template every time the application is recompiled. The instantiated specification is then split into two halves, as its size exceeds the currently available number of eight EPUs on the prototype hardware. The first half hw.tessla filters the high event rate stream of observations on the FPGA. It is translated by the epu-compiler into a configuration file (epu_cfg.txt), and then uploaded to the FPGA by cedar_config. The second half sw.tessla receives the output of the first stage, and does the final processing on a stream that now has a lower event rate in the TeSSLa interpreter.

Then, we run the binary file, which will automatically start sending trace data to the FPGA. The epu-output tool decodes the FPGA output into a TeSSLa event stream. Note that the behaviour of the application is independent of whether the COEMS FPGA is actually connected or not. If not, trace data is silently discarded, but does not affect the timing of the application.

Finally, we analyse this trace with the second part of the TeSSLa specification (sw.tessla) with the TeSSLa interpreter, which will emit race warnings if necessary. Our data race specification uses mostly data trace events, since we require the addresses of memory and locks, except for a control flow event when pthread_create is called and to signal termination of program under test.

In addition to the online (hardware-based) monitoring analysis with the COEMS trace box, the COEMS framework also supports offline (software-based) analysis of execution traces in a personal computer. In the case of software-based analysis, the user only needs the TeSSLa interpreter and the COEMS lock instrumentation tool. Most of the initial steps in Fig. 2 such as the LLVM instrumentation or the instantiation of the TeSSLa template are similar for the software-trace analysis. Instead of compiling the TeSSLa specification for the EPUs, the software TeSSLa interpreter will now run the entire TeSSLa specification for detecting data races on a locally generated software trace-file. Writing the trace data into a file first or piping them into the TeSSLa interpreter has a higher overhead than transmitting them via the AURORA interface.

3.3   Lockset-Based Algorithm in TeSSLa

Conceptually, the algorithm tracks which set of locks is held at every memory access. The current set is intersected with the previous set on a read or write (for simplicity of presentation, we do not distinguish between read- and write accesses, although only read/write and write/write-conflicts are relevant). This defines the alphabet of observations of the algorithm: pairs of reads or writes with a memory address and thread-identifier, and locking or unlocking operations with lock- and thread-identifier. The algorithm initialises the lockset for each memory address with the set containing all locks, and should the intersection ever yield the empty set, then we can conclude that an inconsistent locking discipline has been used. This means that one part of the execution uses no or disjoint locks from another part of the execution when accessing this memory, which hence gives rise to a potential data race if those executions are assumed to be possible concurrently.

As we do not have dynamic memory available to maintain potentially unbounded sets in the TeSSLa-specification on the FPGA, we need to find a static encoding. To achieve this, for each pair of memory location X and lock identifier (also an address) L, we create a boolean stream protecting_X_with_L that is initialised to *true*. The set of all these streams for a given X hence models the lockset as a bit-vector. Note that updates are monotone, i.e., once a stream takes the value *false*, it can no longer revert to *true*. If all these streams for a given X carry *false*, we know that no common lock is protecting the current access, and we emit a race warning on the error_X stream for that memory location. This encoding means that we need to know the set of all memory locations and all lock identifiers before we configure the FPGA, as we cannot declare new streams dynamically.

On every memory access to X, we check if L is being held by the current thread and update the current value if necessary. We track this through the streams holding_L, which carry the identity of the thread currently holding this lock, if any. Again, updating the value on these streams is trivial upon each locking or unlocking operation.

```
1   in threadid: Events[Int]
2   in readaddr: Events[Int]
3   in writeaddr: Events[Int]
4   in mutexlockaddr: Events[Int]
5   in mutexunlockaddr: Events[Int]
6   @FunctionCall("__pthread_create_2_1")
7   in pcreateid: Events[Unit]
8   in line: Events[Int]
9   in dyn_base: Events[Int]
10  in dyn_lock: Events[Int]
```

Fig. 3. Header of the TeSSLa specification, including all the incoming events from the instrumented code.

```
1  def lock_0 := filter(mutexlockaddr ==1, mutexlockaddr ==1)
2  def unlock_0 := filter(mutexunlockaddr ==1, mutexunlockaddr ==1)
3  def lock_1 := filter(mutexlockaddr ==24808, mutexlockaddr
      ==24808)
4  def unlock_1 := filter(mutexunlockaddr ==24808, mutexunlockaddr
      ==24808)
5  def dyn_temp := 4 * (((dyn_lock >> 1) >> 1))
6  def slot := dyn_lock - dyn_temp
7  def dyn_lock_0 = filter(dyn_temp, slot == 0)
8  def lock_4 := filter(mutexlockaddr == dyn_lock_0, mutexlockaddr
      == dyn_lock_0)
9  def unlock_4 := filter(mutexunlockaddr == dyn_lock_0,
      mutexunlockaddr == dyn_lock_0)
10 def read_0 := filter(readaddr ==24532, readaddr ==24532)
11 def write_0 := filter(writeaddr ==24532, writeaddr ==24532)
12 def access_0 := merge(read_0,write_0)
13 def access_after_pc_0 := on(last(pcreateid,access_0),line)
14 def thread_accessing_0 := last(threadid*32768 + line,
      access_after_pc_0)
15 def holding_0 := default(merge(last(threadid, lock_0), last(-1,
      unlock_0)), -1)
16 def protecting_0_with_0 := detect_change(default(
      thread_accessing_0/32768 == last(holding_0,
      thread_accessing_0), true))
17 def error_0 := on(thread_accessing_0,!(protecting_0_with_0 ||
      protecting_0_with_1 || protecting_0_with_2 ||
      protecting_0_with_3 || protecting_0_with_4))
```

Fig. 4. TeSSLa fragment, where lines 1–15 are from the hardware stage, while lines 16–17 are from the software stage.

Figures 3 and 4 show an excerpt of the resulting TeSSLa specification. It has been created for one dynamic lock and three static locks, and tracks accesses to memory address 24532. Static locks are stored at memory addresses 24808, 24528 and 24560 (only lock 24808 is shown in Fig. 4), while the memory address of the dynamic lock is emitted at runtime. The static lock at address 1 is artificial and is used for the main-thread only. TeSSLa built-in stream operations are emphasised. As input streams, we receive instrumented events on mutexlockaddr, mutexunlockaddr, readaddr, writeaddr, threadid, dyn_base and dyn_lock. The pcreateid event reduces false-positives by signalling to only start observing memory accesses after additional threads have actually been created. The annotation @FunctionCall indicates that this is a control flow-event which is triggered by a function call, and not through instrumentation. The symbol name corresponds to the function pthread_create from Linux' system library. To aid in debugging, the instrumentation also emits the current source code line number with each event.

Currently, due to the limited availability of EPUs on the prototype FPGA, the specification is actually split into two halves, with the fast address-filtering done on hardware, and only processing the derived information in the coloured lines 16–17 as a post-processing stage in the interpreter. The multiplication and division are binary left- and right-shifts that reduce the amount of events emitted from the hardware stage to the software stage by encoding the line number of an instruction with its event in the unused lower 16 bits, and encoding dynamically allocated locks (see below).

4   Case Study

In this section, we illustrate our approach with a case study, where we simulate a set of bankers sending random amounts of money from one bank account to another [20]. The bankers lock the source and target bank accounts before committing a transaction, so that transfers are protected against data races and deadlocks. We introduce a special case where one banker (id 0) forgets one lock operation and hence, data may get corrupted. Figure 5 shows the core of the example with locks and memory accesses. The complete example, including source code, execution traces and TeSSLa reports, is available at [1].

```
1  /* get an exclusive lock on both balances before
2     updating (there's a problem with this, see below) */
3  pthread_mutex_lock(transaction_mtx);
4  if( !DATA_RACE || (DATA_RACE & (id != 0)) ){
5     /* In case of DATA_RACE flag is 'on', the thread_id 0
6     forgets to lock the accts[from].mtx mutex */
7     pthread_mutex_lock(&accts[from].mtx);
8        }
9  pthread_mutex_lock(&accts[to].mtx);
10 pthread_mutex_unlock(transaction_mtx);
11 /* Do the actual transfer. */
12 if (accts[from].balance > 0) {
13      payment = 1 + rand_range(accts[from].balance);
14      accts[from].balance -= payment;
15
16 pthread_mutex_unlock(&accts[to].mtx);
17 if( !DATA_RACE || (DATA_RACE & (id != 0)) ){
18     /* For symmetry -- don't unlock if racy: */
19     pthread_mutex_unlock(&accts[from].mtx);
20 }
```

Fig. 5. Example of incorrect locking

TeSSLa Specification. We instantiate the corresponding COEMS data race template (see [2] for all files used here) using the mkDR-script and the instrumented binary, and the names of all mutexes (accts[0].mtx, ...) and shared variables (accts[0].balance, ...) as parameters.

The size of the TeSSLa specification for the Eraser algorithm is proportional to the number of locks and shared memory addresses to monitor, and independent from the number of threads. More precisely, the first half hw.tessla grows linearly with respect to both variables.

For each lock L, the TeSSLa specification includes the lock/unlock pairs and holding_L (plus an additional stream in the case of dynamic locks). For each memory address x, the TeSSLa specification includes a block of five streams (i.e., read_X ... thread_accessing_X). Hence, 3L + 5X streams are generated for the first half, where L is the number of locks and x the number of memory addresses. Regarding the second half, the sw.tessla file, the number of streams grows proportionally to (x+1)*L (i.e., protecting_X_with_L plus error_X).

As the TeSSLa specification is a text file and the size is constrained by the previous parameters, the instantiation of the TeSSLa template for the data race checking is done almost instantaneously, and compilation of the largest specification for the hardware stage into the FPGA completes in around 5 min (see below for detailed measurements) including uploading the configuration to the FPGA, hence a big advantage over approaches that need to translate via VHDL.

Working with Dynamic Allocations. As we have noted above, the addresses of memory locations and locks need to be available at compile-time of the specification. This limits our approach to statically declared resources in a program. However, it fits our application domain in embedded systems for these SoCs, where development may follow the MISRA guidelines [24], which strongly recommends against using e.g., malloc. For more flexibility, we have developed an extension where developers can at runtime send the location of dynamically allocated memory or locks through additional instrumentation.

Conceptually, we parametrise the specification with a placeholder for the argument of the comparison operations above. A write to a particular stream will make the specification use that value in addition to any hard-coded values. A programmer can use the instrumentation to send the address of a (potentially dynamically allocated) lock to the monitor using the function emit_dynamic_lock_event(const short slot,const pthread_mutex_t* addr).

We can encode potentially multiple "slots" into the lower four bits, since these pointers are suitably aligned (see lines 5–8 in Fig. 4). Similarly, the developer can register the base address of dynamically allocated storage for monitoring through emit_dynamic_addr_event(const uintptr_t base). The range of bytes to monitor is given when instantiating the specification.

Due to the size limitation on the FPGA, we currently can only provide this filter for a limited number additional memory addresses or locks. As the number of possible EPUs on the external FPGA increases, these numbers for dynamic allocations should also go up. Note that the number of statically encoded resources underlies different resource constraints, and we report the general numbers below in the performance characteristics.

Running the Experiment. The epu-compiler translates the first part (hw.tessla) into a configuration file (epu_cfg.txt), and then uploads it via USB to the FPGA through cedar_config. The compilation time depends on the number of streams in the TeSSLa specification and, hence, the number of locks and

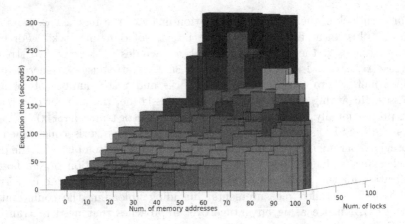

Fig. 6. EPU compilation time for hw.tessla

shared memory addresses in the C code. Figure 6 shows the time required for compiling the TeSSLa specification into the binary configuration format for different scenarios of the bankers example in terms of the number of locks and memory locations. As this involves allocating streams and their operations to the available on-board resources of the FPGA, the following outcomes are possible: (i) successful configuration, (ii) aborted because FPGA-resources have been exceeded, (iii) timeout. Due to the combinatorial growth of the specification, we see that compilation times go up towards the timeout that we have chosen (300 s) for growing numbers of locks/memory locations. After that we reach ranges where it is quickly obvious for the compiler that a configuration cannot be fit onto the FPGA. As compilation is a resource-allocation problem that involves constraint-solving, this slope for compilation time is to be expected: the closer a specification gets to the available resource limits, the harder the constraint-solver has to try searching for a suitable allocation.

After compilation, uploading a new binary configuration into the FPGA after compilation is done in between 3 to 7 s.

The second half of the specification, sw.tessla, receives the output of the first stage, and does the final processing on a stream that now has a lower event rate in the TeSSLa interpreter. Naturally, the interpreter has some startup-cost that also scales with the size of the specification due to parsing and type-checking. Figure 7 shows a similar slope as for the EPU compilation, where startup-time goes up towards the upper right corner, where we also reach up to 300 s.

Since compilation and start-up of the interpreter can be done in parallel and hence lead to the envisioned advantage of quick reconfiguration over approaches going via VHDL.

The COEMS trace box currently supports TeSSLa specifications in the range of hundreds to a few thousands of streams depending on the complexity in the logic of the TeSSLa streams. For our race checker this translates into checking

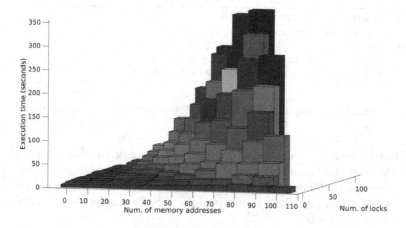

Fig. 7. TeSSLa interpreter startup time for sw.tessla

between around 40 memory locations with 100 locks and 90 memory locations with 20 locks.

```
105923234788: holding_1 = 21653
105923846011: holding_3 = 21653
105923949854: holding_1 = -1
105924265689: holding_1 = 21525
105924621853: thread_accessing_1 = 709525559
105924716727: thread_accessing_1 = 709525559
105924764106: holding_2 = 21525
105924822656: holding_3 = -1
105924872330: holding_1 = -1
105925531285: thread_accessing_0 = 705331255
105925621081: thread_accessing_0 = 705331255
105925674037: holding_1 = 21653
105925731366: holding_2 = -1
105926266497: holding_2 = 21653
```

Fig. 8. Events emitted by the COEMS trace box after processing the hardware half of the TeSSLa specification

```
105847960743: error_0_in_line = 52
105847960743: error_0 = true
105848052196: error_0_in_line = 53
105848052196: error_0 = true
105848316093: error_0_in_line = 54
105848316093: error_0 = true
```

Fig. 9. Race report obtained by processing Fig. 8 including debug information

```
1  for (i = 0; i < N_THREADS; i++)
2        pthread_join(ts[i], NULL);
3  for (total = 0, i = 0; i < N_ACCOUNTS; i++)
4        total += accts[i].balance;
5  printf("Total money in system: %ld\n", total);
```

Fig. 10. Example of false positive after threads have terminated

When we run our C code with the DATA_RACE flag on, the first stage produces the output stream shown in Fig. 8. This stream contains summaries on which thread is holding which lock and accessing any of the selected memory addresses. We then pipe those events into the TeSSLa interpreter with the other half of the specification.

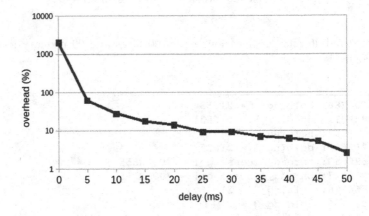

Fig. 11. Overhead introduced by the instrumentation.

The TeSSLa interpreter correctly reports (Fig. 9) the data race errors on the error_X_in_line streams, triggered by the accesses in lines 12–15 in Fig. 5 (corresponding to lines 52, 53 and 54 in the source code). These data race errors are caused by the missing lock of mutex accts[from].mtx by thread id_0. Our tool also detects a false positive in line 4 in Fig. 10 that happens when the main() thread accesses the balance in each account once all banker-threads have terminated. The barrier introduced by pthread_join() cannot be detected by our lockset-based approach, as it does not actually keep track of the threads in use by the program.

Performance. We have so far only obtained partial performance measurements, as currently our instrumentation needs a global lock to serialize transmission of three events per observation to the FPGA. We transmit the thread-id, the address of the relevant datum, and the line number in the source code to aid in debugging. The lock guards against interleaving between the two cores and context-switches on the same core. This leads to a penalty factor of about 20 in execution time over the original uninstrumented code. At least 50% of that overhead can be attributed to the lock, effectively linearising the above example.

Figure 11 shows the overhead in percent of the instrumented version against the original code. To simulate other workloads with less contention (i.e., larger regions where no race checking is required), we have introduced a configurable `usleep()` instruction between both accesses to the bank accounts. The graph shows that the high overhead is due to the tight loop accessing the accounts, and naturally becomes less prominent as contention goes down.

Another factor affecting overhead is that our instrumentation has not yet been optimised and shares code with the software-tracing for prototyping, which among other things means that even when doing hardware-tracing, additional arguments are passed on the stack that the hardware-tracing does not actually consume. Future improvements in the low level runtime support for data trace events may also bring better performance by allowing larger payloads in a single message, which would allow our instrumentation to avoid the explicit global lock.

We have not yet devised a setup that can measure the performance of evaluating the specification, apart from considerations based purely on the use of EPUs and clock rate of the FPGA: our measurements are currently completely dominated by the USB-interface overhead of polling the output events from the FPGA, and do not allow to precisely factor out the processing time. Additionally, intermediate output from the FPGA to the interpreter is transferred in a verbose ASCII-format.

As for memory consumption, our instrumentation does not need to maintain any data structures, and only passes primitive values such as pointer addresses that are already computed and presumably available in registers anyway.

5   Conclusion

In this paper, we followed the path initiated by our guest of honor in the direction of practical approaches for runtime verification. More in detail, we have shown how to use the COEMS technology, a novel platform for online monitoring of multicore systems, and contextualized it to check for potential data races in applications that use locks for synchronisation, one of our guest's research areas.

Through the COEMS platform, developers can observe the control-flow in a digital twin of their application under test on an embedded systems without affecting the behaviour. Additional instrumentation of the application can send more detailed data at negligible cost.

We presented an outline on how the lockset-based Eraser algorithm can be encoded in the TeSSLa-specification language for a given application. This specification is then compiled onto the external COEMS FPGA and uses the data- and control flow trace emitted from the system under test to observe a specified set of locks and memory locations. As the full specification exceeds the capabilities (in terms of size) of the available prototype, we combine a hardware- and a software stage to report on potential races.

Races may still hide in parts of the code that have not been executed, and our checker may report false positives, which is also a general limitation of tools based on the Eraser algorithm. On the positive side, the COEMS hardware race checker does not negatively affect the performance of the application, so potential users need to carefully assess this tradeoff and structure their code to minimize warnings.

The data race analysis uses the LLVM compiler framework, and currently works with threads using `pthread_mutex_lock/unlock` operations for protecting the shared variables. For other ways of synchronization, e.g., through compare-and-swap instructions, or baremetal execution, we do not provide instrumentation and a template yet, but they can easily be adapted from our code.

A practical limitation of the data trace is the currently restricted value-range of the trace messages to 16 bits, which complicates e.g. the use of pointers in the trace. As currently we need multiple messages per event to transmit additional data such as debugging information (the current line number) and the thread identifier, we need to serialize use of the trace bus. This additional locking that is introduced through the instrumentation affects the performance of the application under test, whereas transmitting a single datum in principle has negligible execution overhead.

Our unoptimised performance measurements already puts us in a competitive range with other approaches such as ThreadSanitizer, and we have the advantage that COEMS-based tracing can remain enabled in production. Future developments of the COEMS platform beyond its current prototype will make splitting the specification and post-processing in the interpreter superfluous: 18 (instead of the currently 8) available EPUs will already allow for setups without dynamic values to be handled completely in hardware. In the meantime, we are improving the instrumentation to produce effect summaries for basic blocks of code instead of instrumenting single instructions, which should decrease the overhead especially for tight loops.

We are also preparing additional concurrency patterns that monitor actual deadlocks and so-called lock-order-reversal.

References

1. Ahishakiye, F., Jarabo, J.I.R., Pun, K.I., Stolz, V.: Open data for banker example, December 2020. https://doi.org/10.5281/zenodo.4381982
2. Ahishakiye, F., Jarabo, J.I.R., Stolz, V.: Lock instrumentation tool (2020). https://github.com/selabhvl/coems-racechecker
3. Artho, C., Havelund, K., Biere, A.: High-level data races. Softw. Test. Verif. Reliab. **13**(4), 207–227 (2003). https://doi.org/10.1002/stvr.281
4. Baumeister, J., Finkbeiner, B., Schwenger, M., Torfah, H.: FPGA stream-monitoring of real-time properties. ACM Trans. Embed. Comput. Syst. **18**(5s) (2019). https://doi.org/10.1145/3358220
5. Binkert, N., et al.: The Gem5 simulator. SIGARCH Comput. Archit. News **39**(2), 1–7 (2011). https://doi.org/10.1145/2024716.2024718
6. Bodden, E., Havelund, K.: Aspect-oriented race detection in Java. IEEE Trans. Software Eng. **36**(4), 509–527 (2010). https://doi.org/10.1109/TSE.2010.25

7. Convent, L., Hungerecker, S., Scheffel, T., Schmitz, M., Thoma, D., Weiss, A.: Hardware-based runtime verification with embedded tracing units and stream processing. In: Colombo, C., Leucker, M. (eds.) RV 2018. LNCS, vol. 11237, pp. 43–63. Springer, Cham (2018). https://doi.org/10.1007/978-3-030-03769-7_5

8. Decker, N., et al.: Online analysis of debug trace data for embedded systems. In: Madsen, J., Coskun, A.K. (eds.) Design, Automation & Test in Europe Conference & Exhibition, DATE 2018, pp. 851–856. IEEE (2018)

9. Drzevitzky, S., Kastens, U., Platzner, M.: Proof-carrying hardware: towards runtime verification of reconfigurable modules. In: 2009 International Conference on Reconfigurable Computing and FPGAs, pp. 189–194. IEEE (2009)

10. Filman, R., Havelund, K.: Source-code instrumentation and quantification of events. In: Foundations of Aspect-Oriented Languages (FOAL 2002), No. TR 02-06, April 2002. http://www.cs.ucf.edu/~leavens/FOAL/papers-2002/TR.pdf

11. Flanagan, C., Freund, S.N.: FastTrack: efficient and precise dynamic race detection. In: Hind, M., Diwan, A. (eds.) Proceedings 2009 ACM SIGPLAN Conference on Programming Language Design and Implementation, PLDI 2009, pp. 121–133. ACM (2009)

12. Havelund, K., Reger, G., Roşu, G.: Runtime verification past experiences and future projections. In: Steffen, B., Woeginger, G. (eds.) Computing and Software Science. LNCS, vol. 10000, pp. 532–562. Springer, Cham (2019). https://doi.org/10.1007/978-3-319-91908-9_25

13. Havelund, K., Rosu, G.: Monitoring Java programs with Java PathExplorer. Electron. Notes Theor. Comput. Sci. 55(2), 200–217 (2001). https://doi.org/10.1016/S1571-0661(04)00253-1

14. Havelund, K., Rosu, G.: An overview of the runtime verification tool Java PathExplorer. Formal Methods Syst. Des. 24(2), 189–215 (2004). https://doi.org/10.1023/B:FORM.0000017721.39909.4b

15. Havelund, K., Roşu, G.: Runtime Der. In: Colombo, C., Leucker, M. (eds.) RV 2018. LNCS, vol. 11237, pp. 3–17. Springer, Cham (2018). https://doi.org/10.1007/978-3-030-03769-7_1

16. Hong, S., Kim, M.: A survey of race bug detection techniques for multithreaded programmes. Softw. Test. Verif. Reliab. 25(3), 191–217 (2015)

17. Jahic, J., Jung, M., Kuhn, T., Kestel, C., Wehn, N.: A framework for non-intrusive trace-driven simulation of manycore architectures with dynamic tracing configuration. In: Colombo, C., Leucker, M. (eds.) RV 2018. LNCS, vol. 11237, pp. 458–468. Springer, Cham (2018). https://doi.org/10.1007/978-3-030-03769-7_28

18. Jaksic, S., Bartocci, E., Grosu, R., Kloibhofer, R., Nguyen, T., Nickovic, D.: From signal temporal logic to FPGA monitors. In: 13. ACM/IEEE International Conference on Formal Methods and Models for Codesign, MEMOCODE 2015, pp. 218–227. IEEE (2015)

19. Jakšic, S., Li, D., Pun, K.I., Stolz, V.: Stream-based dynamic data race detection. In: 31st Norsk Informatikkonferanse, NIK 2018. Bibsys Open Journal Systems, Norway (2018). https://ojs.bibsys.no/index.php/NIK/article/view/511

20. Joe, N.: Concurrent programming, with examples, March 2020. https://begriffs.com/posts/2020-03-23-concurrent-programming.html

21. Leucker, M., Sánchez, C., Scheffel, T., Schmitz, M., Schramm, A.: TeSSLa: runtime verification of non-synchronized real-time streams. In: ACM Symposium on Applied Computing (SAC), pp. 1925–1933. ACM (2018)

22. Lucia, B., Ceze, L., Strauss, K., Qadeer, S., Boehm, H.: Conflict exceptions: simplifying concurrent language semantics with precise hardware exceptions for dataraces. In: Seznec, A., Weiser, U.C., Ronen, R. (eds.) 37th International Symposium on Computer Architecture (ISCA 2010), pp. 210–221. ACM (2010)
23. Matar, H.S., Tasiran, S., Unat, D.: EmbedSanitizer: runtime race detection tool for 32-bit embedded ARM. In: Lahiri, S., Reger, G. (eds.) RV 2017. LNCS, vol. 10548, pp. 380–389. Springer, Cham (2017). https://doi.org/10.1007/978-3-319-67531-2_24
24. MIRA Ltd.: MISRA C:2012 Guidelines for the use of the C language in critical systems (2013)
25. Moosbrugger, P., Rozier, K.Y., Schumann, J.: R2U2: monitoring and diagnosis of security threats for unmanned aerial systems. Formal Methods Syst. Design **51**(1), 31–61 (2017). https://doi.org/10.1007/s10703-017-0275-x
26. Preußer, T., Weiss, A.: The CEDARtools platform - massive external memory with high bandwidth and low latency under fine-granular random access patterns. In: Sourdis, I., Bouganis, C., Álvarez, C., Díaz, L.A.T., Valero-Lara, P., Martorell, X. (eds.) 29th International Conference on Field Programmable Logic and Applications, FPL 2019, pp. 426–427. IEEE (2019)
27. Savage, S., Burrows, M., Nelson, G., Sobalvarro, P., Anderson, T.E.: Eraser: a dynamic data race detector for multithreaded programs. ACM Trans. Comput. Syst. **15**(4), 391–411 (1997)
28. Serebryany, K., Potapenko, A., Iskhodzhanov, T., Vyukov, D.: Dynamic race detection with LLVM compiler. In: Khurshid, S., Sen, K. (eds.) RV 2011. LNCS, vol. 7186, pp. 110–114. Springer, Heidelberg (2012). https://doi.org/10.1007/978-3-642-29860-8_9
29. Watterson, C., Heffernan, D.: Runtime verification and monitoring of embedded systems. IET Softw. **1**(5), 172–179 (2007)
30. Yu, Z., Yang, Z., Su, X., Ma, P.: Evaluation and comparison of ten data race detection techniques. Int. J. High Perform. Comput. Network. **10**(4–5), 279–288 (2017)

Comparing Two Methods for Checking Runtime Properties

Gerard J. Holzmann$^{(\boxtimes)}$

Nimble Research, Monrovia, CA, USA
gholzmann@acm.org

Abstract. A number of tools for runtime verification have been developed over the years, and just as many different formalisms for specifying the types of properties that they can check over the runs of a system. Though there have been some attempts to develop them, there are as yet no general benchmark suites available with event logs of a realistic size, together with the relevant properties to check. This makes it hard to compare the expressiveness and ease of use of different specification formalisms, or even the relative performance of the available tools. In this paper we try to address this to some extent by considering a formal logic and its supporting tool, and compare both ease of formalization and tool performance with a tool that was designed for an entirely different domain of application, namely interactive source code analysis. The static analysis tool needs just a few small adjustments to support runtime verification of event streams. The results of the comparison are surprising in that they unexpectedly show the static analysis tool outperforming the tool that was designed for runtime verification, both in accuracy and in performance.

Keywords: Runtime verification · Interactive static analysis · Interval logic · Performance · Formal specification

1 Introduction

For a comparison of options for runtime verification we consider a recent paper describing a new tool called $nfer$ [1,2]. The goal of the $nfer$ tool was to simplify the analysis of event-logs by making it easier to accurately specify properties of interest and making it possible to efficiently monitor event streams for those properties. In this paper we compare the results from $nfer$ with runtime checks that can be performed with an extended version of the Cobra tool [4], which was developed to support interactive static analysis of large code archives, and consider what we can learn from any differences we find.

A driving example for the development of $nfer$ was its application to the analysis of event logs from NASA/JPL's Mars Science Laboratory (MSL) mission, specifically from the Curiosity Rover. As a specific example of this analysis the $nfer$ authors describe a scenario where a specific type of error event, named

© Springer Nature Switzerland AG 2021
E. Bartocci et al. (Eds.): Havelund Festschrift, LNCS 13065, pp. 127–133, 2021.
https://doi.org/10.1007/978-3-030-87348-6_7

TLM_TR_ERROR, must be ignored when it appears within the bounds of a known type of safe interval, but must be flagged as an error if it appears outside these intervals.

A formalization of the concept of an event interval can provide a useful abstraction for reasoning about event streams in general. It should then be possible to define interval sequences that overlap, are adjacent, or nested hierarchically, depending on application. To capture these notions, the *nfer* tool adopts a logic framework for expressing properties of intervals known as Allen Interval algebra [5]. The operators from Allen interval algebra include, for example, *"i1 before i2"*, *"i1 overlaps i2"*, *"i1 during i2"*, and *"i1 meets i2"*. where *i1* and *i2* refer to specific intervals of events.

2   Event Intervals

Allen algebra allows one to reason about event intervals and draw logical conclusions from relations between intervals. This assumes, of course, that everything of interest can indeed be formalized as an event interval. A standalone event, like the TLM_TR_ERROR event, can be considered as a special type of zero-length interval, which would then allow us to reason about its appearance inside or outside other intervals. Using zero-length intervals, though, does introduce some peculiarities in the logic that turn out to be important.

3   Formalization in Interval Logic

The formalization of the TLM_TR_ERROR property in Allen logic, as given in [1,2], is as follows:

```
cmdExec :- CMD_DISPATCH before CMD_COMPLETE
      where CMD_DISPATCH.cmd = CMD_COMPLETE.cmd
      map cmd -> CMD_DISPATCH.cmd
okRace :- TLM_TR_ERROR during cmdExec
      where cmdExec.cmd = MOB_PRM | cmdExec.cmd = ARM_PRM
```

This formalization defines an interval of interest named *cmdExec*, which starts with a CMD_DISPATCH event and ends with CMD_COMPLETE. Each event in the target log has a name and a *cmd* field, which can hold a device identifier. The *where* clause in the formalization specifies that these fields must match for the events to be considered part of the same interval.

The second part of the specification states that if event TLM_TR_ERROR (taken as a pseudo interval of zero length) occurs inside the *cmdExec* interval as defined here, then it is to be tagged *okRace* (meaning it is not an error) provided that the device identifier on the interval was either MOB_PRM or ARM_PRM.

4   Some Complicating Factors

The test lends itself naturally to an alternate formalization as a state machine, with state changes indicating whether or not we are inside an interval of interest. In that case we can check what the current state in the processing of the log is when TLM_TR_ERROR events occur. But there are some complicating factors that we must take care of to perform the check correctly.

A first complicating factor is that the target event-log captures an *interleaved* series of timestamped events originating from *different* sources. Specifically, the TLM_TR_ERROR events come from a different source than the events named CMD_DISPATCH and CMD_COMPLETE, and although all events carry a timestamp that is ordered chronologically for each source separately, events from different sources can appear *out of order* with respect to events from other sources in the log. Specifically, the timestamps on TLM_TR_ERROR events can lag those delimiting the *cmdExec* intervals.

A second complicating factor is that the target log also contains *zero − length* intervals for *pairs* of events: the log shows that CMD_DISPATCH and the matching CMD_COMPLETE events often carry the same timestamp. This can be a problem especially for the *nfer* specification because the key operators from Allen logic have a formal semantics that does not match what is needed to handle the zero-length intervals. Specifically, the semantics of the *during* operator state that the timestamp on the *first* event of the interval must precede the timestamp of the *second*. This means that it requires a < (less than) relation on timestamps, and not a ≤ relation (less than or equals).

5   A Cobra Script

The property can be formulated in Cobra's interactive scripting language as a textual description of a small finite state machine. The check can be written in about 25 lines of text if we can assume that all events are ordered chronologically. Since this is not the case for the target log, some more information must be remembered, and the extended checker script now grows to about 30 lines, plus some helper functions. Both versions are of course longer than the 5-line version formalized in Allen logic, but have a fairly simple straightforward structure.

The Cobra version of the query is shown in Fig. 1, handling each of the three types of relevant events in the log separately, using small helper functions, *new_interval*, *close_interval*, and *check_interval*, to create, close, and check the relevant intervals. Timestamps follow the event name and command identifier field in the log, in a standard comma-separated values (csv) format. An example is:

```
CMD_DISPATCH, SEQ_WAIT_FOR, 517525760
CMD_COMPLETE, DAN_ABORT,    517525760
```

The Cobra tool turns names and commas into token fields that can be navigated by following standard .nxt or .prv references to the immediately following or

```
%{
    if (#CMD_DISPATCH)
    {   id = .nxt;          # comma separator
        id = id.nxt;        # cmd id field
        if (id.txt == "ARM_PRM_SETDMP")
        {       A = new_interval(id.nxt, A);
        }
        if  (id.txt == "MOB_NAV_PRM_SET")
        {       M = new_interval(id.nxt, M);
        }
        Next;
    }
    if (#CMD_COMPLETE)
    {   id = .nxt;
        id = id.nxt;
        if (id.txt == "ARM_PRM_SETDMP")
        {       close_interval(id.nxt, A);
        }
        if (id.txt == "MOB_NAV_PRM_SET")
        {       close_interval(id.nxt, M);
        }
        Next;
    }
    if (#TLM_TR_ERROR)
    {   id = .nxt;          # ,
        id = id.nxt;        # command identifier
        ts = id.nxt;        # ,
        ts = ts.nxt;        # timestamp

        a = A;
        while (check_interval(a, "ARM")) { a = a.nxt; }
        m = M;
        while (check_interval(m, "MOB")) { m = m.nxt; }
    }
%}
```

Fig. 1. Cobra script for the interval property.

preceding token, respectively. For the above two lines, for instance, a sequence of 10 tokens is generated, four of which are names, two are numbers, and four are the commas used to separate the fields.

For handling a CMD_DISPATCH event, the script checks if the command identifier is of the right type and then builds a new token sequence as a linked list of intervals (named A or M) for each type of interval, preserving the timestamps.

To handle TLM_TR_ERROR events, the script checks the currently open intervals, traversing the linked list for each type, and check if the property is violated. We have to handle the fact that TLM_TR_ERROR events can appear in the log long after the intervals in which they appear were marked closed.

An interval can therefore only be deleted as soon as TLM_TM_ERROR events are seen that are beyond the CMD_COMPLETE timestamp of that interval. In our version of the check, though, we did not delete any closed interval to simplify the processing.

The helper functions are defined in an initialization segment that ends with a Stop command to shortcut the processing over all tokens, as shown in Fig. 2.

The initialization also initializes the two linked lists and declares a global variable named inside to indicate whether we are within the bounds one of the tracked intervals. Variables need not be declared in the scripting language, with the data types determined by the context in which the variables are used. A detailed description of the Cobra scripting language can be found online [3]. The source code for the tool is available on Github [6].

The traversal of the lists of open intervals when handling a TLM_TR_ERROR event uses function check_interval to check if the new timestamp appears within, or is coinciding with, the stored intervals. The function returns zero either when the end of the list is seen, or when the timestamp being checked is found to be within a stored open or closed interval.

Earlier we extended the Cobra tool to allow the analysis of not just source code but also arbitrary inputs, using a new streaming input option that allows the tool to read and process live event streams from the standard input, for indefinite periods of time. This is the option we used for this application.

6   Comparison

Running the *nfer* version of the check on the target MSL event log of 50,000 events, as reported in [1,2], labels 4 of 45 TLM_TR_ERROR events as appearing within the designated types of intervals, and the remaining 41 occurrences to appear outside these intervals, requiring warnings to be generated.

When we repeat the verification with an independent check using the formalization in a Cobra script, we find that 6 of the 45 TLM_TR_ERROR events fall within designated intervals, and the remaining 39 are outside. Closer inspection of the intervals shows this to be the correct result. The reason for the incorrect *nfer* result is that the *before* operator from Allen logic only detects intervals where the CMD_COMPLETE events appears *later* in time than the CMD_DISPATCH event. This results in the tool pairing CMD_DISPLATCH events with CMD_COMPLETE events from later, unrelated, intervals in the event stream, that do have higher timestamps.

Performance numbers for the *nfer* checks are included in [1], and show a runtime of 251.1 s. Various heuristics were defined in [1] to see how they affected the accuracy of the analysis in return for a reduced runtime. From the approximate runs that give the same (but incorrect) results as the original run without the heuristics, the fastest run with the *nfer* tool took 28.5 s. In contrast, the Cobra result is obtained in just 0.25 s, or two to three orders of magnitude faster than the *nfer* run on the same event log.

```
%{
    A = newtok();
    M = newtok();
    inside = 0;
    function new_interval(x, S) {
        y = newtok();
        x = x.nxt;
        y.seq = x.seq;
        y.txt = x.txt;
        y.lnr = x.lnr;
        y.nxt = S;
        return y;
    }
    function close_interval(x, S) {
        x = x.nxt;
        S.prv = x;
    }
    function check_interval(y, x) {
        if (y.seq == 0)
        {      return 0;        # end of list
        }
        b = y.prv;
        if (b.seq == 0           # interval not closed
        ||  (y.txt <= ts.txt
        &&   b.txt >= ts.txt))
        {      y.mark++;
            if (y.mark == 1)
            {   print x " interval " y.txt;
                print " contains TLM_TR_ERROR\n";
            }
            inside++;
            return 0;
        }
        return 1;
    }
    Stop;
%}
```

Fig. 2. Definitions of Cobra helper functions for processing intervals.

7 Conclusion

This experiment illustrates how difficult it can be to correctly interpret complex statements, especially when they are expressed in a less commonly used logic. In this case, the semantics of Allen Interval logic included some surprises, but the same type of problem can cause problems with the formalization of complex properties in more mainstream logics like LTL [7] as used in the Spin model checker [8]. This can lead to inaccuracies that can remain undetected for long periods of time. The flaw that our comparison revealed was unknown to the authors of the *nfer* tool, until we tried to find out why the results of our verification runs differed. A simpler formalization of queries can not only be more robust, but as our comparison showed, it can be significantly more efficient to check.

Acknowledgment. The author gratefully acknowledges the help of Klaus Havelund for access to the event log that was used for the *nfer* verification, and for his insights in understanding the difference in the results obtained.

References

1. Kauffman, S., Havelund, K., Joshi, R.: nfer – a notation and system for inferring event stream abstractions. In: Falcone, Y., Sánchez, C. (eds.) RV 2016. LNCS, vol. 10012, pp. 235–250. Springer, Cham (2016). https://doi.org/10.1007/978-3-319-46982-9_15
2. Kauffman, S., Havelund, K., Joshi, R., Fischmeister, S.: Inferring event stream abstractions. Formal Methods Syst. Des. **53**, 54–82 (2018). https://doi.org/10.1007/s10703-018-0317-z (Journal version of [1])
3. http://spinroot.com/cobra/
4. Holzmann, G.J.: Cobra: a light-weight tool for static and dynamic program analysis. Innov. Syst. Softw. Eng. **13**(1), 35–49 (2016). https://doi.org/10.1007/s11334-016-0282-x
5. https://en.wikipedia.org/wiki/Allen's_interval_algebra
6. https://github.com/nimble-code/Cobra/
7. Pnueli, A.: The temporal logic of programs. In: Proceedings FOCS, pp. 46–57 (1977)
8. Holzmann, G.J.: The Spin Model Checker - Primer and Reference Manual. Addison-Wesley, Reading Mass (2004)

Dynamic Assurance

Confidence Monitoring and Composition for Dynamic Assurance of Learning-Enabled Autonomous Systems
Position Paper

Ivan Ruchkin[✉], Matthew Cleaveland[✉], Oleg Sokolsky[✉], and Insup Lee[✉]

University of Pennsylvania, Philadelphia, USA
{iruchkin,sokolsky,lee}@cis.upenn.edu, mcleav@seas.upenn.edu

Abstract. Design-time approaches to safety assurance for autonomous systems are limited because they must rely on assumptions about the behaviors of learned components in previously unseen environments. These assumptions may be violated at run time, thus invalidating the guarantees produced at design time. To overcome this limitation, we propose to complement design-time assurance with run-time monitoring that calculates the confidence that those assumptions are satisfied and, therefore, design-time guarantees continue to hold. As the first step in our vision, we elicit the logical relationship between assumption violations and safety violations. Then, we develop a probabilistic confidence monitor for each design-time assumption. Finally, we compose these assumption monitors based on their logical relation to safety violations, producing a system-wide assurance monitor. Our vision is illustrated with a case study of an autonomous underwater vehicle that performs pipeline inspection.

1 Introduction and Motivation

A clear technological trend emerged in the past decade: safety-critical systems, such as cars, airplanes, and other vehicles, are becoming increasingly autonomous. The assurance for these systems is becoming increasingly complex for two reasons. First, safety-critical systems often operate in environments that have not been anticipated at design time. The systems now have to understand these newly encountered environments and respond to them in a safe manner. Second, these systems rely on machine learning in various modules, including perception, planning, and control, yielding black-box implementations with high-dimensional inputs. Traditionally, design-time guarantees of safety require modeling the system and its environment, and models are carefully validated

This work is supported in part by the Air Force Research Laboratory and the Defense Advanced Research Projects Agency as part of the Assured Autonomy program under Contract No. FA8750-18-C-0090.

E. Bartocci et al. (Eds.): Havelund Festschrift, LNCS 13065, pp. 137–146, 2021.
https://doi.org/10.1007/978-3-030-87348-6_8

to ensure sufficient fidelity. However, the models of the learning-enabled components as well as detailed environment models cannot be fully validated at design time.

We certainly cannot abandon design-time assurance, but we can *complement* it with run-time assurance techniques. Several arguments for run-time assurance articulated the need for comprehensive self-assessment of mission progress by an autonomous system [2, 9]. It is typical to deploy safety monitoring systems across the system, supported by rigorous systems of monitor generation [6, 10]. Such safety monitors tend to be defined in terms of thresholds over the system's state variables, with a fixed tolerance margin. For example, a collision warning monitor may, in effect, say "you are close to an obstacle and moving too fast towards it." The confidence in such warnings is derived from the pre-determined margin and does not account for unpredictable situations and noisy/missing inputs. This confidence can be improved by predictive safety monitoring [1, 12], which takes into account future behaviors, and combining monitors with state estimators [15], which account for perception/control uncertainties within a limited time horizon.

The challenge is that such advanced monitors also rely on the very models of the system dynamics and perception that we are trying to validate in the first place. The drawback we see in these monitoring approaches is that they do not take into account all of the hard work that went into design-time assurance of those models; instead, they try to estimate the confidence in the mission progress directly from the observations. In this paper, we are advocating for a different approach to run-time assurance, one that builds upon modern model-based verification technologies. The question we are asking at run time is: based on what we observe, how confident are we that our verification guarantees still imply that the system will succeed in its mission?

Our approach investigates, at design time, how the design-time verification guarantees can be invalidated at run time. The process of eliciting these potential problems is similar to the traditional hazard analysis [5, 11], but instead of hazards introduced by component failures, we consider the hazards introduced by the limitations of design-time verification technologies. Specifically, we focus on the *assumptions* that are by necessity made at design time to enable verification. If an assumption is violated, the guarantee may become invalid as well. We consider examples of such assumptions below in the running example.

We note that a violated assumption does not, by itself, mean that the mission is compromised. However, as long as the assumptions are not violated, we know that design-time guarantees hold. Therefore, if we identify all the assumptions subject to violation, our confidence in them can be used as a *lower bound on the probability* that the system's mission is on track.

Illustrative Example. Consider a simple example of an autonomous underwater vehicle (AUV) that inspects a pipeline on an ocean floor. This example was used as a case study in the Assured Autonomy program funded by DARPA.

Figure 1 illustrates a typical mission of follow the pipe while avoiding an obstacle. The mission specification is as follows: *If no obstacles ahead are present, the AUV should follow the pipeline at a constant distance that allows it to obtain the best resolution of the sonar image. When an obstacle is encountered, the AUV needs to maintain a specified separation from the obstacle without losing the pipeline.* The AUV is equipped with a front-looking sonar to detect obstacles and a side-looking synthetic-aperture sonar to track the pipeline. In order to perform the mission autonomously, the AUV is also equipped with three learning-enabled components. First, an *obstacle detector* discovers obstacles in the front sonar image and calculates the distance to the nearest obstacle, as well as its size. Second, a *perception component* detects the pipeline in the side sonar image and calculates the distance to the pipeline and the vehicle's heading relative to the pipeline. Finally, a *neural-network controller* takes in the relative heading, the distance to the pipeline, and the obstacle information, and calculates control commands for the actuators on the vehicle.

We assume a scenario where design-time assurance for such a mission is provided by formal closed-loop verification. In our case study, we modeled the AUV and its environment as a hybrid system and used the tool Verisig [7] to perform reachability analysis of the system model and verify that the mission requirements are satisfied. Such analysis is subject to a number of assumptions. In particular, we had to assume that the physical dynamics of the AUV have been accurately captured by the model; that is, the response of the vehicle to an actuation command is within a certain error bound of the model's prediction. Further, the perception component, itself implemented using a neural network, was too complex to be included in the model for verification. Instead, we assumed that it always provides an accurate readings—also up to an error bound—of the AUV's distance and heading relative to the pipeline. These assumptions are likely to be violated at run time.

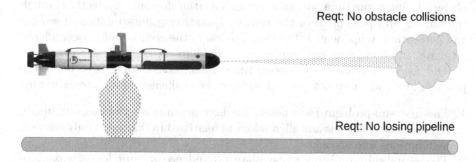

Reqt: No obstacle collisions

Reqt: No losing pipeline

Fig. 1. Requirements for underwater pipeline inspection with an AUV.

2   Problem Statement and Challenges

We aim to address the following problem: given run-time observations of the system's operation, determine the level of confidence that the guarantees of satisfaction of the safety requirements, established at design time, still hold. A low confidence in these guarantees does not necessarily mean that a violation of safety requirements is imminent. However, a probabilistic interpretation of this confidence would serve as a lower bound on the probability that the mission is safe. To make this confidence useful, however, we should make the gap between our estimate and the probability of being safe as small as possible.

Revisiting our AUV example, we intend to monitor the operation of learning-enabled components that process the readings from the forward and side sonars and compute control commands, as well as how the vehicle responds to the control commands. From these observations, we intend to compute an estimate of the probability that the design-time verification results apply; namely, that the AUV will neither lose the pipeline nor collide with an obstacle.

Verification results may become invalid if the verification models were inaccurate or if assumptions used in constructing these models are violated at run time. In the case of the AUV, some possible causes of invalid guarantees are that (1) the sonars are less reliable that we expected (e.g., because the water has more dust particles, which degrade sonar images) and (2) the vehicle responds to control commands differently that expected (e.g., because there is a strong current). In either of those cases, the AUV may collide with an obstacle despite the safety proven by design-time verification. Thus, our goal is to estimate our confidence that neither of these two causes (nor other possible ones) are currently applicable.

This estimation faces two major challenges. First, as mentioned above, a violation of assumptions does not necessarily imply a safety violation. In order for the confidence estimate to be useful, the connection should be as tight as possible, excluding assumption violations that currently do not affect safety. Second, both safety requirements and assumptions typically refer to the actual relationship between the system and its environment (e.g., the actual distance from the obstacle). But at run time, we can assess this relationship only indirectly, through the sensing and perception of the vehicle. Quantifying uncertainties in sensors and perception components is therefore critical to the accuracy of our confidence estimate, and more than one component may be involved in this assessment.

Our focus on violations of design-time assumptions allows us to break the problem into two sub-problems and address the challenges in a systematic way.

1. The first sub-problem is to determine how assumption violations influence requirement violations and elicit a logical relationship that takes only relevant assumptions into account.
2. The second sub-problem is to calculate a confidence measure for each assumption, reflecting the probability that the assumption holds, and to compose these confidence measures into an overall assurance measure for the current mission, according to the logical relationship in the first sub-problem.

Addressing these two sub-problems in a coordinated fashion forms the core of our approach, which we discuss in the next section.

3 Outline of the Approach

We consider formal verification as a design-time assurance technique. Verification—in our example, closed-loop reachability analysis—is typically performed on a model of the system and its environment, constructed in a modular fashion. Each module represents either a particular component in the system or a part of the system environment. Unavoidably, models rely on assumptions about the system behavior, which stem either from insufficient knowledge about the actual system or its operating environment, or from simplifications needed to scale up the verification. If these assumptions are violated, the verification results may not hold for the actual system. In our experience, modeling assumptions reflect the modularity of the verification model: each assumption concerns the operation of a component in the system, or some interaction of a component with other components or the system environment. This observation allows us to monitor for assumption violations by focusing on individual components or specific interactions.

As discussed at the end of Sect. 2, we decompose the problem of computing the confidence estimate into two sub-problems. One is a problem of establishing a relationship between assumption violations and violations of system requirements. We elicit this relationship using the *assumption effect analysis*, establishing a logical structure for composing confidence monitors of individual assumptions into a system-wide *assurance monitor*. The other is a problem of developing confidence monitors for the assumptions based on observed behaviors of system components. Produced by our *probabilistic analysis*, each of the assumption monitors outputs a logical verdict $\mathbf{v}$ (i.e., whether the assumption is satisfied), as well as a level of confidence $\mathbf{c}$ in the verdict. Both of these sub-problems are addressed at design time. At run time, assumption monitors are deployed alongside the components they monitor. Confidence outputs of the assumption monitors are fed into the assurance monitor, which outputs the overall confidence measure. Figure 2 illustrates our overall approach.

3.1 Logical Structure of the Assurance Monitor

The first step in designing an assurance monitor is to establish a relationship between design-time modeling assumptions and verification guarantees. We capture this relationship as a logical formula over Boolean variables that represent the satisfaction of each assumption. Naively, we can always represent this relationship as a conjunction over all assumptions. That is, verification guarantees hold only if all assumptions are satisfied. This formula would often be too conservative, resulting is a much lower confidence than necessary. Some assumptions may be relevant only to certain safety properties and in certain modes of operation; hence, by making this relation explicit in the formula, we can build a more accurate assurance monitor and thus tightening the lower bound on the probability of mission success.

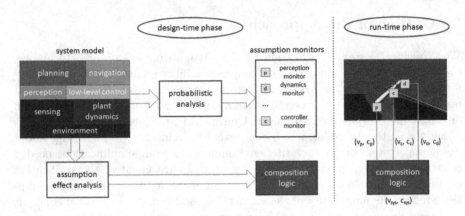

Fig. 2. Overview of the confidence composition approach.

Assumption Effect Analysis. In order to identify assumptions and analyze the effects of their violations on safety guarantees, we follow a process similar to traditional hazard analysis [5,11]. Hazard analysis is an important step in the design of safety-critical system that identifies potential failures in system components and reasons about their effect on system safety and mitigations against these failures. Similarly, our *assumption effect analysis* determines which component models and which assumptions need to be monitored—and how. To perform this analysis, we consider each assumption in turn and analyze the effect of its violation on the system behavior. Ultimately, we identify the logical condition under which violation of the assumption can lead to the safety violation.

Example: Assumption Effect Analysis for AUV Missions. Consider a subset of assumptions that are made during the verification of the AUV model:

A1 The current true state is the set of initial states for which verification passed

A2 Vehicle behavior is consistent with the dynamics model used in verification

A3 Obstacle detector has bounded error on the obstacle distance

A4 Perception module has bounded errors on the range/heading to the pipeline

A5 No false-negative obstacle detections

A6 No false-positive obstacle detections

Assumptions A1, A2, and A4 always need to be satisfied. However, if an obstacle is currently detected, assumption A5 is irrelevant. This is because A5 deals with false negative detections of obstacles, but we would currently have a positive detection. Conversely, if an obstacle is not detected, assumption A6 would be irrelevant; furthermore, assumption A3 would also be irrelevant, because the distance to the obstacle is not used in computing the control command. As a result of this analysis, we obtain the following logical specification for the assurance monitor in terms of assumption monitors:

$$(\neg obstDet \wedge S_1) \vee (obstDet \wedge S_2),$$

where $obstDet$ is a Boolean flag indicating that the obstacle is detected, $S_1 = A1 \wedge A2 \wedge A4 \wedge A6$ is the set of assumptions relevant in the absence of detected obstacles, and $S_2 = A1 \wedge A2 \wedge A3 \wedge A4 \wedge A5$ is the set of assumptions relevant in the presence of detected obstacles.

3.2   Assumption Monitors

Most of the assumptions we encounter in practice are either associated with a particular system component or can be trivially decomposed into component-based sub-assumptions. For example, assumption A1, which concerns the physical state of the vehicle, naturally decomposes into an assumption A1o, which constrains the true distance from an obstacle and its size and is associated with the forward sonar and the obstacle detector—and an assumption A1p, which constrains the true distance from the pipeline and its heading and is associated with the side sonar and the pipeline detector. Such sub-assumptions are often stochastically independent, allowing us to monitor assumptions associated with each component independently of other components and compose the outcomes based on the logical structure elicited above. A single component may be associated with multiple assumptions. For example, assumptions A1o, A3, A5, and A6 are all associated with the same component—the obstacle detector.

   Many assumptions can be specified as assertions over the true values of physical variables (e.g., the distance to an obstacle) and the observable values produced by a component. For example, if DT is the true distance from an obstacle, DO is the observed distance from the obstacle, and $obstDet$ is the flag denoting an obstacle detection, then assumption A3 is $|DT - DO| \leq \epsilon$ and assumption A6 is $obstDet \implies DT < \delta$, for some positive constants ϵ and δ. Since DT is not observable directly, these assumptions can be ascertained only in a probabilistic fashion, with a measure of confidence representing the probability that the assumption is indeed satisfied.

   The assumptions associated with one component need to be monitored together, because they are almost always correlated. For example, if the obstacle detector encounters a blurry sonar image, due to murky water or sensor noise, the detector may suffer a false positive or false negative, and the distance projection it produces is likely to be meaningless as well. To account for such dependencies, we create a *probabilistic confidence model* for each component, the nature of which depends on the circumstances. Generally, a broad range of state estimators, such as Kalman and particle filters, and probabilistic models, such as Bayesian nets, can be used for this purpose. In some cases, a component may already have a monitor that produces a confidence estimate in its correct operation. For example, neural network classifiers often produce a confidence in the classification outcome. In this case, our probabilistic confidence model would relate this value to confidence estimates of related assumptions. In other cases, e.g., to check whether a dynamics model is valid, we may need to apply a statistical detection method that would yield a distribution over the unknown variables.

For our AUV case study, we concentrated on the assumptions about vehicle dynamics and perception components. For the vehicle dynamics, we plan to use a lightweight technique for model invalidation [3], which applies classification-based techniques to conclude that observed responses of the vehicle to a sequence of actuator commands do not comply with a dynamics model. The technique provides us with a level of confidence, which, if properly calibrated, corresponds to a probability that the assumed model is not valid. For monitoring perception, we will apply our recent work on confidence calibration for neural network classifiers [8], which would allow us to derive confidence in perception outputs.

In general, we would require a taxonomy of approaches to produce calibrated confidence for different kinds of assumptions by monitoring a variety of system components. For now, it remains a part of our future work.

3.3 Composition of Assumption Monitors

As discussed in Sect. 3.1, the outcome of the assumption effect analysis is a logical formula that describes the composition of assumption monitors to obtain the assurance monitor for the whole system. However, we are composing monitors that produce not just a Boolean-valued verdict, but also a value that describes the confidence in the verdict. The challenge is to perform this composition in a way that the resulting assurance monitor provides a confidence value in the formula turning into "true". In particular, since the assumptions in sub-formulas f_1 and f_2 are neither independent nor mutually exclusive, the composition is not as simple as replacing $P(f_1 \wedge f_2)$ with $P(f_1) \cdot P(f_2)$ and $P(f_1 \vee f_2)$ with $P(f_1) + P(f_2)$. Instead, the composition should be based on the dependencies between the monitors.

To address this challenge, we plan to extend our recent work on logical composition of stochastic detectors [13], which are run-time monitors that deliver Boolean verdicts with probabilistic guarantees in terms of false positive and false negative rates. This framework allows us to develop composite detectors that are based on formulas of a temporal logic—and derive probabilistic estimates of their performance. Since assurance monitors also perform logic-based composition, we expect them to be realizable in our framework. In addition, we intend to represent the framework with fitting representations of dependencies between monitors, such as covariances/correlations, conditional probabilities, odds ratios, and copula functions. These representations can be learned at design time from training data and simulations or possibly estimated at run time.

4 Summary and Discussion

We have proposed a technique to dynamically estimate our confidence in the operation of an autonomous system by leveraging design-time safety guarantees. Our first step is to identify the assumptions underlying these guarantees and develop run-time monitors of probabilistic confidence in these assumptions. We then consider ways in which violations of these assumptions can lead to safety violations and use this relationship to compose assumption monitors into a system-wide assurance monitor.

We are currently in the process of implementing this vision in case studies of autonomous systems. These case studies will help us better understand the kinds of assumptions that can be effectively monitored and improve confidence composition techniques, as well as evaluate the utility of the proposed vision.

Open Questions. There are several aspects of dynamic assurance that the described approach does not yet handle.

Confidence-Based Adaptation. For autonomous systems it is not enough to detect that the confidence in the mission progress is unacceptably low. Ideally, the system needs to react to the potential problem in a way that would restore the confidence or potentially abort the mission in order to save the vehicle from being lost. Several approaches loosely based on Simplex architecture [14] have been proposed [4]. The difference in our case is that reactions are triggered not by fault detection but by a drop in confidence. Such a reaction requires that we not only detect the problem, but also identify its causes. Here, this identification may be supported by the multi-level compositional structure of the assurance monitor. Extending our framework to support confidence-driven adaptation is another important research direction.

Predictive Confidence. The meaning of confidence introduced above relies on the satisfaction of design-time assumptions up to the current moment. However, if the assumptions are confidently satisfied now, we should intuitively be confident in safety in the immediate future. So far we have not explored the relationship between the level of confidence and the time horizon for safety. It also will be an important avenue of our future work.

Making an explicit connection to a time horizon for safety may also allow us to reduce conservatism in our confidence estimate. As discussed in the first two sections, a violation of design-time assumption does not necessarily mean that a safety violation is imminent. Thus, the confidence in the satisfaction of the assumptions is expected to be lower than the confidence in system safety. This lower bound may turn out to be quite conservative and cause false alarms. One possible way to achieve a tighter connection between assumptions and safety confidence is to incorporate predictive monitors [1,12] in our confidence calculation.

Confidence vs. Robustness. We may be able to establish a connection between our notion of confidence and robustness of safety satisfaction. The idea is that, if the system operates near the boundary of the safety region, a small perturbation can make it unsafe. And since we cannot reliably observe small perturbations, our confidence cannot be too high in this situation. Therefore, a high confidence may probabilistically guarantee some minimal distance from the boundary. This is a promising yet challenging direction of research because formally, confidence and robustness are related through complex verification and monitoring models.

References

1. Althoff, M., Dolan, J.M.: Online verification of automated road vehicles using reachability analysis. IEEE Trans. Robot. **30**(4), 903–918 (2014)
2. Alves, E.E., Bhatt, D., Hall, B., Driscoll, K., Murugesan, A., Rushby, J.: Considerations in assuring safety of increasingly autonomous systems. Technical Report NASA/CR-2018-220080, NASA, July 2018
3. Carpenter, T.J., Ivanov, R., Lee, I., Weimer, J.: ModelGuard: Runtime Validation of Lipschitz-continuous Models. In: 7th IFAC Conference on Analysis and Design of Hybrid Systems (ADHS 2021). arXiv: 2104.15006 (2021)
4. Desai, A., Ghosh, S., Seshia, S.A., Shankar, N., Tiwari, A.: SOTER: a runtime assurance framework for programming safe robotics systems. In: 2019 49th Annual IEEE/IFIP International Conference on Dependable Systems and Networks (DSN), pp. 138–150 (2019)
5. Ericson, C.: Hazard Analysis Techniques for System Safety. Wiley, New York (2005)
6. Haupt, N.B., Liggesmeyer, P.: A runtime safety monitoring approach for adaptable autonomous systems. In: Romanovsky, A., Troubitsyna, E., Gashi, I., Schoitsch, E., Bitsch, F. (eds.) SAFECOMP 2019. LNCS, vol. 11699, pp. 166–177. Springer, Cham (2019). https://doi.org/10.1007/978-3-030-26250-1_13
7. Ivanov, R., Weimer, J., Alur, R., Pappas, G.J., Lee, I.: Verisig: verifying safety properties of hybrid systems with neural network controllers. In: Proceedings of the 22nd ACM International Conference on Hybrid Systems: Computation and Control, pp. 169–178 (2019)
8. Jang, S., Ivanov, R., Lee, I., Weimer, J.: Confidence calibration with bounded error using transformations. In: Proceedings of the 24th International Conference on Artificial Intelligence and Statistics (AISTATS 2021), February 2021
9. Koopman, P., Wagner, M.: Autonomous vehicle safety: an interdisciplinary challenge. IEEE Intell. Transp. Syst. Mag. **9**(1), 90–96 (2017)
10. Machin, M., Guiochet, J., Waeselynck, H., Blanquart, J.-P., Roy, M., Masson, L.: SMOF - a safety monitoring framework for autonomous systems. IEEE Trans. Syst. Man Cybern. Syst. **48**(5), 702–715 (2018)
11. Pumfrey, D.J.: The principled design of computer system safety analyses. Ph.D. thesis, University of York (1999)
12. Royo, V.R., Fridovich-Keil, D., Herbert, S.L., Tomlin, C.J.: A classification-based approach for approximate reachability. In: International Conference on Robotics and Automation (ICRA), pp. 7697–7704 (2019)
13. Ruchkin, I., Sokolsky, O., Weimer, J., Hedaoo, T., Lee, I.: Compositional probabilistic analysis of temporal properties over stochastic detectors. IEEE Trans. Comput. Aided Des. Integrated Circuits Syst. **39**, 3288 (2020)
14. Sha, L.: Using simplicity to control complexity. IEEE Softw. **18**(4), 20–28 (2001)
15. Stoller, S.D., et al.: Runtime verification with state estimation. In: Khurshid, S., Sen, K. (eds.) RV 2011. LNCS, vol. 7186, pp. 193–207. Springer, Heidelberg (2012). https://doi.org/10.1007/978-3-642-29860-8_15

Collision-Free 3D Flocking Using the Distributed Simplex Architecture

Usama Mehmood[1(✉)], Scott D. Stoller[1(✉)], Radu Grosu[2(✉)], and Scott A. Smolka[1(✉)]

[1] Department of Computer Science, Stony Brook University, Stony Brook, USA
{umehmood,stoller,sas}@cs.stonybrook.edu
[2] Department of Computer Engineering, Technische Universität Wien, Vienna, Austria
radu.grosu@tuwien.ac.at

Abstract. The *Distributed Simplex Architecture* (DSA) extends the Simplex control architecture of Sha et al. to provide runtime safety assurance for multi-agent systems under distributed control. In this paper, we show how DSA can be used to ensure collision-free 3D flocking behavior, such that agents avoid colliding with each other and with cuboid-shaped obstacles.

Keywords: Runtime assurance · Simplex architecture · Control Barrier Functions · Flocking · Collision avoidance

1 Introduction

The *Distributed Simplex Architecture* (DSA), is a new runtime assurance technique that provides safety guarantees for multi-agent systems (MASs) under distributed control [1]. DSA is inspired by Sha et al.'s Simplex Architecture [2,3], but differs from it in significant ways. The Simplex Architecture provides runtime assurance of safety by switching control from an unverified (hence potentially unsafe) *advanced controller* (AC) to a verified-safe *baseline controller* (BC), if the action produced by the AC could result in a safety violation in the near future. The switching logic is implemented in a verified *decision module* (DM).

The applicability of the traditional Simplex architecture is limited to systems with a centralized control architecture, or to those under decentralized control to ensure a "local" safety property that does not depend on the outputs of other controllers. DSA addresses this limitation by re-engineering the traditional Simplex architecture to widen its scope to include MASs. Also, as in [4], it implements *reverse switching* by reverting control back to the AC when it is safe to do so.

This paper provides a brief overview of DSA and then presents a significant DSA application: collision-free 3D flocking, where agents form a flock and navigate through an obstacle field to reach a target location without colliding with each other nor with cuboid-shaped obstacles. Figure 1 highlights some of the key findings of the case study, showing how a flock of eight agents, initially

E. Bartocci et al. (Eds.): Havelund Festschrift, LNCS 13065, pp. 147–156, 2021.
https://doi.org/10.1007/978-3-030-87348-6_9

positioned near the origin, is able to safely navigate around a cuboid to reach a target location. In particular, our results show that DSA prevents all potential collisions. A much simpler version of this case study (2D, no obstacles, no target location) was considered in [1].

We conducted this case study in conjunction with the Klaus Havelund Festschrift. Klaus is an esteemed colleague and friend, and a pioneer in the run-time verification community. We are honored to contribute to the proceedings.

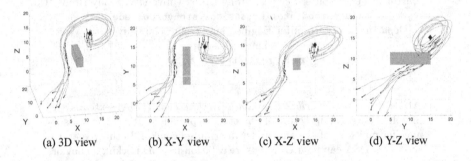

(a) 3D view   (b) X-Y view   (c) X-Z view   (d) Y-Z view

Fig. 1. DSA ensures inter-agent collision avoidance and obstacle avoidance. A flock of eight agents, initialized near the origin, is able to safely navigate to the target location shown as a blue diamond. We represent initial and final positions as red dots, velocities as blue lines, and the trajectory segments where the AC/BC is in control are shown in grey/blue. They grey cuboid is the obstacle. (Color figure online)

2   Distributed Simplex Architecture

This section provides a brief overview of the Distributed Simplex Architecture (DSA). For further details please refer to [1]. We formally introduce the MAS safety problem and then briefly discuss the main components of DSA, namely, the distributed baseline controller (BC) and the distributed decision module (DM).

Consider a MAS consisting of k homogeneous agents, denoted as $\mathcal{M} = \{1, ..., k\}$, where the nonlinear control affine dynamics for the ith agent are:

$$\dot{x}_i = f(x_i) + g(x_i)u_i \tag{1}$$

where $x_i \in D \subset \mathbb{R}^n$ is the state of agent i and $u_i \in U \subset \mathbb{R}^m$ is its control input. For an agent i, we define the set of its *neighbors* $\mathcal{N}_i \subseteq \mathcal{M}$ as the agents whose state is accessible to i either through sensing or communication. We denote a combined state of all of the agents in the MAS as the vector $\mathbf{x} = \{x_1^T, x_2^T, ...x_k^T\}^T$ and denote a state of the neighbors of agent i (including i itself) as $x_{\mathcal{N}_i}$. DSA uses discrete-time control: the DMs and controllers execute every η seconds. We assume that all agents execute their DM and controllers simultaneously; this assumption simplifies the analysis.

The set of admissible states $\mathcal{A} \subset \mathbb{R}^{kn}$ consists of all states that satisfy the safety constraints. A constraint $C : D^k \to \mathbb{R}$ is a function from k-agent MAS states to the reals. In this paper, we are primarily concerned with *binary constraints* (between

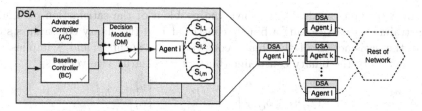

Fig. 2. DSA for the MAS on the right. Agents are homogeneous and operate under DSA; the figure zooms in on DSA components for agent i. Sensed state of agent i's j^{th} neighbor is denoted as $S_{i,j}$. AC, BC, and DM take as input the state of the agent and its neighbors.

neighboring agents) of the form $C_{ij} : D \times D \rightarrow \mathbb{R}$, and *unary constraints* of the form $C_i : D \rightarrow \mathbb{R}$. Hence, the set of admissible states, $\mathcal{A} \subset \mathbb{R}^{kn}$ are the MAS states of $\mathbf{x} \in \mathbb{R}^{kn}$ such that all of the unary and binary constraints are satisfied.

Formally, DSA is solving the following problem. Given a MAS defined as in Eq. (1) and $\mathbf{x}(0) \in \mathcal{A}$, design a BC and DM to be used by all agents such that the MAS remains safe; i.e. $\mathbf{x}(t) \in \mathcal{A}, \forall\, t > 0$.

In DSA, illustrated in Fig. 2, for each agent, there is a verified-safe BC and a verified switching logic such that if all agents operate under DSA, then safety of the MAS is guaranteed. The BC and DM along with the AC are distributed and depend only on local information. DSA itself is *distributed* in that it involves one local instance of traditional Simplex per agent such that the conjunction of their respective safety properties yields the desired safety property for the entire MAS. For example, consider our flocking case study, where we want to establish collision-freedom for the entire MAS. This can be accomplished in a distributed manner by showing that each local instance of Simplex, say for agent i, ensures collision-freedom for agent i and its neighboring agents. Moreover, DSA allows agents to switch their mode of operation independently. At any given time, some agents may be operating in AC mode while others are operating in BC mode.

2.1   Baseline Controller

Our approach to the design of the BC and DM leverages *Control Barrier Functions* (CBFs), which have been used to synthesize safe controllers [5–7], and are closely related to Barrier Certificates used for safety verification of closed dynamical systems [8,9]. A CBF is a mapping from the system's (i.e., plant's) state space to a real number, with its zero level-set partitioning the state space into safe and unsafe regions. If certain inequalities on the derivative of the CBF in the direction of the state trajectories (also known as the Lie derivative) are satisfied, then the corresponding control actions are considered safe (admissible). For binary safety constraints, the corresponding inequalities on the Lie derivative of the CBF are conditions on the control actions of a pair of agents. The distributed control of the two agents cannot independently satisfy the binary constraint without running an agreement protocol.

In accordance with [7], we solve the problem of the satisfaction of binary constraints by partitioning a binary constraint into two unary constraints such that the satisfaction of the unary constraints by agents i and j implies the satisfaction of the binary constraint (but not necessarily vice versa).

$$\left.\begin{array}{c} P_{ij}u_i \leq b_{ij}/2 \\ Q_{ij}u_j \leq b_{ij}/2 \end{array}\right\} \Rightarrow \begin{bmatrix} P_{ij} & Q_{ij} \end{bmatrix} \begin{bmatrix} u_i \\ u_j \end{bmatrix} \leq b_{ij} \tag{2}$$

In DSA, the BC is designed as an optimal controller with the goal of increasing a utility function based on the Lie derivatives of the CBFs. As CBFs are a measure of the safety of a state, optimizing for control actions with higher Lie derivative values provides a direct way to make the state safer. The safety of the BC is further guaranteed by constraining the control action to remain in a set of admissible actions that satisfy certain inequalities on the Lie derivatives of the CBFs. CBFs are also used in the design of the switching logic, as they provide an efficient method for checking whether an action could lead to a safety violation during the next time step.

2.2   Decision Module

Each agent's DM implements the switching logic for both forward and reverse switching. Control is switched from the AC to the BC if the *forward switching condition* (FSC) is true. Similarly, control is reverted back to the AC (from the BC) if the *reverse switching condition* (RSC) is true.

We derive the switching conditions from the CBFs as follows. To ensure safety, the FSC must be true in a state $x_{\mathcal{N}_i}(t)$ if an unrecoverable state is reachable from $x_{\mathcal{N}_i}(t)$ in one time step η. For a CBF in a given state, we define a *worst-case action* to be an action that minimizes the CBF's Lie derivative. The check for one-step reachability of an unrecoverable state is based on the minimum value of the Lie derivative of the CBFs, which corresponds to the worst-case actions by the agents. Hence, for each CBF h, we define a minimum threshold value $\lambda_h(x_{\mathcal{N}_i})$ equal to the magnitude of the minimum of the Lie derivative of the CBF times η, and we switch to the BC if, in the current state, the value of any CBF h is less than $\lambda_h(x_{\mathcal{N}_i})$. This directly ensures that none of the CBFs can decrease enough to become negative during the next control period.

We derive the RSC using a similar approach, except the inequalities are reversed and an m-time-step reachability check with $m > 1$ is used; the latter prevents frequent back-and-forth switching between the AC and BC. The RSC holds if in the current state, the value of each CBF h is greater than the threshold $m\lambda_h(x_{\mathcal{N}_i})$. This results in an FSC and RSC of the following form:

$$FSC(x_{\mathcal{N}_i}) = (h_i < \lambda_{h_i}(x_{\mathcal{N}_i})) \vee (\exists j \in \mathcal{N}_i \mid h_{ij} < \lambda_{h_{ij}}(x_{\mathcal{N}_i})) \tag{3}$$

$$RSC(x_{\mathcal{N}_i}) = (h_i > m\lambda_{h_i}(x_{\mathcal{N}_i})) \wedge (\forall j \in \mathcal{N}_i \mid h_{ij} > m\lambda_{h_{ij}}(x_{\mathcal{N}_i})) \tag{4}$$

3   Collision-Free Flocking

We evaluate DSA on the distributed flocking problem with the goal of preventing inter-agent collisions and collisions with stationary cuboid-shaped obstacles.

Consider a MAS consisting of k robotic agents with double integrator dynamics, indexed by $\mathcal{M} = \{1, \ldots, k\}$:

$$\begin{bmatrix} \dot{p}_i \\ \dot{v}_i \end{bmatrix} = \begin{bmatrix} 0 & I_{3\times3} \\ 0 & 0 \end{bmatrix} \begin{bmatrix} p_i \\ v_i \end{bmatrix} + \begin{bmatrix} 0 \\ I_{3\times3} \end{bmatrix} a_i \tag{5}$$

where p_i, v_i, $a_i \in \mathbb{R}^3$ are the position, velocity and acceleration of agent $i \in \mathcal{M}$, respectively. The magnitudes of velocities and accelerations are bounded by $\bar{v}$ and $\bar{a}$, respectively. Acceleration a_i is the control input for agent i. There are l static cuboid-shaped obstacles, indexed by $\mathcal{O} = \{1, ..., l\}$.

As DSA is a discrete-time protocol, the state of the DM and the a_i's are updated every η seconds. The *state* of an agent i is denoted by the vector $s_i = [p_i^T v_i^T]^T$. The *state* of the entire flock at time t is denoted by the vector $\mathbf{s}(t) = [\mathbf{p}(t)^T \ \mathbf{v}(t)^T]^T \in \mathbb{R}^{6k}$, where $\mathbf{p}(t) = [p_1^T(t) \cdots p_k^T(t)]^T$ and $\mathbf{v}(t) = [v_1^T(t) \cdots v_k^T(t)]^T$ are the vectors respectively denoting the positions and velocities of the flock at time t. For ease of notation, we sometimes use $\mathbf{s}$ and $\mathbf{s}_i$ to refer to the state variables $\mathbf{s}(t)$ and $\mathbf{s}_i(t)$, respectively, without the time index.

We assume that an agent can accurately sense the positions and velocities of objects in a sphere of radius r. The sensed objects include the other agents and the static cuboid-shaped obstacles. The set of *spatial neighbors* of agent i is defined as $\mathcal{N}_i(\mathbf{p}) = \{j \in \mathcal{M} \mid j \neq i \wedge \|p_i - p_j\| < r\}$, where $\|\cdot\|$ denotes the Euclidean norm. The obstacles which are completely or partially within the sensing range of agent i are denoted by the set $\mathcal{O}_i$.

The MAS is characterized by a set of operational constraints which include physical limits and safety properties. States that satisfy the operational constraints are called *admissible*, and are denoted by the set $\mathcal{A} \in \mathbb{R}^{6k}$. The desired safety property is that no agent is in a "state of collision" with any other agent or any obstacle. A pair of agents is considered to be in a *state of collision* if the Euclidean distance between them is less than a threshold distance $d_\alpha \in \mathbb{R}^+$, resulting in binary safety constraints of the form: $\|p_i - p_j\| - d_\alpha \geq 0 \ \forall \ i \in \mathcal{M}, j \in \mathcal{N}_i$. Similarly, an agent is considered to be in a state of collision with an obstacle if the shortest Euclidean distance between the agent and the obstacle is less than a threshold distance $d_\beta \in \mathbb{R}^+$, resulting in unary safety constraints of the form: $\|p_i - p_o\| - d_\beta \geq 0 \ \forall \ i \in \mathcal{M}, o \in \mathcal{O}$. A state $\mathbf{s}$ is *recoverable* if all agents can brake (de-accelerate) relative to each other and relative to the stationary obstacles without colliding. Otherwise, $\mathbf{s}$ is considered *unrecoverable*.

3.1   Synthesis of Control Barrier Function

For an agent i, CBFs are defined for all its neighboring agents and for all the obstacles in its sensing range. We assume the following two conditions on the sensing range:

$$r > \bar{v}\eta + \frac{\bar{v}^2}{4\bar{a}} + d_\alpha$$

$$r > \bar{v}\eta + \frac{\bar{v}^2}{2\bar{a}} + d_\beta \tag{6}$$

These conditions ensure collision freedom, during the next decision period η, with the agents and obstacles outside the sensing range, respectively. Hence CBFs are not needed for objects outside the sensing range.

For each agent i, the local admissible set $\mathcal{A}_i \subset \mathbb{R}^6$ is the set of states $s_i \in \mathbb{R}^6$ which satisfy all the unary obstacle avoidance constraints. The set $\mathcal{S}_i \subset \mathcal{A}_i$ is defined as the super-level set of the CBF $h_i : \mathbb{R}^6 \to \mathbb{R}$, which is designed to ensure forward-invariance of $\mathcal{A}_i$. Similarly, for a pair of neighboring agents i, j where $i \in \mathcal{M}, j \in \mathcal{N}_i$, the pairwise admissible set $\mathcal{A}_{ij} \subset \mathbb{R}^{12}$ is the set of pairs of states which satisfy all the binary inter-agent collision avoidance constraints. The set $\mathcal{S}_{ij} \subset \mathcal{A}_{ij}$ is defined as the super-level set of the CBF $h_{ij} : \mathbb{R}^{12} \to \mathbb{R}$ designed to ensure forward-invariance of $\mathcal{A}_{ij}$. The recoverable set $\mathcal{R}_{ij} \subset \mathbb{R}^{12}$, for a pair of neighboring agents i, j where $i \in \mathcal{M}, j \in \mathcal{N}_i$, is defined in terms of $\mathcal{S}_i$, $\mathcal{S}_j$ and $\mathcal{S}_{ij}$.

$$\mathcal{S}_i = \{s_i \in \mathbb{R}^6 | h_i(s_i) \geq 0\} \tag{7}$$

$$\mathcal{S}_{ij} = \{(s_i, s_j) \in \mathbb{R}^{12} | h_{ij}(s_i, s_j) \geq 0\} \tag{8}$$

$$\mathcal{R}_{ij} = (\mathcal{S}_i \times \mathcal{S}_j) \cap \mathcal{S}_{ij} \tag{9}$$

The recoverable set $\mathcal{R} \subset \mathcal{A}$ for the entire MAS is defined as the set of system states in which $(s_i, s_j) \in \mathcal{R}_{ij}$ for every pair of agents i, j.

In accordance with [10], the inter-agent collision avoidance CBF function $h_{ij}(s_i, s_j)$ is based on a safety constraint over a pair of neighboring agents i, j. The safety constraint ensures that for any pair of agents, the maximum deceleration can always keep the agents at a distance greater than d_α from each other. As introduced earlier, d_α is the threshold distance that defines an inter-agent collision. Considering that the tangential component of the relative velocity, denoted by Δv, causes a collision, the constraint regulates Δv by application of maximum acceleration to reduce Δv to zero. Hence, the safety constraint can be represented as the following condition on the inter-agent distance $\|\Delta \mathbf{p}_{ij}\| = \|p_i - p_j\|$, the stopping distance $(\Delta v)^2/4\bar{a}$, and the safety threshold distance d_α:

$$\|\Delta \mathbf{p}_{ij}\| - \frac{(\Delta v)^2}{4\bar{a}} \geq d_\alpha \tag{10}$$

$$h_{ij}(s_i, s_j) = \sqrt{4\bar{a}(\|\Delta \mathbf{p}_{ij}\| - d_\alpha)} - \Delta v \geq 0 \tag{11}$$

The stopping distance is the distance covered while the relative speed reduces from Δv to zero under a deceleration of $2\bar{a}$. As introduced earlier, $\bar{a}$ is the upper limit on the magnitude of accelerations for all agents. The constraint in Eq. (10) is re-arranged to get the CBF h_{ij} given in Eq. (11). Similarly, the obstacle avoidance CBF $h_i^{(j)}(s_i)$ is defined for the agent i and (stationary) obstacle j where the obstacle is within the sensing range of the agent:

$$h_i^{(j)}(s_i) = \sqrt{2\bar{a}(\|O_{ij}\| - d_\beta)} - v_i^T \frac{O_{ij}}{\|O_{ij}\|} \geq 0 \tag{12}$$

where $\|O_{ij}\|$ is the shortest distance between the agent i and the obstacle j. The vector $O_{ij} = p_i - o_j^{(i)}$, where $o_j^{(i)}$ is the point on obstacle j closest to the agent *i*. The zero-level set of $h_i^{(j)}$ separates the states from which the agent can brake to a stop, maintaining a distance of at least d_β from the obstacle j.

The admissible control space for the BC is defined by constraining the Lie derivatives of the CBFs. For the CBF h_{ij}, linear constraint on the accelerations for agents i and j, are obtained by constraining the Lie derivative of the CBF h_{ij} to be greater than $-\alpha(h_{ij})$, where $\alpha : \mathbb{R} \to \mathbb{R}$ is an extended class $\mathcal{K}$ function i.e., strictly increasing and $\alpha(0) = 0$. We set $\alpha(h_{ij}) = \gamma h_{ij}^3$, as in [10], where $\gamma \in \mathbb{R}^+$, resulting in the following constraint on the accelerations of agents i, j:

$$\frac{\Delta \mathbf{p}_{ij}^T (\Delta \mathbf{a}_{ij})}{\|\Delta \mathbf{p}_{ij}\|} - \frac{(\Delta \mathbf{v}_{ij}^T \Delta \mathbf{p}_{ij})^2}{\|\Delta \mathbf{p}_{ij}\|^3} + \frac{\|\Delta \mathbf{v}_{ij}\|^2}{\|\Delta \mathbf{p}_{ij}\|}$$
$$+ \frac{2\bar{a}\Delta \mathbf{v}_{ij}^T \Delta \mathbf{p}_{ij}}{\|\Delta \mathbf{p}_{ij}\| \sqrt{4\bar{a}(\|\Delta \mathbf{p}_{ij}\| - d_\alpha)}} \geq -\gamma h_{ij}^3 \qquad (13)$$

where the left-hand side is the Lie derivative of the CBF h_{ij} and $\Delta \mathbf{p}_{ij} = p_i - p_j$, $\Delta \mathbf{v}_{ij} = v_i - v_j$, and $\Delta \mathbf{a}_{ij} = a_i - a_j$ are the vectors representing the relative position, the relative velocity, and the relative acceleration of agents i and j, respectively. We further note that the binary constraint (13) can be reformulated as $\begin{bmatrix} P_{ij} & Q_{ij} \end{bmatrix} \begin{bmatrix} a_i \\ a_j \end{bmatrix} \leq b_{ij}$, and hence can be split into two unary constraints $P_{ij} u_i \leq b_{ij}/2$ and $Q_{ij} u_j \leq b_{ij}/2$, following the convention in Eq. (2). Constraints similar to Eq. (13) are also computed for the obstacle avoidance CBF $h_i^{(j)}$ which can be denoted as $B_i^{(j)} u_i \leq c_i^{(j)}$. The set of safe accelerations for an agent i, denoted by $\mathcal{K}_i(\mathbf{s}_i) \subset \mathbb{R}^3$, is defined as the intersection of the half-planes defined by the Lie-derivative-based constraints, where each neighboring agent and each obstacle within the sensing range contributes a single constraint:

$$\mathcal{K}_i(\mathbf{s}_i) = \left\{ a_i \in \mathbb{R}^2 \mid P_{ij} u_i \leq b_{ij}/2 \ \forall j \in \mathcal{N}_i \wedge B_i^{(j)} u_i \leq c_i^{(j)} \ \forall j \in \mathcal{O}_i \right\} \qquad (14)$$

With the CBFs for collision-free flocking defined in (11) and (12) and the admissible control space defined in (14), the FSC, and RSC follow from (3), and (4), respectively. The BC is designed as a constrained optimal controller as defined in Sect. 2.1.

3.2   Advanced Controller

We extend the Reynolds flocking model [11] to include target seeking behaviour and use it as the AC. In the Reynolds model, the acceleration a_i for an agent is a weighted sum of three acceleration terms based on simple rules of interaction with neighboring agents: *separation* (move away from your close-by neighbors), *cohesion* (move towards the centroid of your neighbors), and *alignment* (match your velocity with the average velocity of your neighbors). We add two more terms for the target seeking behaviour: A *goto target* term which forces the agent to move towards the fixed target location, and a *velocity damping term*, which brings the agent to a stop at the target location, preventing it from overshooting the target and oscillating about it. The mathematical expressions for the acceleration terms are

$$a_i^s = \frac{1}{|\mathcal{N}i|} \cdot \left(\sum_{j \in \mathcal{N}i} \frac{p_i - p_j}{\|p_i - p_j\|^2} \right)$$

$$a_i^c = \left(\frac{1}{|\mathcal{N}i|} \cdot \sum_{j \in \mathcal{N}i} p_j \right) - p_i$$

$$a_i^{al} = \left(\frac{1}{|\mathcal{N}i|} \cdot \sum_{j \in \mathcal{N}i} v_j \right) - v_i$$

$$a_i^{gt} = \frac{t - p_i}{\|t - p_i\|}$$

$$a_i^{dp} = -\frac{v_i}{\|t - p_i\|^2} \tag{15}$$

where $t \in \mathbb{R}^3$ is the target location and $a_i^s, a_i^c, a_i^{al}, a_i^{gt}, a_i^{dp} \in \mathbb{R}^3$ are the acceleration terms corresponding to separation, cohesion, alignment, goto target, and velocity damping, respectively.

The acceleration for agent i is $a_i = w_s a_i^s + w_c a_i^c + w_{al} a_i^{al} + w_{gt} a_i^{gt} + w_{dp} a_i^{dp}$, where $w_s, w_c, w_{al}, w_{gt}, w_{dp} \in \mathbb{R}^+$ are scalar weights. We note that the Reynolds model does not guarantee collision avoidance; see Fig. 3(a). Nevertheless, when the flock stabilizes, the average distance between an agent and its closest neighbors is determined by the weights of the interaction terms.

3.3   Experimental Results

The number of agents in the MAS is $k = 8$. The other parameters used in the experiments are $r = 4$, $\bar{a} = 5$, $\bar{v} = 2.5$, $d_\alpha = d_\beta = 2$, $\eta = 0.2$ s, $\gamma = 0.5$, and $m = 2$. There are three cuboid-shaped obstacles in the path to the target location. The length of the simulations is 50 s. The initial positions and the initial velocities are uniformly sampled from $[-10, 10]^2$ and $[0, 1]^2$, respectively, and we ensure that the initial state is recoverable. The weights of the Reynolds model terms are chosen experimentally to ensure that no pair of agents are in a state of collision in the steady state. They are set to $w_s = 3.0$, $w_c = 1.5$, $w_{al} = 1.2$, $w_t = 0.3$, and $w_{dp} = 3.0$.

We performed two simulations, starting from the same initial configuration. In the first simulation, Reynolds model is used to control all of the agents for the duration of the simulation. In the second simulation, Reynolds model is wrapped with a verified safe BC and DM designed using DSA.

To recall, the safety property is that agents maintain a distance greater than d_α from each other and distance greater than d_β from the obstacles. Figures 3(a) and (b) plot, for the duration of the simulations, the distance between each agent and its closest neighbor. As evident from Fig. 3(a), Reynolds model results in safety violations. In contrast, as shown in Fig. 3(b), DSA preserves safety, maintaining a separation greater than d_α between all agents. Figures 3(c) and 3(d) plot, for the duration of the simulations, the distance between each agent and

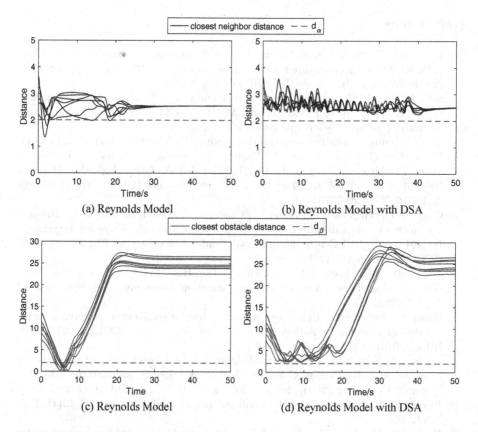

Fig. 3. DSA is able to avoid all inter-agent collisions and obstacle collisions for a flock of eight agents.

the closest point on the closest obstacle. As Reynolds model is not designed for obstacle avoidance, it results in a number of agent-obstacle collisions, whereas DSA completely prevents them. We further observe that the average time the agents spent in BC mode is only 7.8% of the total duration of the simulation, demonstrating that for this case study, DSA is largely non-invasive.

4   Conclusion

The Distributed Simplex Architecture is a runtime safety assurance technique for multi-agent systems. DSA is distributed in the sense that it involves one local instance of traditional Simplex per agent such that the conjunction of their respective safety properties yields the desired safety property for the entire MAS. In this paper, we have demonstrated the effectiveness of the DSA approach by successfully applying it to collision-free 3D flocking.

References

1. Mehmood, U., Stoller, S.D., Grosu, R., Roy, S., Damare, A., Smolka, S.A.: A distributed simplex architecture for multi-agent systems. CoRR, vol. abs/2012.10153 (2020). http://arxiv.org/abs/2012.10153
2. Seto, D., Sha, L.: A case study on analytical analysis of the inverted pendulum real-time control system. Technical Report CMU/SEI-99-TR-023, Software Engineering Institute, Carnegie Mellon University, Pittsburgh (1999)
3. Sha, L.: Using simplicity to control complexity. IEEE Softw. 18(4), 20–28 (2001)
4. Phan, D.T., Grosu, R., Jansen, N., Paoletti, N., Smolka, S.A., Stoller, S.D.: Neural simplex architecture. In: Lee, R., Jha, S., Mavridou, A., Giannakopoulou, D. (eds.) NFM 2020. LNCS, vol. 12229, pp. 97–114. Springer, Cham (2020). https://doi.org/10.1007/978-3-030-55754-6_6
5. Gurriet, T., Singletary, A., Reher, J., Ciarletta, L., Feron, E., Ames, A.: Towards a framework for realizable safety critical control through active set invariance. In: 2018 ACM/IEEE 9th International Conference on Cyber-Physical Systems (ICCPS), pp. 98–106 (2018)
6. Egerstedt, M., Pauli, J.N., Notomista, G., Hutchinson, S.: Robot ecology: constraint-based control design for long duration autonomy. Ann. Rev. Control 46, 1–7 (2018)
7. Wang, L., Ames, A.D., Egerstedt, M.: Safety barrier certificates for heterogeneous multi-robot systems. In: 2016 American Control Conference (ACC), pp. 5213–5218. IEEE (2016)
8. Prajna, S., Jadbabaie, A.: Safety verification of hybrid systems using barrier certificates. In: Alur, R., Pappas, G.J. (eds.) HSCC 2004. LNCS, vol. 2993, pp. 477–492. Springer, Heidelberg (2004). https://doi.org/10.1007/978-3-540-24743-2_32
9. Prajna, S.: Barrier certificates for nonlinear model validation. Autom. 42(1), 117–126 (2006)
10. Borrmann, U., Wang, L., Ames, A.D., Egerstedt, M.: Control barrier certificates for safe swarm behavior. IFAC-PapersOnLine 48(27), 68–73 (2015)
11. Reynolds, C.W.: Flocks, herds and schools: a distributed behavioral model. SIGGRAPH Comput. Graph. 21(4), 25–34 (1987)

Automata Learning

A Context-Free Symbiosis of Runtime Verification and Automata Learning

Markus Frohme$^{(\boxtimes)}$ and Bernhard Steffen$^{(\boxtimes)}$

Chair of Programming Systems, Faculty of Computer Science,
TU Dortmund University, Dortmund, Germany
{markus.frohme,steffen}@cs.tu-dortmund.de

Abstract. We present an approach for efficient life-long learning of systems modeled in terms of our recently developed formalism of systems of procedural automata (SPAs). SPAs describe context-free/procedural systems in which entering and exiting procedures is observable. Key to the efficiency of our life-long learning approach is an SPA-based monitor that verifies individual procedures without having to consider the complete trace of the global system. This in itself allows for an efficient monitor implementation that is able to detect runtime verification errors and—if such a behavioral mismatch is observed—an efficient extraction of on-the-fly reduced counterexamples, thus further boosting performance in the life-long learning context. Our experimental evaluation based on (synthetic) scenarios of various profiles indicates the tractability of counterexamples of lengths of billions of symbols, a number that we believe suffices for most practical applications.

Keywords: Context-free languages · Procedural automata ·
Instrumentation · Runtime monitoring · Runtime verification · Active
automata learning · Never-stop learning

1 Introduction

Klaus Havelund, Dane, blonde (now almost white), male, formal methodist and prize-winner. Two developments, (1) model checking of software and the corresponding development of Java PapthFinder (cf. [55] and related [25,26,32]), and (2) Monitoring of Java programs with Java PathExplorer (cf. [28,29] and related [27,30]) were awarded prizes for their long-term impact. Personally, I (Bernhard) became friends with Klaus through our ISoLA-related collaboration for preparing two tracks entitled *Towards a Unified View of Modeling and Programming* [13,14] and one entitled *Programming: What is Next?* [31]. The contribution of this paper addresses the monitoring aspect of Klaus' research agenda. Whereas Klaus typically assumes that the source code is available as a basis for monitoring construction, we discuss a black-box approach where the monitor is incrementally learned in the course of monitoring.[1]

---

[1] Even though the learning process itself does not touch the code, we require a coding style that enables learnability as discussed in more detail in the course of the paper.

© Springer Nature Switzerland AG 2021
E. Bartocci et al. (Eds.): Havelund Festschrift, LNCS 13065, pp. 159–181, 2021.
https://doi.org/10.1007/978-3-030-87348-6_10

The lack of up-to-date formal models of software programs is an ongoing problem for quality assurance [52]. Initiated by [24, 36, 48, 51], *active automata learning* (AAL) has gained a lot of traction in this context. In a practical AAL setting, a *learner* interacts with a system under learning (SUL) by means of testing to explore its behavioral traits and to infer an (automaton-based) formal model of the system [35, 44, 50]. Many extensions to the original approach by Angluin [6] covering input/output behavior [36], data [1, 12, 19, 33, 34, 38, 43], probability [21], additional computational structures like hierarchy/recursion [37, 42] and parallelism have contributed to extending the practical application of AAL.

The driving force in AAL are *equivalence queries* (EQs) which check whether the SUL and the learner's current hypothesis model (or just *hypothesis*) of the system are equivalent. In case of in-equivalence, EQs yield a *counterexample*—a sequence of actions for which the SUL and hypothesis behave differently—which can be used by the learner to refine the current hypothesis of the system. The inherent problem with EQs in practice is that the black-box equivalence problem is undecidable [46], which makes AAL in general neither correct nor complete. However, there are plenty of techniques and heuristics, especially from the field of model-based testing [9, 10, 15], which allow AAL to be successfully applied in practice.

A particularly interesting approach to this problem is called *never-stop* or *life-long* learning [11]: In comparison to classic AAL, there exists an additional monitor for the system (under learning) that can record interactions with the system. One starts with learning a hypothesis model of the SUL using the conventional methods for finding counterexamples. Once these equivalence tests no longer expose any inequalities, the latest hypothesis model of the learner is passed to the system monitor and used as a reference model of the SUL. The monitor then observes user inputs to the (potentially in-production) system and continuously validates the observed behavior with the expected behavior of the reference (hypothesis). If the monitor observes a mismatch, one of two scenarios has occurred:

(1) If the monitored trace constitutes an invalid system interaction, the monitor has revealed an error in the system. This is similar to classic *runtime verification* and the monitored trace can be used to reproduce the error in order to fix the system.

(2) If the monitored trace constitutes a valid system interaction, the monitor has revealed an error in the reference model (hypothesis). In this case, the observed trace constitutes a counterexample for the current hypothesis and therefore can be regarded as an answer to an equivalence query. The counterexample can be used to refine the hypothesis and the new hypothesis can be used to update the monitor.

Here, we especially focus on the second case. From a learning perspective, this approach can be seen as a never-stopping, user-driven counterexample search that has shown promising results in a number of software projects in the past [11, 40, 47, 56].

The downside of this approach is that counterexamples may be very long as mismatches could potentially be detected only after a system has been in service for weeks or months. For regular systems, the TTT algorithm [39] has been developed that is capable to deal with counterexamples consisting of tenths of thousands of symbols. This is one or two orders of magnitude larger than for competing algorithms, but may still not be enough to cope with counterexamples that have been built up in the course of weeks.

In this paper, we present an approach for efficient life-long learning of systems modeled in terms of our recently developed formalism of *systems of procedural automata* (SPAs). SPAs describe context-free/procedural systems in which entering and exiting procedures is observable. Essentially, any program or system can be lifted to this formalism via a lightweight instrumentation that makes calls and returns visible. Moreover, there exist wide-spread formalisms such as (DTD-based) XML documents or JSON documents that can be described by SPAs without the need of any instrumentation at all. This allows for especially fruitful applications in *document-driven system modeling* scenarios akin to [22,54].

Key to the efficiency of our life-long learning approach is an SPA-based monitor that verifies individual procedures without having to consider the complete trace of the global system. This in itself allows for an efficient monitor implementation that is able to detect runtime verification errors and—if such a behavioral mismatch is observed—an efficient extraction of efficient counterexamples, thus boosting performance in the life-long learning context. The inherent compositionality of SPAs allows one to implement the monitor in an online fashion which makes this approach attractive for network/security scenarios as well. Our experimental evaluation based on (synthetic) scenarios of various profiles indicates the tractability of counterexamples of lengths of billions of symbols, a number that we believe suffices for most practical applications.

To summarize our contributions, we present in this paper

- a formal definition of an efficient monitor mechanism that verifies SPA-based system behavior given an SPA reference model in an online fashion,
- a definition of how our monitor can be used inside a life-long learning scenario to efficiently provide efficient counterexamples to an SPA-based active automata learning process and
- an evaluation on (synthetic) benchmarks to show the characteristics of both our presented monitor and its provided counterexamples.

Outline. Section 2 continues to introduce preliminary terminology and concepts and discusses related work. In Sect. 3 we present the main contribution of the paper: a formal definition of our context-free runtime monitor as well as an analysis of its properties that allows us to efficiently monitor, verify and extract counterexamples for SPAs. Section 4 presents a performance evaluation of our approach and discusses its impact on the practicability of life-long learning. Section 5 concludes the paper and gives an outlook on future work.

```
F -> a | a F a | b | b F b | G | ε
G -> c | c G c | F
```
```
F' -> F a R | F a F' a R | F b R | F b F' b R | F G' R | F R
G' -> G c R | G c G' c R | G F' R
```

Listing 1.1. Production rules in BNF for a system of palindromes over the three characters a, b and c. On top: the original system, on bottom: the instrumented system.

2 Preliminaries and Related Work

We continue with presenting the key concepts of [23] and discussing related work.

2.1 Preliminaries

Our concept of procedural systems revolves around the idea of procedural *actions* and procedural *invocations*, where procedural actions represent atomic actions of the currently active procedure and procedural invocations delegate the execution (potentially recursively) to different procedures. When describing procedural systems via context-free grammars, one gets a nice correspondence between procedural actions and terminal symbols as well as procedural invocations and non-terminal symbols. Listing 1.1 (top) shows an example of such a procedural system resembling palindrome semantics.

Core to our learning and (in this paper) monitoring approach is an instrumentation, that makes *calls to* and *returns from* a procedure visible. On a formal level, this is achieved by introducing observable symbols (or actions) that are executed at the beginning and the end of each procedure. Listing 1.1 (bottom) shows the instrumented version of the palindrome system.

In order to differentiate between the different roles of the respective symbols, we introduce the notion of an *SPA alphabet*.

Definition 1 (SPA alphabet). *An SPA alphabet $\Sigma = \Sigma_{call} \uplus \Sigma_{int} \uplus \{r\}$ is the disjoint union of three finite sets, where Σ_{call} denotes the* call *alphabet, Σ_{int} denotes the* internal *alphabet and r denotes the* return *symbol.*

For the example in Listing 1.1 the SPA alphabet is given by $\Sigma = \{F, G\} \uplus \{a, b, c\} \uplus \{R\}$. Key to our learning and monitoring approach is a translation between a global (system) context and a local (procedural) context. In order to differentiate between the two contexts, we use $\hat{\ }$ to denote the local context and add (or remove) $\hat{\ }$ to switch between the two contexts. A word w over an alphabet Σ—denoted as $w \in \Sigma^*$—is given by the concatenation ($\cdot$) of individual symbols. We write $|w|$ to denote the length of a word and for $1 \leq i \leq j \leq |w|$, we write $w[i, j]$ to denote the sub-sequence of w starting at the symbol at position i and ending at position j (inclusive). For any $i > j$, $w[i, j]$ denotes the empty word ε. We write $w[i,]$ ($w[, j]$) to denote the suffix starting at position i (prefix up to and including position j). We continue to introduce *procedural automata*.

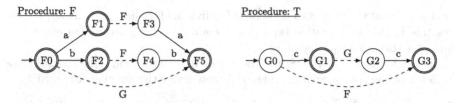

Fig. 1. An SPA representation of the procedural system of Listing 1.1. Sink states and corresponding transitions of the DFAs are omitted for readability.

Definition 2 (Procedural automaton). *Let Σ be an SPA alphabet and $c \in \Sigma_{call}$ denote a procedure. A procedural automaton for procedure c over Σ is a deterministic finite automaton $P^c = (Q^c, q_0^c, \delta^c, Q_F^c)$, where*

- *Q^c denotes the finite, non-empty set of states,*
- *$q_0^c \in Q^c$ denotes the initial state,*
- *$\delta^c \colon Q^c \times (\widehat{\Sigma}_{call} \cup \widehat{\Sigma}_{int}) \to Q^c$ denotes the transition function, and*
- *$Q_F^c \subseteq Q^c$ denotes the set of accepting states.*

We define $L(P^c)$ as the language of P^c, i.e. the set of all accepted words of P^c.

In essence, procedural automata resemble regular DFAs over the joined alphabet of call symbols and internal symbols and accept the (non-instrumented) language of right-hand sides of the production rules of a non-terminal. Here, we use accepting states to express that a procedure can terminate after a sequence of actions instead of using the (artificial) return symbol. We call the aggregation of procedural automata a *system* of procedural automata (SPA).

Definition 3 (System of procedural automata). *Let Σ be an SPA alphabet with $\Sigma_{call} = \{c_1, \ldots, c_q\}$. A system of procedural automata S over Σ is given by the tuple of procedural automata $(P^{c_1}, \ldots, P^{c_q})$ such that for each call symbol there exists a corresponding procedural automaton. The initial procedure of S is denoted as $c_0 \in \Sigma_{call}$.*

An example of an SPA for the procedural system of Listing 1.1 is shown in Fig. 1.

To formally define the behavior and *language* of an SPA, we use structural operational semantics (SOS [49]). We use a slightly modified notation that allows us to label state transformations in order to describe the generation process of words that constitute the language of an SPA. We write

$$\frac{guard}{(s_1, \sigma_1) \xrightarrow{o} (s_2, \sigma_2)}$$

for some states s_1, s_2 and some control components σ_1, σ_2 to denote that this transformation (if applicable) *emits* an output symbol o. We generalize this notation to output *sequences* by writing

$$(s_1, \sigma_1) \xrightarrow{w}{}^* (s_2, \sigma_2)$$

to denote, that there exists a sequence of individual (applicable) transformations starting in the configuration (s_1, σ_1) and ending in configuration (s_2, σ_2) whose concatenation of output symbols yields w.

For defining an SPA-SOS, we first define a *stack* to model the control components of the transformation rules and then define the language of an SPA.

Definition 4 (Generator stack). *Let Σ be an SPA alphabet. We define $\Gamma_G = \widehat{\Sigma}^* \uplus \{\bot\}$ as the stack domain, with $\bot$ $(\neq \varepsilon)$ as the unique bottom-of-stack symbol. We use $\bullet$ to denote the stacking of elements of Γ_G, where writing elements left-to-right displays the stack top-to-bottom and we write $ST(\Gamma_G)$ to denote the set of all possible stack configurations.*

Definition 5 (Language of an SPA). *Let Σ be an SPA alphabet and S be an SPA over Σ. Using tuples from $\widehat{\Sigma}^* \times ST(\Gamma_G)$ to denote a system configuration, we define three kinds of SOS transformation rules:*

1. *call-rules:*

$$\frac{\widehat{w} \in L(P^c)}{(\widehat{c} \cdot \widehat{v}, \sigma) \xrightarrow{c} (\widehat{w} \cdot \widehat{r}, \widehat{v} \bullet \sigma)}$$

   for all $\widehat{c} \in \widehat{\Sigma}_{call}, \widehat{v} \in \Sigma^*, \widehat{w} \in (\widehat{\Sigma}_{call} \cup \widehat{\Sigma}_{int})^*, \sigma \in ST(\Gamma_G)$.
2. *int-rules:*

$$\frac{}{(\widehat{i} \cdot \widehat{v}, \sigma) \xrightarrow{i} (\widehat{v}, \sigma)}$$

   for all $\widehat{i} \in \widehat{\Sigma}_{int}, \widehat{v} \in \widehat{\Sigma}^*, \sigma \in ST(\Gamma_G)$.
3. *ret-rules:*

$$\frac{}{(\widehat{r}, \widehat{v} \bullet \sigma) \xrightarrow{r} (\widehat{v}, \sigma)}$$

   for all $\widehat{v} \in \widehat{\Sigma}^*, \sigma \in ST(\Gamma_G)$.

We define the language of an SPA as

$$L(S) = \{w \in \Sigma^* \mid (\widehat{c}_0, \bot) \xrightarrow{w}{}^* (\varepsilon, \bot)\}.$$

Definition 5 "implements" SPAs as a stack-machine where the state (left part of the configuration tuple) represents the workload of the currently active procedure and the configuration (right part of the configuration tuple) represents the call stack. Upon encountering a procedural invocation (call-rule) the corresponding global version of the call symbol is emitted, the remaining workload is pushed onto the stack and a new, admissible workload from the invoked procedure (including its observable termination) is selected. int-rules simply emit atomic actions and ret-rules terminate the current procedure (while emitting the return symbol) and continue from where the currently active procedure was invoked.

An inherent property of words in $L(S)$ is that they are *well-matched*, i.e. every call-symbol is at some point followed by a matching return symbol and vice versa. We can formally define well-matched words using the notion of a call-return balance.

Definition 6 (Call-return balance). *Let Σ be an SPA alphabet. The call-return balance is a function $\beta\colon \Sigma^* \to \mathbb{Z}$, defined as*

$$\beta(\varepsilon) = 0$$

$$\beta(u \cdot v) = \beta(v) + \begin{cases} 1 & \text{if } u \in \Sigma_{call} \\ 0 & \text{if } u \in \Sigma_{int} \\ -1 & \text{if } u = r \end{cases}$$

for all $u \in \Sigma, v \in \Sigma^*$.

We call a word $w \in \Sigma^*$ *well-matched*, if and only if every prefix u satisfies $\beta(u) \geq 0$ and every suffix v satisfies $\beta(v) \leq 0$. We denote the set of all well-matched words over Σ as $WM(\Sigma)$. We call a well-matched word *rooted*, if it begins with a call symbol and ends with a return symbol. All words in $L(S)$ are rooted in c_0.

Well-matchedness allows one to decompose a word of the (global) SPA into its (local) procedural sub-components. To switch between these two views, one needs a form of abstraction to the procedural level because the concept of *calling* other procedures is not expressible by procedural automata. We formalize this concept by a *projection* which essentially replaces each nested invocation with its respective procedural call symbol. To do so, we use an auxiliary *find-return function* to determine the termination of the current procedure.

Definition 7 (Find-return function). *Let Σ be an SPA alphabet and $w \in \Sigma^*$. We define the* find-return function $\rho_w\colon \mathbb{N} \to \mathbb{N}$ *as*

$$\rho_w(x) = \min\{i \in \{x, \ldots, |w|\} \mid \beta(w[x, i]) < 0\}$$

Definition 8 (Alpha projection). *Let Σ be an SPA alphabet. The alpha projection $\alpha\colon WM(\Sigma) \to (\widehat{\Sigma}_{call} \cup \widehat{\Sigma}_{int})^*$ is defined as*

$$\alpha(\varepsilon) = \varepsilon$$

$$\alpha(u \cdot v) = \begin{cases} \widehat{u} \cdot \alpha(v) & \text{if } u \in \Sigma_{int} \\ \widehat{u} \cdot \alpha(v[\rho_v(1) + 1,]) & \text{if } u \in \Sigma_{call} \end{cases}$$

for all $u \in (\Sigma_{call} \cup \Sigma_{int}), v \in \Sigma^*$.

The alpha projection replaces nested (well-matched) invocations with a single call symbol that is parseable by a procedural automaton. This leads the way to Theorem 1 which provides an equivalent, procedural characterization of the language of an SPA.

Definition 9 (Instances set). *Let Σ be an SPA alphabet and $w \in \Sigma^*$. We define the* instances set $Inst_w \subseteq \Sigma_{call} \times \mathbb{N}$ *as*

$$(c, i) \in Inst_w \Leftrightarrow w[i] = c \in \Sigma_{call}$$

Theorem 1 (Localization theorem). *Let Σ be an SPA alphabet, S be an SPA over Σ and $w \in WM(\Sigma)$ be rooted in c_0. Then we have*

$$w \in L(S) \Leftrightarrow \forall (c, i) \in Inst_w : \alpha(w[i + 1, \rho_w(i + 1) - 1]) \in L(P^c)$$

Proof. This equivalence is based on the fact that for every emitted call symbol c of the SPA, there needs to exist a corresponding word $\hat{v} \in L(P^c)$. One can verify this property for each call symbol by checking the membership of the projected, procedural trace in the language of the respective procedural automaton. For details, see [23].

From an AAL perspective, this equivalence allows one to decompose the learning of SPAs into a simultaneous inference of individual procedures. We exploit this property in [23] to formalize an AAL algorithm for SPAs. For refining an SPA hypothesis, our algorithm reduces a global counterexample of the SPA to a local counterexample of the affected procedural automaton. In the context of life-long learning, this allows a monitor to operate on a very fine-grained (per-procedure) level which allows us to boost performance twofold: First, the monitoring process can be improved because the monitor only needs to verify the current procedure and only needs to store information about how the current procedure has been accessed instead of managing the complete (global) trace. Second, if the monitor observes a violating behavior when verifying a procedure, the relevant (local) information can be passed directly to the respective learner of the concerned procedure without requiring further analysis, thus improving the performance of the (life-long) learning process. Based on these two characteristics, we formalize an efficient monitor for efficient counterexample extraction in Sect. 3.

2.2   Related Work

The idea of SPAs was originally introduced under the name *Context-Free Process Systems* (CFPSs) in [16] for model checking and has since then been adapted to similar formalisms such as *Recursive State Machines* (RSMs) in [3] or extensions for dealing with pushdown processes [17]. Calling them *Systems of Procedural Automata* here and focusing on deterministic automata is meant to better address the automata learning community.

Our learning approach integrates into the *minimum adequate teacher* (MAT) framework proposed by Angluin [6], which describes the process of inferring a system's behavior by an iterative loop of *exploration* (via testing) to construct a formal (automaton-based) hypothesis and *verification* (via searching for evidence of in-equality with the SUL) to successively refine the hypothesis. We expect the reader to be familiar with the basic concepts of AAL—see e.g. [53] or [41,

Chapter 8] for an introduction. Important for this paper is that AAL requires so-called *counterexamples*, i.e. input traces for which the system and the current hypothesis behave differently, to refine the current hypothesis. One of the key challenges for AAL in practice is finding these counterexamples.

Similar to [11], we pursue a (life-long) monitoring-based approach for searching counterexamples, which consists of monitoring the (possibly in-production) system and verifying its behavior against a previously provided hypothesis. The concepts of monitoring and verifying behavior are part of the broader field of *runtime verification* (see e.g. [8,20] for an introduction/current overview). An approach for *practical* context-free runtime verification has previously been presented in [45]. [2] proposes the CARET logic which—similar to our approach—explicitly includes calls to and returns from procedures to reason about their scopes (e.g. pre and post conditions) and may also be used in a runtime verification context. However, both approaches only cover the plain verification of properties on a given model and do not focus on the simultaneous inference of a model (by means of AAL) by extracting information of the system.

Moreover, our proposed monitoring approach is novel in the sense that it exploits properties of our recently established notion of SPAs [23]. SPAs and their instrumentation are similar to *visibly pushdown languages* (VPLs) [4,5] where specific call and return symbols determine the stack behavior of the corresponding *visibly pushdown automaton* (VPA). In fact, our instrumented systems can also be modeled by (and learned as) VPAs. However, when given our proposed instrumentation (cf. Listing 1.1), general-purpose VPLs exhibit additional complexity that we do not require. We have observed in [22,23] that the simplicity of SPAs improves the performance of the learning process by multiple orders of magnitude. In the context of monitoring, SPAs allow us to verify individual procedures without having to monitor the complete (well-matched) trace. With VPAs this would only be possible by altering the semantics of the system, e.g. by inferring prefix-closed VPLs, which is a more complex task than inferring well-matched VPLs. Thus, when applicable, SPAs can be considered the more practical solution, in particular for live-long learning.

3 Efficient Context-Free Runtime Monitoring

In the following, we assume the existence of an SPA alphabet Σ such that interactions with the SUL can be described by words of an SPA language over Σ. We use Σ and our learning algorithm to learn initial hypotheses up to the point where we decide to run the SUL in a (possibly production) environment where arbitrary clients (users, external services, etc.) interact with the SUL. We assume to have a monitoring mechanism that is capable of both monitoring the system (runtime monitoring) and—for our application in the context of AAL—verifying properties (runtime verification).

Monitoring properties: For each client (user, external service, etc.) the monitor is able to observe successfully performed actions and associate a symbol

$s \in \Sigma$ with said action. Consequently, a *trace* of the monitor $t \in \Sigma^*$ resembles a sequence of admissible interactions with the system starting from some unique initial state. This can be considered common practice in the runtime monitoring community (see e.g. [20] for different characterizations of monitoring and a comparison of current tools).

Verification properties: We provide the monitor with a formal (SPA) model from previous AAL runs, which the monitor uses to compare the actual behavior of the system with the expected behavior of the model on the fly. As discussed in Sect. 1, we focus here on the case that mismatching behavior indicates an error in the model.

To concretize our understanding of *efficiently* monitoring an SPA, we propose the following three core goals of our monitor:

(1) The resources for maintaining the information of t should be kept as low as possible.
(2) Once the monitor observes a mismatch, analyzing the trace t to extract critical information should require as least effort as possible.
(3) Especially in the context of AAL, the extracted counterexample should be as concise as possible.

In the following, we present our monitor and analyze it regarding these properties.

3.1   An SOS-Based SPA Monitor

Similar to Definition 5, we use SOS to specify the behavior of the monitor. For this, we first introduce an auxiliary (monitor) stack.

Definition 10 (Monitor stack). *Let Σ be an SPA alphabet. We define $\Gamma_M = (\Sigma_{call} \times \widehat{\Sigma}^*) \uplus \{\bot\}$ as the stack domain, with $\bot$ $(\neq \varepsilon)$ as the unique bottom-of-stack symbol. We use $\bullet$ to denote the stacking of elements of Γ_M, where writing elements left-to-right displays the stack top-to-bottom and we write $ST(\Gamma_M)$ to denote the set of all possible stack configurations.*

Definition 11 (SPA monitor). *Let Σ be an SPA alphabet, S be an SPA over Σ and let $Procs = \Sigma_{call} \uplus \{\theta\}$ denote a set of procedures, where $\theta \notin \Sigma$ denotes the main procedure with $L(P^\theta) = \{\widehat{c_0}\}$. Using tuples from $(\Sigma^* \times Procs \times (\widehat{\Sigma}_{call} \cup \widehat{\Sigma}_{int})^* \times ST(\Gamma_M))^2$ to denote a system configuration, we define three kinds of SOS transformation rules:*

1. *call-rules:*

$$\frac{\exists \widehat{u} \in (\widehat{\Sigma}_{call} \cup \widehat{\Sigma}_{int})^* : \widehat{v} \cdot \widehat{c} \cdot \widehat{u} \in L(P^p)}{(c \cdot w, p, \widehat{v}, \sigma) \to (w, c, \varepsilon, (p, \widehat{v} \cdot \widehat{c}) \bullet \sigma)}$$

for all $c \in \Sigma_{call}, w \in \Sigma^*, p \in Procs, \widehat{v} \in (\widehat{\Sigma}_{call} \cup \widehat{\Sigma}_{int})^*, \sigma \in ST(\Gamma_M)$.

---

[2] Trace to process × current procedure × locally processed × current stack.

2. *int-rules:*

$$\frac{\exists \widehat{u} \in (\widehat{\Sigma}_{call} \cup \widehat{\Sigma}_{int})^* : \widehat{v} \cdot \widehat{i} \cdot \widehat{u} \in L(P^p)}{(i \cdot w, p, \widehat{v}, \sigma) \to (w, p, \widehat{v} \cdot \widehat{i}, \sigma)}$$

for all $i \in \Sigma_{int}, w \in \Sigma^*, p \in \Sigma_{call}, \widehat{v} \in (\widehat{\Sigma}_{call} \cup \widehat{\Sigma}_{int})^*, \sigma \in ST(\Gamma_M)$.

3. *ret-rules:*

$$\frac{\widehat{v}_1 \in L(P^{p_1})}{(r \cdot w, p_1, \widehat{v}_1, (p_2, \widehat{v}_2) \bullet \sigma) \to (w, p_2, \widehat{v}_2, \sigma)}$$

for all $w \in \Sigma^*, p_1, \in \Sigma_{call}, p_2 \in Procs, \widehat{v}_1, \widehat{v}_2 \in (\widehat{\Sigma}_{call} \cup \widehat{\Sigma}_{int})^*, \sigma \in ST(\Gamma_M)$.

An *SPA monitor* M accepts a trace $w \in \Sigma^*$ if and only if there exist $p \in Procs, \widehat{v} \in (\widehat{\Sigma}_{call} \cup \widehat{\Sigma}_{int})^*, \sigma \in ST(\Gamma_M)$ such that

$$(w, \theta, \varepsilon, \bot) \to^* (\varepsilon, p, \widehat{v}, \sigma).$$

The main idea of the monitor is to check for each observed input symbol, if the currently active procedure can still reach an accepting state after parsing the symbol. (To implement this efficiently, one can pass the monitor a system of *reduced*[3] procedural automata and simply check whether they would traverse undefined transitions.)

When reading a valid call symbol (call-rule) the monitor places the current context on top of the stack, switches to the context of the invoked procedure and continues to read future inputs in the context of the just-invoked procedure. Valid internal actions (int-rules) are simply processed and appended to the locally processed input sequence of the current procedure. When reading a return symbol (ret-rules) the monitor checks if the recorded local trace is accepted by the currently active procedure. If this is the case, the monitor resumes the previous context from which the just-terminated procedure was invoked. If any of the guards is not satisfied (or no applicable rule exists) no further SOS transformations are possible and the monitor rejects the trace because it cannot reach an accepting configuration.

Note that each rule of the monitor SOS only reads a single symbol of the input trace and does not require any further look-ahead. This allows one to implement the SOS-based monitor both as online or offline monitor, as each input symbol can be processed as soon as it is observed.

3.2   Correctness and Complexity

For detecting errors in the monitored system, the monitor needs to validate that for every observed input there needs to exist an applicable rule in the SOS system of the reference model that emits the observed symbol. Here, we face the challenge of when to detect the correct (or incorrect) applications of SOS rules.

---

[3] We call an automaton *reduced* if it contains no transitions to states that cannot reach an accepting state anymore (e.g. the two automata in Fig. 1).

The behavior of an SPA is inherently determined by its procedural automata when emitting call symbols (cf. Definition 5). The call-rules, which are guarded by the membership condition of the respective procedural words, decide future configurations of the SOS system. The monitor, however, cannot check the validity of the call-rule upon observing the call symbol alone because neither can the monitor look into the internal configuration of a black-box system nor can the monitor predict future actions as they are only observed once they have been successfully executed.

The monitor can (and does), however, check this property when observing a return symbol. For call and internal symbols the monitor checks whether there still exists an admissible continuation of the currently parsed trace, which, if not, would unavoidably answer the membership question negatively when parsing the matching return symbol. If the guards of the transformation rules do not hold, the monitor has in both situations observed enough of the procedural word (execution of the procedure) to reliably disprove the membership of the projected run (cf. Definition 8) in the language of the corresponding procedural automaton. Theorem 1 guarantees that this condition is sufficient because the existence of a single (projected) procedural run that is rejected by its corresponding procedural automaton means that the complete trace cannot belong to the language of the SPA model. Hence the monitored trace is a witness of an in-equivalence.

Our requirements to the monitor are very simple as only successfully executed actions need to be observed. Consequently, when used in the context of AAL, this means that the monitor is only able to observe positive counterexamples, i.e. traces that are possible in the monitored system but should not be possible according to the reference model. This is not a vital restriction for two reasons: First, negative counterexamples for SPAs can be nicely detected using context-free model checking [16]. Second, with a small extension of the monitor to be able to also detect *unsuccessful* actions, one can easily capture if returning from a state of a procedural automaton would fail, thus providing negative counterexamples. Even more powerful extensions are discussed in Sect. 5.

Reflecting on our performance requirements, we can see that the SOS-based characterization of the monitor meets all of them:

(1) When successfully terminating a procedural invocation, i.e. applying a ret-rule of the monitor (cf. Definition 11), the context information about the just-terminated procedure is discarded, as it no longer holds any value for detecting invalid behavior. This on-the-fly cleanup mechanism ensures that at any time only the minimal amount of required information (the *reproduction sequence* to the current system state) is stored in the monitor's stack.

(2) If the monitor observes conflicting behavior, the procedural information about the error (which procedure, which procedural input sequence) can be accessed in constant-time by extracting the relevant data from the top-of-stack element. The trace for reproducing the error in the (global) system is directly given by a (linear) bottom-to-top traversal of the monitor's stack.

(3) When monitoring call symbols, the monitor directly stores the projected invocation in its context. This means, when detecting in-equivalent behavior,

the procedural counterexample required for the local (procedural) learner can be directly extracted from the locally processed input sequence of the top-of-the-stack element. No further (global) counterexample analysis is required.

The next section elaborates on these properties with empirical data.

4 Benchmarks and Performance Evaluation

To analyze the performance properties of our approach and gauge its potential for the AAL process, we simulated our monitor on randomly generated systems. For a single system, we first constructed an SPA alphabet consisting of 10 call symbols, 25 internal symbols and the single return symbol. For each of the call symbols, we constructed a corresponding procedural automaton consisting of 50 states with accepting/non-accepting states and successors randomly chosen according to a uniform distribution. These automata were then aggregated to an SPA and passed to the monitor as the supposed reference model.

We used the same SPA model to generate random traces (cf. Sect. 4.1) to simulate client interaction with the system. At specific times, we probed the monitor for behavioral properties and analyzed its current stack $\sigma_* \in ST(\Gamma_M)$ to determine its resource consumption and the properties of a potential counterexample, if a mismatch was to be observed at this point. We measured the following properties:

Reproduction Length (RL): The sum of the length of the locally processed input sequences over all stack elements, i.e. $\sum_{(p,w) \in \sigma_*} |w|$. This value gives the length of the input trace required for reproducing the observed faulty behavior.

Maximum Resource Consumption (MRC): The maximum RL value during monitoring. This value gives an indication for the maximum amount of memory required while monitoring the current trace.

Local Counterexample Length (LCEL): The length of the processed trace of the top-of-stack element, i.e. $|w|$ for $\sigma_* = (p, w) \bullet \cdots$. This value gives the length of the local counterexample that would be passed to the procedural learner of p.

Stack Height (SH): The number of elements of σ_*. This supplementary value gives an intuition for the structure of the generated traces.

4.1 Experimental Setup

In order to generate input sequences for the monitored system, we took the generated SPA and randomly (see below) generated input sequences. Similar to the SPA monitor (cf. Definition 11), the trace generator kept track of the current stack $\sigma_* \in ST(\Gamma_M)$ to only emit symbols that are valid in the current configuration.

The generator emitted symbols according to the following rules: The first symbol was always the initial procedure to ensure a valid entry point into the system. Afterwards the generator checked for every symbol of Σ if it was *admissible* in the current configuration (p, w) (where $\sigma_* = (p, w) \bullet \cdots$).

- A call symbol $c \in \Sigma_{call}$ is admissible, iff $\exists \widehat{v} \in (\widehat{\Sigma}_{call} \cup \widehat{\Sigma}_{int})^* : \widehat{w} \cdot \widehat{c} \cdot \widehat{v} \in L(P^p)$.
- An internal action $i \in \Sigma_{int}$ is admissible, iff $\exists \widehat{v} \in (\widehat{\Sigma}_{call} \cup \widehat{\Sigma}_{int})^* : \widehat{w} \cdot \widehat{i} \cdot \widehat{v} \in L(P^p)$.
- The return symbol r is admissible iff $\widehat{w} \in L(P^p)$ and $|\sigma_*| > 1$ (to prevent an accidental early termination of the main procedure).

The property of admissibility guarantees, that irrespective of which (admissible) symbol is chosen, one can always reach an accepting state and therefore guarantee that the symbol is part of a valid run in the system. From the set of admissible symbols we then randomly sampled a symbol according to a weighted uniform distribution:

- Internal symbols are weighted with 1.
- Call symbols are weighted with $x \in \{0.01, 0.1, 0.5, 1, 2, 5\}$ for simulating different system configurations ranging from rather "flat", regular systems to highly nested systems.
- The return symbol is weighted with the current stack size $|\sigma_*|$.

The chosen symbol was then emitted by the generator and observed by the monitor as user interaction. We conducted 25 independent experiment runs (i.e. 25 different SPA systems) and probed the monitor after each 10^x steps, with $x \in \{0, \ldots, 9\}$. The source code for reproducing the benchmark results is available at https://github.com/mtf90/havelund65.

4.2 Threats to the Validity of the Experimental Results

Random generation as a basis of experimental evaluation is often criticized to be unrealistic and biased. On the other hand, there are situations where there is no good alternative: Live-long learning is meant to capture executions of real-world systems that run for many hours if not days and may produce traces of length 10^9 and more. A systematic investigation of corresponding real-world scenarios with multiple of such runs is unfeasible (cf. Sect. 4.3).

In order to still get some indication of the scalability effects of our approach, we decided to systematically construct runs on synthetic systems in a profile-oriented way using a parameter-based generation process. For example, to simulate scenarios where procedural interactions (calls and returns) are seldom used, we chose a low call symbol weight when generating runs. Here, it is mainly the parameter that determines the structure of the trace and not so much the (random) structure of the system. In fact, the generated trace may be seen as a "normal" interaction on a real-world system that utilizes very few procedures.

As we will see in the next subsection, based on this generation process we are able to reveal/confirm the impact of the structure of the considered scenarios on the scalability of our approach. Of course, these in our eyes quite promising observations would still have to be confirmed in real-world settings.

4.3   Experimental Results

Figures 2 and 3 show the averaged and median results of our benchmark. We present these two values, because the arithmetic mean is not outlier resistant and therefore presenting the median data allows additional insight into the data's structure.

Figures 2d and 3d show the data for the stack height. In Fig. 3d we can see, that after a small "warm-up" phase, the median stack height remains mostly constant due to the self-adjusting weight of the return symbol during sampling. The (median) stack height correlates with the weight of the call symbols: the higher the call weight, the higher the stack height. As Fig. 2d shows, we can see similar behavior for the averaged values with the exception of the highest call weight. Here, there were two runs where the generation process predominantly selected call symbols (i.e. other symbols were not admissible), which caused the stack to continuously increase with growing trace length. This outlier also affects other results.

Figures 2a and 3a show the data for the reproduction length. Here, we can see that the reproduction length for configurations with a call weight below 1 (0.5 with a slight delay) increases almost linear with a slope of 1. This is due to the low call probability resulting in very "flat" trace structures where the majority of (internal) interactions happen in a single procedure and therefore cannot be abstracted by procedural invocations. Figure 2a suggests that this is (on average) also the case for the highest call weight. Looking at the individual benchmark data shows that this outlier corresponds to the two runs of Fig. 2d and therefore shows an interesting effect of out-of-control systems (a potentially overflowing nesting of procedures which cannot be abstracted). For the more moderate weight configurations (and the median data of the highest weight), we can see that the reproduction length increases very slowly.

Figures 2b and 3b show the data for the maximum resource consumption. Comparing the data to Figs. 2a and 2b, one sees that they exhibit mostly similar characteristics. Overall, the MRC value is a little bit higher than the RL value, which was to be expected since the monitor can compact the internal representation only after observing procedural returns. However, the resource consumption is mainly determined by the amount of (required) reproduction information and not affected by any external overhead, which empirically supports our claims regarding the efficiency of our monitor (cf. Sect. 3.2).

Figures 2c and 3c show the data for the local counterexample length. Here, the "flat" traces of the lowest weight result in long local counterexamples as these traces predominately stay in the main procedure (cf. Figs. 2d and 3d). Due to five extreme points this is (on average) also the case for the second lowest procedural weight. However, comparing the median data for weights 0.01 and 0.1, we see that already a slight increase in affinity towards calling (and consequently returning from) procedures often allows to break a trace into much more manageable procedural contexts and to significantly reduce the local counterexample length. The more often procedures change, the shorter the local counterexamples

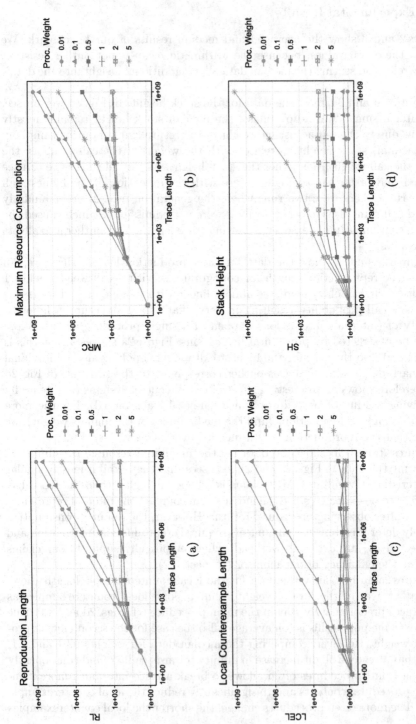

Fig. 2. Averaged benchmark results.

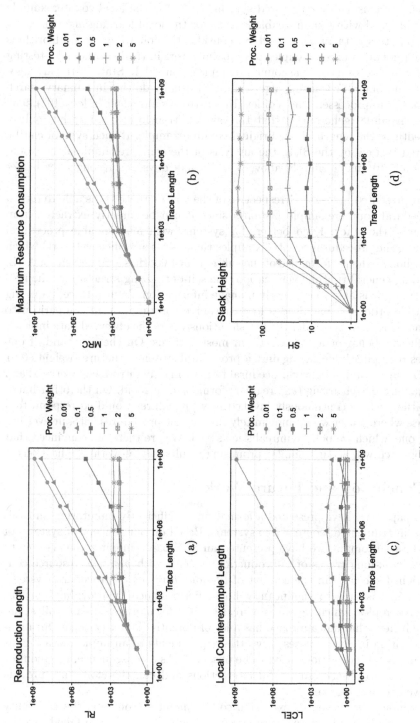

Fig. 3. Median benchmark results.

become. For reasonably structured systems ($p > 0.1$) the local counterexample lengths are well within manageable lengths for the local learning algorithms.

To put this data into perspective, consider the following: AAL algorithms analyze (global) counterexamples to pinpoint errors in the hypothesis by testing (transformed versions of) the counterexample on the SUL. State-of-the-art algorithms (and our SPA learning algorithm [23]) usually do this in a binary-search fashion. For unprocessed traces of length 10^9 this would result in $\log_2(10^9) \approx 30$ queries. Assume (generously) that the average transformed query has only a hundredth of the length of the original counterexample. If each symbol can be answered in $1\,\mathrm{ms}$ by the SUL, the analysis of the counterexample alone would require $30 \cdot 10^7\,\mathrm{ms}$ or slightly above 3 and a half days—even longer for bigger traces.

Our presented monitor—irrespective of the trace structure—is able to return a procedural counterexample *instantly* since it can be directly extracted from the top of the stack. Even better, for systems with a reasonable procedural structure, the procedural counterexamples themselves are efficient (short) which further boosts the performance of the subsequent hypothesis refinement of AAL. Regarding general runtime verification, the self-optimizing structure of the proposed monitor is able to efficiently manage information about a trace, requiring a multiple orders of magnitudes lower resource consumption in comparison to the trace length. We consider the few situations where the observed data indicate non-efficient behavior as unrealistic in most systems: On the one hand, if one chooses to explicitly decide against a procedural system structure (weights 0.01 and 0.1), using an inherently procedural formalism only introduces overhead and one may use better fitting (e.g. regular) formalisms instead. On the other hand, the outliers which continuously invoked new procedures would correspond to a use-case where a user would indefinitely invoke new procedures without ever finishing one, which we believe unrealistic as well. We are therefore convinced that our approach will achieve similar promising results in real-world applications.

5   Conclusion and Future Work

In this paper, we have presented a formalism for efficiently monitoring and validating instrumented, context-free systems. Based on our concept of systems of procedural automata, we have presented an SOS-based monitor that is able to process week-long traces of in-production systems with *practical* resource consumption. Especially in the context of *life-long learning* of procedural systems our monitor is able to significantly boost performance by providing efficient counterexamples, which we see as a great enabler for more practical application.

We believe that our approach has a lot of potential for extensions: Our monitor definition in Sect. 3 poses very little requirements to an implementation, as only successful interactions need to be observed. As a consequence, the monitor is only able to observe successful interactions and can therefore only provide positive counterexamples.

A simple, yet powerful, extension to the monitor would be the capability to detect if observed actions were executed successfully or have failed, e.g. by checking whether or not an exception was thrown. This would allow the monitor at each return symbol to not only check if the action was illegitimately possible in the system, but also (in case of a failed return) check if it was illegitimately *not* possible in the system. Consequently, this monitor would also be able to provide negative counterexamples and therefore increase the amount of feedback the monitor can give to the AAL process.

This concept may be expanded even further by validating *every* recorded interaction, as opposed to only non-admissible actions. This is already possible with the presented approach if one can guarantee that each procedure of the monitored system is prefix-closed. For the more general case, one would need to extend the SPA specification to allow for immediate feedback for an interaction, similar to, e.g., Mealy machines. The benefit of this extension would be that a discrepancy between the monitored system and the specification could be observed as soon as it happens, hence further reducing the length of local counterexamples. We are currently working on extending our approach to Mealy-based SPAs in order to describe systems with context-free input/output behavior and to further boost the efficiency of monitoring-based counterexample search.

An orthogonal line of research concerns the expressive power of the underlying automata formalism. It would be interesting to see under which conditions extensions as proposed in [7,18,38] can be leveraged to improve our learning-based monitoring approach.

References

1. Aarts, F., Fiterau-Brostean, P., Kuppens, H., Vaandrager, F.: Learning register automata with fresh value generation. In: Leucker, M., Rueda, C., Valencia, F.D. (eds.) ICTAC 2015. LNCS, vol. 9399, pp. 165–183. Springer, Cham (2015). https://doi.org/10.1007/978-3-319-25150-9_11

2. Alur, R., Etessami, K., Madhusudan, P.: A temporal logic of nested calls and returns. In: Jensen, K., Podelski, A. (eds.) TACAS 2004. LNCS, vol. 2988, pp. 467–481. Springer, Heidelberg (2004). https://doi.org/10.1007/978-3-540-24730-2_35

3. Alur, R., Etessami, K., Yannakakis, M.: Analysis of recursive state machines. In: Berry, G., Comon, H., Finkel, A. (eds.) CAV 2001. LNCS, vol. 2102, pp. 207–220. Springer, Heidelberg (2001). https://doi.org/10.1007/3-540-44585-4_18

4. Alur, R., Kumar, V., Madhusudan, P., Viswanathan, M.: Congruences for visibly pushdown languages. In: Caires, L., Italiano, G.F., Monteiro, L., Palamidessi, C., Yung, M. (eds.) ICALP 2005. LNCS, vol. 3580, pp. 1102–1114. Springer, Heidelberg (2005). https://doi.org/10.1007/11523468_89

5. Alur, R., Madhusudan, P.: Visibly pushdown languages. In: Proceedings of the 36th Annual ACM Symposium on Theory of Computing, pp. 202–211. ACM (2004)

6. Angluin, D.: Learning regular sets from queries and counterexamples. Inf. Comput. **75**(2), 87–106 (1987)

7. Barringer, H., Falcone, Y., Havelund, K., Reger, G., Rydeheard, D.: Quantified event automata: towards expressive and efficient runtime monitors. In: Giannakopoulou, D., Méry, D. (eds.) FM 2012. LNCS, vol. 7436, pp. 68–84. Springer, Heidelberg (2012). https://doi.org/10.1007/978-3-642-32759-9_9

8. Bartocci, E., Falcone, Y. (eds.): Lectures on Runtime Verification. LNCS, vol. 10457. Springer, Cham (2018). https://doi.org/10.1007/978-3-319-75632-5
9. Beizer, B.: Black-Box Testing: Techniques for Functional Testing of Software and Systems. Wiley, New York (1995)
10. Berg, T., Grinchtein, O., Jonsson, B., Leucker, M., Raffelt, H., Steffen, B.: On the correspondence between conformance testing and regular inference. In: Cerioli, M. (ed.) FASE 2005. LNCS, vol. 3442, pp. 175–189. Springer, Heidelberg (2005). https://doi.org/10.1007/978-3-540-31984-9_14
11. Bertolino, A., Calabrò, A., Merten, M., Steffen, B.: Never-stop learning: continuous validation of learned models for evolving systems through monitoring. ERCIM News **2012**(88), 28–29 (2012). http://ercim-news.ercim.eu/en88/special/never-stop-learning-continuous-validation-of-learned-models-for-evolving-systems-through-monitoring
12. Bollig, B., Habermehl, P., Leucker, M., Monmege, B.: A fresh approach to learning register automata. In: Béal, M.-P., Carton, O. (eds.) DLT 2013. LNCS, vol. 7907, pp. 118–130. Springer, Heidelberg (2013). https://doi.org/10.1007/978-3-642-38771-5_12
13. Broy, M., Havelund, K., Kumar, R., Steffen, B.: Towards a unified view of modeling and programming (track summary). In: Margaria, T., Steffen, B. (eds.) ISoLA 2016, Part II. LNCS, vol. 9953, pp. 3–10. Springer, Cham (2016). https://doi.org/10.1007/978-3-319-47169-3_1
14. Broy, M., Havelund, K., Kumar, R., Steffen, B.: Towards a unified view of modeling and programming (ISoLA 2018 track introduction). In: Margaria, T., Steffen, B. (eds.) ISoLA 2018, Part I. LNCS, vol. 11244, pp. 3–21. Springer, Cham (2018). https://doi.org/10.1007/978-3-030-03418-4_1
15. Broy, M., Jonsson, B., Katoen, J.-P., Leucker, M., Pretschner, A. (eds.): Model-Based Testing of Reactive Systems. LNCS, vol. 3472. Springer, Heidelberg (2005). https://doi.org/10.1007/b137241
16. Burkart, O., Steffen, B.: Model checking for context-free processes. In: Cleaveland, W.R. (ed.) CONCUR 1992. LNCS, vol. 630, pp. 123–137. Springer, Heidelberg (1992). https://doi.org/10.1007/BFb0084787
17. Burkart, O., Steffen, B.: Composition, decomposition and model checking of pushdown processes. Nordic J. Comput. **2**(2), 89–125 (1995). http://dl.acm.org/citation.cfm?id=642068.642070
18. Cassel, S., Howar, F., Jonsson, B., Steffen, B.: Extending automata learning to extended finite state machines. In: Bennaceur, A., Hähnle, R., Meinke, K. (eds.) Machine Learning for Dynamic Software Analysis: Potentials and Limits. LNCS, vol. 11026, pp. 149–177. Springer, Cham (2018). https://doi.org/10.1007/978-3-319-96562-8_6
19. Drews, S., D'Antoni, L.: Learning symbolic automata. In: Legay, A., Margaria, T. (eds.) TACAS 2017, Part I. LNCS, vol. 10205, pp. 173–189. Springer, Heidelberg (2017). https://doi.org/10.1007/978-3-662-54577-5_10
20. Falcone, Y., Krstić, S., Reger, G., Traytel, D.: A taxonomy for classifying runtime verification tools. In: Colombo, C., Leucker, M. (eds.) RV 2018. LNCS, vol. 11237, pp. 241–262. Springer, Cham (2018). https://doi.org/10.1007/978-3-030-03769-7_14
21. Feng, L., Kwiatkowska, M., Parker, D.: Compositional verification of probabilistic systems using learning. In: Proceedings of the 2010 Seventh International Conference on the Quantitative Evaluation of Systems, QEST 2010, Washington, DC, USA, pp. 133–142. IEEE Computer Society (2010). https://doi.org/10.1109/QEST.2010.24

22. Frohme, M., Steffen, B.: Active mining of document type definitions. In: Howar, F., Barnat, J. (eds.) FMICS 2018. LNCS, vol. 11119, pp. 147–161. Springer, Cham (2018). https://doi.org/10.1007/978-3-030-00244-2_10

23. Frohme, M., Steffen, B.: Compositional learning of mutually recursive procedural systems. Int. J. Softw. Tools Technol. Transf. (STTT) (2021, to appear). https://doi.org/10.1007/s10009-021-00634-y

24. Hagerer, A., Hungar, H., Niese, O., Steffen, B.: Model generation by moderated regular extrapolation. In: Kutsche, R.-D., Weber, H. (eds.) FASE 2002. LNCS, vol. 2306, pp. 80–95. Springer, Heidelberg (2002). https://doi.org/10.1007/3-540-45923-5_6

25. Havelund, K.: Java PathFinder a translator from Java to promela. In: Dams, D., Gerth, R., Leue, S., Massink, M. (eds.) SPIN 1999. LNCS, vol. 1680, pp. 152–152. Springer, Heidelberg (1999). https://doi.org/10.1007/3-540-48234-2_11

26. Havelund, K., Pressburger, T.: Model checking JAVA programs using JAVA PathFinder. Int. J. Softw. Tools Technol. Transf. 2(4), 366–381 (2000). https://doi.org/10.1007/s100090050043

27. Havelund, K., Reger, G., Roşu, G.: Runtime verification past experiences and future projections. In: Steffen, B., Woeginger, G. (eds.) Computing and Software Science. LNCS, vol. 10000, pp. 532–562. Springer, Cham (2019). https://doi.org/10.1007/978-3-319-91908-9_25

28. Havelund, K., Rosu, G.: Monitoring Java programs with Java PathExplorer. Electron. Notes Theor. Comput. Sci. 55(2), 200–217 (2001). https://doi.org/10.1016/S1571-0661(04)00253-1

29. Havelund, K., Rosu, G.: Monitoring programs using rewriting. In: 16th IEEE International Conference on Automated Software Engineering (ASE 2001), Coronado Island, San Diego, CA, USA, 26–29 November 2001, pp. 135–143. IEEE Computer Society (2001). https://doi.org/10.1109/ASE.2001.989799

30. Havelund, K., Roşu, G.: Efficient monitoring of safety properties. Int. J. Softw. Tools Technol. Transf. 6(2), 158–173 (2003). https://doi.org/10.1007/s10009-003-0117-6

31. Havelund, K., Steffen, B.: Programming: what is next? In: Proceedings of the 9th International Symposium on Leveraging Applications of Formal Methods, Verification and Validation (ISoLA 2021). LNCS, Springer (2021, to appear)

32. Havelund, K., Visser, W.: Program model checking as a new trend. Int. J. Softw. Tools Technol. Transf. 4(1), 8–20 (2002). https://doi.org/10.1007/s10009-002-0080-7

33. Howar, F., Steffen, B., Jonsson, B., Cassel, S.: Inferring canonical register automata. In: Kuncak, V., Rybalchenko, A. (eds.) VMCAI 2012. LNCS, vol. 7148, pp. 251–266. Springer, Heidelberg (2012). https://doi.org/10.1007/978-3-642-27940-9_17

34. Howar, F., Steffen, B., Merten, M.: Automata learning with automated alphabet abstraction refinement. In: Jhala, R., Schmidt, D. (eds.) VMCAI 2011. LNCS, vol. 6538, pp. 263–277. Springer, Heidelberg (2011). https://doi.org/10.1007/978-3-642-18275-4_19

35. Hungar, H., Margaria, T., Steffen, B.: Test-based model generation for legacy systems. In: Proceedings of the 2003 International Test Conference, ITC 2003, vol. 1, pp. 971–980, October 2003. https://doi.org/10.1109/TEST.2003.1271205

36. Hungar, H., Niese, O., Steffen, B.: Domain-specific optimization in automata learning. In: Hunt, W.A., Somenzi, F. (eds.) CAV 2003. LNCS, vol. 2725, pp. 315–327. Springer, Heidelberg (2003). https://doi.org/10.1007/978-3-540-45069-6_31

37. Isberner, M.: Foundations of active automata learning: an algorithmic perspective. Ph.D. thesis, Technical University Dortmund, Germany (2015). http://hdl.handle.net/2003/34282
38. Isberner, M., Howar, F., Steffen, B.: Learning register automata: from languages to program structures. Mach. Learn. **96**(1), 65–98 (2013). https://doi.org/10.1007/s10994-013-5419-7
39. Isberner, M., Howar, F., Steffen, B.: The TTT algorithm: a redundancy-free approach to active automata learning. In: Bonakdarpour, B., Smolka, S.A. (eds.) RV 2014. LNCS, vol. 8734, pp. 307–322. Springer, Cham (2014). https://doi.org/10.1007/978-3-319-11164-3_26
40. Issarny, V., et al.: CONNECT challenges: towards emergent connectors for eternal networked systems. In: ICECCS, pp. 154–161. IEEE Computer Society, June 2009
41. Kearns, M.J., Vazirani, U.V.: An Introduction to Computational Learning Theory. MIT Press, Cambridge (1994)
42. Kumar, V., Madhusudan, P., Viswanathan, M.: Minimization, learning, and conformance testing of Boolean programs. In: Baier, C., Hermanns, H. (eds.) CONCUR 2006. LNCS, vol. 4137, pp. 203–217. Springer, Heidelberg (2006). https://doi.org/10.1007/11817949_14
43. Maler, O., Mens, I.-E.: Learning regular languages over large alphabets. In: Ábrahám, E., Havelund, K. (eds.) TACAS 2014. LNCS, vol. 8413, pp. 485–499. Springer, Heidelberg (2014). https://doi.org/10.1007/978-3-642-54862-8_41
44. Margaria, T., Niese, O., Raffelt, H., Steffen, B.: Efficient test-based model generation for legacy reactive systems. In: HLDVT 2004: 2004 Ninth IEEE International Proceedings of the High-Level Design Validation and Test Workshop, Washington, DC, USA, pp. 95–100. IEEE Computer Society (2004). https://doi.org/10.1109/HLDVT.2004.1431246
45. Meredith, P.O., Jin, D., Chen, F., Roşu, G.: Efficient monitoring of parametric context-free patterns. Autom. Softw. Eng. **17**(2), 149–180 (2010). https://doi.org/10.1007/s10515-010-0063-y
46. Moore, E.F.: Gedanken-experiments on sequential machines. Ann. Math. Stud. **34**, 129–153 (1956)
47. Neubauer, J., Windmüller, S., Steffen, B.: Risk-based testing via active continuous quality control. Int. J. Softw. Tools Technol. Transf. **16**(5), 569–591 (2014). https://doi.org/10.1007/s10009-014-0321-6
48. Peled, D., Vardi, M.Y., Yannakakis, M.: Black box checking. In: Wu, J., Chanson, S.T., Gao, Q. (eds.) Proceedings of the FORTE 1999, pp. 225–240. Kluwer Academic (1999)
49. Plotkin, G.D.: A structural approach to operational semantics. Technical report, University of Aarhus (1981). dAIMI FN-19
50. Raffelt, H., Merten, M., Steffen, B., Margaria, T.: Dynamic testing via automata learning. Int. J. Softw. Tools Technol. Transf. (STTT) **11**(4), 307–324 (2009). https://doi.org/10.1007/s10009-009-0120-7
51. Raffelt, H., Steffen, B.: LearnLib: a library for automata learning and experimentation. In: Baresi, L., Heckel, R. (eds.) FASE 2006. LNCS, vol. 3922, pp. 377–380. Springer, Heidelberg (2006). https://doi.org/10.1007/11693017_28
52. Rozier, K.Y.: Specification: the biggest bottleneck in formal methods and autonomy. In: Blazy, S., Chechik, M. (eds.) VSTTE 2016. LNCS, vol. 9971, pp. 8–26. Springer, Cham (2016). https://doi.org/10.1007/978-3-319-48869-1_2

53. Steffen, B., Howar, F., Merten, M.: Introduction to active automata learning from a practical perspective. In: Bernardo, M., Issarny, V. (eds.) SFM 2011. LNCS, vol. 6659, pp. 256–296. Springer, Heidelberg (2011). https://doi.org/10.1007/978-3-642-21455-4_8
54. Tegeler, T., Murtovi, A., Frohme, M., Steffen, B.: Product line verification via modal meta model checking. In: ter Beek, M.H., Fantechi, A., Semini, L. (eds.) From Software Engineering to Formal Methods and Tools, and Back. LNCS, vol. 11865, pp. 313–337. Springer, Cham (2019). https://doi.org/10.1007/978-3-030-30985-5_19
55. Visser, W., Havelund, K., Brat, G.P., Park, S.: Model checking programs. In: The Fifteenth IEEE International Conference on Automated Software Engineering, ASE 2000, Grenoble, France, 11–15 September 2000, pp. 3–12. IEEE Computer Society (2000). https://doi.org/10.1109/ASE.2000.873645
56. Windmüller, S., Neubauer, J., Steffen, B., Howar, F., Bauer, O.: Active continuous quality control. In: 16th International ACM SIGSOFT Symposium on Component-Based Software Engineering, CBSE 2013, pp. 111–120. ACM, New York (2013). https://doi.org/10.1145/2465449.2465469

Reverse Engineering Through Automata Learning

Doron Peled[✉]

Department of Computer Science, Bar Ilan University, Ramat Gan, Israel

Abstract. We suggest a method for constructing a system that needs to satisfy some given formal specification φ. In our setting, a black box system satisfying φ is given; we can only interface with the system through experiments and cannot duplicate it or modify its design. Instead of developing a system satisfying φ from scratch, either manually or through algorithmic synthesis, we use a reverse engineering method based on a combination of Angluin's automata learning algorithm and model checking.

1 Introduction

Following centuries in which increasingly sophisticated mechanical tools that extend human capabilities were developed, the recent decades were characterised by the development of computer-controlled systems for performing tasks that mimic human-like capabilities. This includes decision making, vision and speech. A challenging task is to automate parts of the process of computer programming and hardware design. An emerging research area is software and hardware synthesis, where a specification, given in a human-friendly logical formalism, e.g., temporal logic, needs to be converted into code, or a form that is easily implementable, usually finite automata [11].

We suggest a reverse engineering (RE) method based on automata learning and model checking to elicit from a black box system that is known to satisfy a property φ, and with which we can interface only through experiments, a finite state automaton that satisfies φ. We do not have access to the structure (states, transitions) of this black box system, and, furthermore, we are not interested in (or capable of) copying it precisely. Instead, we only want to reverse engineer, through learning based on experiments with the black box, a model in a form of a finite automaton that would satisfy φ. The obtained model can then be the basis for further refinement of the desired system.

The technique studied here inherits elements from *black box checking* (BBC) [9], where model checking is applied to a black box system. Angluin's automata learning algorithm [1] is used to incrementally learn models of the system. As part of BBC, one sometimes needs to compare the learned model

The research was partially funded by Israeli Science Foundation grant 1464/18: "Efficient Runtime Verification for Systems with Lots of Data and its Applications."

© Springer Nature Switzerland AG 2021
E. Bartocci et al. (Eds.): Havelund Festschrift, LNCS 13065, pp. 182–192, 2021.
https://doi.org/10.1007/978-3-030-87348-6_11

with the black box. These comparisons, called *equivalence queries*, are provably exponential in the size of the black box, which limits the practicality of the methods.

For reverse engineering, we are given a specification φ and a black box system that already satisfies it, and want to learn an automaton model that satisfies φ. This makes equivalence queries redundant, which allows polynomial complexity in the size of the black box automaton.

One application of the method presented here is to reverse engineer a system that is based on a recurrent neural network (RNN), i.e., a neural network whose output depends on the input sequence so far. This can be used during a process where an RNN is trained to reproduce some task that involves aspects of human perception, instincts and habits, e.g., as part of one of the greatest challenges of this era: autonomous driving. After the deep learning phase that obtains an RNN, using our reverse engineering process can be used to obtain an automaton model for at least part of the tasks; then one can further refine this model using automata-based method.

2   Angluin's L^* Learning Algorithm

Angluin's L^* algorithm [1] learns a finite black box automaton B through experiments. It returns the smallest deterministic finite automaton (DFA) that produced the same behavior as B.

A Mealy machine $B = (Q, v_0, \Sigma, \mathcal{T}, \Delta, O)$ is an automaton with output on the states, where

- Q is a finite set of *states*.
- $v_0 \in Q$ the *initial state*.
- Σ is the finite *input alphabet*.
- $\mathcal{T}$ is a *transition function* $\mathcal{T} : Q \times \Sigma \mapsto Q$.
- Δ is a set of *outputs*.
- $O : Q \mapsto \Delta$ is a mapping from states to *outputs*.

We assume for simplicity that the output is either a 0 or a 1. An *execution* of an automaton B is a prefix closed alternating sequence of states and inputs on transitions: $v_0 \sigma_0 v_1 \sigma_1 \ldots$ such that

- v_0 is the initial state,
- for each $i \geq 0$, $v_{i+1} = \mathcal{T}(v_i, \sigma_i)$.

The executions are often denoted as sequence of inputs, ignoring the states (the states can be uniquely recovered due to the deterministic nature of the automaton).

The automata learning algorithm assumes the existence of a *teacher* that answers two kinds of queries about the black box system B:

- A *membership query* tests whether a given execution has the expected output on B.

- *An equivalence query* asks whether a candidate automaton M produces the same outputs as B on all sequences of input. If not, an execution sequence where M and B differ on the outputs is returned for further learning.

The teacher can be automated as a procedure that provides answers to such queries. Membership queries can be implemented as simple tests to the black box. Equivalence queries require testing a comprehensive set of sequences, e.g., using the Chow-Vasilewski algorithm [2,15], which requires time exponential in the size of the black box.

The algorithm uses two finite sets of finite sequences:

- S is a prefix closed set of *accessibility sequences*. Each such sequence serves to transfer the candidate learned automaton from its initial state to a particular state. Several sequences in S may transfer the initial state of B to the same state.
- E is a suffix closed set of *distinguishing sequences*. They are used to distinguish the states of a candidate automaton from each other; a candidate automaton gives different outputs w.r.t. at least one of the distinguishing sequences in E when applied as input from two distinct states.

Both sets, S and E contain the empty sequence λ. Further elements are added to the sets S and E as the algorithm progresses.

The algorithm creates a table T. The rows of the table are the sequences in $S \cup (S.\Sigma)$, while the columns are the sequences in E. The table T is defined so that $T(s,e)$ is the last output of the black box after applying $s \in S \cup (S.\Sigma)$ from the initial state followed by $e \in E$. It is convenient to think of the table as consisting of two parts: The *top* part corresponding to the states S, and the *bottom* part corresponding to the successors $(S.\Sigma) \setminus S$.

We define an equivalence relation $\equiv_{mod(E)}$ over sequences in S as follows: $s_1 \equiv_{mod(E)} s_2$ if for each $e \in E$, $T(s_1, e) = T(s_2, e)$. This means that we cannot distinguish the state of B reached after s_1 from the state reached after s_2 by executing any of the sequences in E. Let $[s]$ denote the equivalence class that includes s. When the learning algorithm suggests a candidate automaton, these equivalence classes become the states of the automaton.

Definition 1. A table T is *closed* if for each $s.a \in (S.\Sigma) \setminus S$ there is some $s' \in S$ such that $s.a \equiv_{mod(E)} s'$.

In other words, T is closed if each row in $S.\Sigma$ has the same entries as a row that is in S. If a table is not closed then there is some $s.a \in (S.\Sigma) \setminus S$ that can be distinguished from any sequence in S by appending some sequence in E. We move the row $s.a$ from the bottom part $(S.\Sigma) \setminus S$ to the top part S and add a row $s.a$ to the table. We then add to the bottom part rows of the form $s.a.b$ for each $b \in \Sigma$. Then we update the table entries $T(s.a.b, e)$, for every $e \in E$, by checking the membership query with the sequence $s.a.b.e$.

Definition 2. A table is *consistent* if for all s_1, $s_2 \in S$ such that $s_1 \equiv_{mod(E)} s_2$ it holds that for each $a \in \Sigma$, $s_1.a \equiv_{mod(E)} s_2.a$.

That is, a table is consistent if whenever two sequences are equivalent, so are all their successors. If the table is inconsistent, then there are $s_1, s_2 \in S$, $a \in \Sigma$ and $e \in E$, such that $s_1 \equiv_{mod(E)} s_2$, but the outputs in the $a.e$ entries of the rows s_1 and s_2 are different. In order to distinguish between s_1 and s_2 we add $a.e$ to E and update the table T by checking the membership queries for every sequence in $S \cup (S.\Sigma)$ followed by $a.e$.

Given a closed and consistent table T over the sets S and E, we construct the *candidate automaton* $M = (Q, q_0, \Sigma, \delta, F)$ as follows:

- The set of states Q is $\{[s] \mid s \in S\}$.
- The initial state q_0 is $[\lambda]$, where λ is the empty sequence.
- The transition relation δ is defined as follows: for $s \in S, a \in \Sigma, \delta([s], a) = [s.a]$.
- $O([s]) = T(s, \lambda)$. O is well defined since the outputs on each row equivalent to s, found under the column $\lambda \in E$, is the same.

Two basic steps are used in the learning algorithms for extending the table T:

add_rows(s) : Add s to S. Update the table by moving the row s to the top part of T and adding a row $s.a$ to the bottom part of T for each $a \in \Sigma$ (if not already present). Update $T(s.a, e)$ for each $e \in E$ according to the membership query for $s.a.e$.

add_column(e) : Add e to E. Update the table T by adding the column e. Set $T(s, e)$ for each $s \in S \cup (S.\Sigma)$, according to the membership query for $s.e$.

Using *add_rows* and *add_column*, we give pseudo-code for the algorithm L^* in Fig. 1. The algorithm updates the sets S and E and the table T until a consistent and closed table is obtained. It then constructs from the table the corresponding candidate automaton M, and generates an equivalence query for the teacher. If M is not equivalent to B then a minimal counterexample μ differentiating between M and B is returned. The algorithm then extends the top part of the table with rows corresponding to all the prefixes of μ, and extends the lower part of the table accordingly. This is repeated until an equivalence query affirms that a candidate automaton that is equivalent to B is obtained.

The algorithm is in time polynomial in n, the size of B, when not taking into account the time for the oracle to answer equivalence queries. However, automating the equivalence queries takes time exponential in n. Optimized automata learning algorithms appear in [5,8].

Example. Consider an automaton that accepts the regular language $L = a^*b^+$ over the $\Sigma = \{a, b\}$. A minimal automaton B for this language appears in Fig. 2. The outputs are $\Delta = \{0, 1\}$, where 1 signals an accepting state and 0 a nonaccepting state. Initially, $S = E = \{\lambda\}$.

Table 1 is the initial table, with $S = E = \{\lambda\}$. This requires to check the output for the empty word, and the words $a, b \in S.\Sigma$. The table is consistent but not closed: $b \in S.\Sigma$ is not equivalent to λ, the only element in S. We thus add b to S and ba and bb to $S.\Sigma$. We obtain Table 2 by checking the output for the latter sequences. This table is closed and consistent and therefore we construct

Initialize S and E to $\{\lambda\}$
Ask membership queries for λ and each $a \in \Sigma$
Construct the initial table (S, E, T)

Repeat
    while (S, E, T) is not consistent or not closed do
        if (S, E, T) is not consistent then
            find $s_1, s_2 \in S$, $a \in \Sigma$, $e \in E$, such that
              $s_1 \equiv_{mod(E)} s_2$ and $T(s_1.a, e) \neq T(s_2.a, e)$;
            add_column$(a.e)$;
        else
            find $s \in S$, $a \in \Sigma$, such that
              $s.a \notin [s']$ for any $s' \in S$;
            add_rows$(s.a)$;
    end while
    Construct the candidate automaton M
    Generate an equivalence query for M and B
    If the teacher returns a counterexample η then
        add η and all its prefixes to S;
        extend T to $(S \cup (S.\Sigma)) \times E$ using membership queries;
Until the teacher has returned ''yes'' to the equivalence query;
Halt and output M

Fig. 1. The L^* algorithm

Table 3.   Table 4.

Table 2.

Table 1.

Table 1	λ
λ	0
a	0
b	1

Table 2	λ
λ	0
b	1
a	0
ba	0
bb	1

Table 3	λ
λ	0
b	1
ba	0
bab	0
a	0
bb	1
baa	0
baba	0
babb	0

Table 4	λ	b
λ	0	1
b	1	1
ba	0	0
bab	0	0
a	0	1
bb	1	1
baa	0	0
baba	0	0
babb	0	0

a conjecture automaton M^1, where $S^1 = \{[\lambda], [b]\}$, $q_0^1 = [\lambda]$ and $F^1 = \{[b]\}$, $\delta^1([\lambda], a) = [\lambda]$, $\delta^1([\lambda], b) = [b]$, $\delta^1([b], a) = [\lambda]$, and $\delta^1([b], b) = [b]$

Since $\mathcal{L}(M^1) \neq L$, an equivalence query results in a counterexample in their symmetric difference that distinguishes between. Assume the counterexample is bab, where the output according to B is 0100, while according to M^1 it is 0101. Then, bab and all its prefixes are added to S, and $S.\Sigma$ is extended accordingly. This is demonstrated in Table 3. This table is closed but not consistent. For instance, $\lambda \equiv_{mod(E)} ba$, but $b \not\equiv_{mod(E)} bab$. This means that the states $[\lambda]$ and $[ba]$

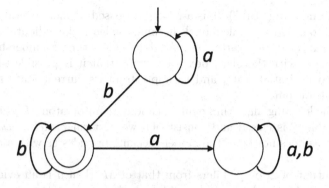

Fig. 2. A minimal automaton for $L = a^*b^+$

should be distinguished, since the word b differentiates between them. We thus add b to E and extend Table 3 with another column. Table 4 is the result of this extension. This table is closed and consistent. The candidate automaton M^2 is thus $S^2 = \{[\lambda], [b], [ba]\}$, $v_0^2 = [\lambda]$ and $F^2 = \{[b]\}$. $\delta^2([\lambda], a) = [\lambda]$, $\delta^2([\lambda], b) = [b]$, $\delta^2([b], a) = [ba]$, $\delta^2([b], b) = [b]$ $\delta^2([ba], a) = [ba]$, and $\delta^2([ba], b) = [ba]$. This is a minimal DFA recognizing $L = a^*b^+$.

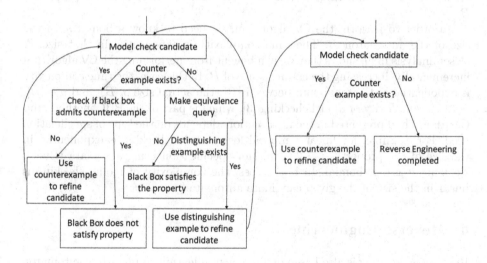

Fig. 3. Black box checking (left) Vs. reverse engineering (right)

3   Black Box Checking

The reverse engineering procedure that is presented in the next section, inherits some components of black box checking [7,9]. Figure 3 presents a flow diagram for both procedures, side by side, for comparison.

Black box checking (BBC) [9] is a procedure based on incremental learning a black box automaton B, while model checking the learned candidates satisfy the specification φ. Learning starts using Angluin's algorithm. Membership queries are experiments with the black box: we assume that it is possible to *reset* the black box to its initial state, and to apply from its current state any input, observing the output.

When the learning algorithm emits a candidate automaton M (this happens when the table T is closed and consistent), we perform *model checking* [3] for $M \models \varphi$. If this does not hold, the model checking provides us with a counterexample μ.

If the output of B on μ differs from that of M, then μ is an evidence that distinguishes between the candidate M and B. Let η be the minimal prefix of μ that causes a difference in the outputs between M and B. We perform *add_rows(η)* and continue the learning process. If B admits μ, it means that $B \not\models \varphi$, and we can just stop and inform about this.

The case where model checking results in that $M \models \varphi$ does not provide a counterexample that can help deciding whether M and B can be distinguished or gives evidence to show that $B \not\models \varphi$. In this case, we use the Chow-Vasilewski (CV) [2,15] algorithm as an equivalence query, to find whether a distinguishing sequence exists. If so, we use it to continue the learning. Otherwise, the languages of M and B are indistinguishable, thus, we can conclude from $M \models \varphi$ that $B \models \varphi$.

In order to perform the CV algorithm, we need to know a bound n on the size of the automaton B. The time complexity is exponential in that size. A closer analysis in [9] shows that we can benefit from performing the CV algorithm incrementally, increasing the assumed size of B. In this case, the time complexity is exponential in the maximum between $|B|$ (the actual size of B), and $n - |B|$.

The complexity of model checking [3], which is part of the BBC method, and the RE method presented in the next section, depends on the type of specification used. For example, for linear temporal logic, model checking is exponential in the size of the property φ [13], while for specification using automata (Büchi, Regular) it is polynomial. In both cases, the complexity of model checking is linear in the size of the given candidate automata.

4   Reverse Engineering

Reverse engineering is also based on incremental learning a black box automaton B. It is assumed that B satisfies the specification φ. Learning starts with using Angluin's algorithm. Again, membership queries are experiments to the black box, and we assume the capability of resetting the black box to its initial state.

As in BBC, when the learning algorithm emits a candidate automaton M, we perform *model checking* for $M \models \varphi$. If this holds, we are done, as M can be used as the model that we need, although M may not be the same as B. Finishing the learning process before B is completely learned is an advantage rather than a problem: all we seek is a model that satisfies φ.

If $M \not\models \varphi$, then model checking returns a counterexample μ. Since B is known to satisfy φ, μ distinguishes between B and M. Let η be the minimal prefix of μ that causes a difference between the outputs by M and B. We perform $add\_rows(\eta)$ and continue the learning process. RE does not use the expensive equivalence queries. The complexity of RE is thus polynomial in the size of the automaton B.

Consider now the case where $B \models \varphi$ is not guaranteed. We use a variant of the previously described RE algorithm, shown in Fig. 4. Each time that a counterexample for $M \models \varphi$ for a candidate automaton M is found using model checking, it is also tested against the black box B using a membership query. If B produces the same outputs on η, then $B \not\models \varphi$, contrary to what we assumed, and we can just stop and inform about this. Thus, in this case, we either generate a model that satisfies φ, or show that $B \not\models \varphi$. Note that it is possible that a model satisfying φ is generated in this way, while B itself does not satisfy it. Thus, this variant of the algorithm cannot be used to replace the **BBC** algorithm (which has a higher complexity) in deciding whether $B \models \varphi$.

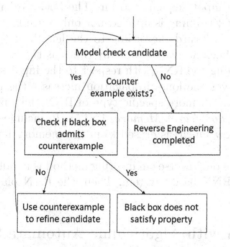

Fig. 4. Reverse engineering with verification

Deep Learning. Deep learning is a collection of methods for training *neural networks*, which can be used to perform various tasks such as image and speech recognition or playing games at an expert level. A neural network consists of a collection of nodes, the *neurons*, arranged in several layers, each neuron connected to all the neurons in the previous and the next layer. The first layer is the *input layer* and the last layer is the *output layer*. The other layers are *hidden*.

The value x_i of the ith neuron at layer $j + 1$ is computed from the column vector $\mathbf{y} = (y_1, \ldots, y_m)$ of all the neurons at layer j. To compute x_i, we first apply a transformation $t_i = \mathbf{w}_i \mathbf{y} + b_i$ where $\mathbf{w}_i$ is a line vector of *weights*, and b_i

a number called *bias*. Then we apply to the vector $\mathbf{t} = (t_1, \ldots, t_n)$ an *activation function*, which is usually non-linear, making the value of each neuron a function of the values of neurons at the preceding layer. Typical activation functions include the sigmoid and tanh functions, as well as the softmax.

Given values for all neurons in the input layer, we can compute the values for all neurons in the network, and overall a neural network represents a function $\mathbb{R}^n \rightarrow \mathbb{R}^m$ where n is the size of the input layer, and m the size of the output layer.

The values of the weights w_i and the biases b_i are initially random, and modified through *training*. A *loss function* provides a measurement on the distance between the actual output of the neural net and the desired output. The goal of training is to minimize the loss function.

For applications where sequences of inputs are analyzed, as e.g. in natural language recognition, one often uses a form of network called *Recurrent Neural Network* (RNN). An RNN maintains a feedback loop, where values of some neurons are returned to the network as additional inputs to the next step. In this way an RNN has the capability of maintaining some long term memory that summarizes the input sequence so far. The backward propagation of the *gradient descent* based training is applied not only once to the RNN, but continues to propagate backwards according to the length of the input sequence, where the RNN has been activated as many times as the length of the input so far. This allows training the RNN with respect to the input sequence instead of the last input. However the long propagation increases the problem of *vanishing/exploding* gradient. A more specific type of RNN that intends to solve this problem is a *Long Short-Term Memory*, LSTM. It includes components that control what (and how much) is erased from the memory layer of the network and what is added.

One application of our reverse engineering method is in obtaining an automaton model from an RNN based system. Then, the RNN plays the role of the black box.

5   Comparison with Algorithmic Automata Synthesis

Algorithmic synthesis of an automaton from a temporal specification [11] consists of the following steps:

1. Converting the (temporal) specification φ into a Büchi automaton.
2. Determinizing the automaton (this may require transforming from one type of automata to another).
3. Finding a game strategy that restricts all the behaviours of the resulted (finite deterministic) automaton to those that satisfy the specification.

The complexity of the synthesis is exponential given an automaton specification, and doubly exponential given a temporal specification.

Consider now a classical synthesis example of a family of specifications, where the size of the realization grows doubly exponential with he size of the specification when written in linear temporal logic [6]. The required realization is an automaton that accepts sequences of the form $x_1 \# x_2 \# \ldots \# x_m \# \# y$, where $x_1, \ldots x_m, y$ are bitstrings over $\{0, 1\}$ of length n. The system emits a 1 at the end (accept) exactly if y is the same as one of the x_i's.

A temporal logic specification can describes this property in quadratic space [6]. A nondeterministic automaton specification guesses the sequence u that will repeat and verify that (a) it appears as one of the x_i's and (b) checks that it appears betwen the $\#\#$ and the end of the sequence. An execution satisfies the specification in the following way: it must emit an output of 1 at the end of the execution, if there is at least one run of the nondeterministic automaton that accepts that execution. This is a bit of a non-standard way to denote the specification, however, our aim is to simplify the presentation, and avoid the details of dealing with a temporal logic specification.

The size of this automaton is determined by the number of possible y's, which is 2^n. The realization, a finite deterministic automaton, will need $\mathcal{O}(2^{2^n})$ states, to remember all the possible sets of values of x_i's that appeared so far, and before the $\#\#$ symbols so that we can compare the sequence y against it. Now, for this example, this is also the lower bound on the size of B, and consequently, the reverse engineering procedure will also have doubly exponential time and space complexity.

For specifications whose realization require a number of states that is proportional to the complexity measure, the comparison between the algorithmic synthesis and the reverse engineering approach depends on the optimizations used.

Consider again the above family of properties. Now, assume that the x_i's and the y are restricted to some sparse set of sequences with n characters 0 or 1, such that only $O(n)$ among the 2^n possible sequences can appear. The black box B is obtained, e.g., through experimentation or using deep learning, and we do not have the exact characterization of the set of possible values in advance. In this case, the B can be of size $\mathcal{O}(2^n)$ and construction by learning can be exponentially more efficient (both in time and space) than the algorithmic synthesis approach. However, the learned system is more restricted than the one obtained algorithmically, not admitting sequences that were not foreseen by the black box B.

A subtle deficiency of using learning in this case stems from the fact that B may satisfy φ, yet does not admit *all* the executions satisfying φ, even under the restriction on the input sequences. For example, B may restrict the inputs such that some sequence x_i may appear only after k repeated occurrences of some x_j, but not before. A learned candidate automaton M may thus satisfy φ, however, it does not necessarily allow all the inputs of B: some of them are "hidden" after long inputs that were not queried during the Angluin learning process. This is a consequence of the fact that our learning procedure stops once we found a candidate automaton (through a closed and consistent table) that satisfies φ, *without* applying the (computationally expensive) equivalence query. Adding the (proven exponentially complex in the size of B) equivalence query will make the overall complexity of the RE algorithm worse than the algorithmic synthesis.

Acknowledgement. First and foremost, I would like to thank Klaus Havelund for years of fruitfull and pleasant collaboration. I would also like to thank Yu-Fang Chen and Roi Fogler for inspiring discussions on the subject of this paper.

References

1. Angluin, D.: Learning regular sets from queries and counterexamples. Inf. Comput. **75**, 87–106 (1987)
2. Chow, T.S.: Testing software design modeled by finite-state machines. IEEE Trans. Softw. Eng. **3**, 178–187 (1978)
3. Clarke, E.M., Grumberg, O., Peled, D.: Model Checking. MIT Press, Cambridge (2000)
4. Gerth, R., Peled, D., Vardi, M.Y., Wolper, P.: Simple on-the-fly automatic verification of linear temporal logic. In: PSTV 1995. IAICT, pp. 3–18. Springer, Boston (1996). https://doi.org/10.1007/978-0-387-34892-6_1
5. Kearns, M.J., Vazirani, U.V.: An Introduction to Computational Learning Theory. MIT Press, Cambridge (1994)
6. Kupferman, O., Vardi, M.Y.: Model checking of safety properties. Formal Methods Sys. Des. **19**(3), 291–314 (2001)
7. Groce, A., Peled, D., Yannakakis, M.: Adaptive model checking. In: Katoen, J.-P., Stevens, P. (eds.) TACAS 2002. LNCS, vol. 2280, pp. 357–370. Springer, Heidelberg (2002). https://doi.org/10.1007/3-540-46002-0_25
8. Isberner, M., Howar, F., Steffen, B.: The TTT algorithm: a redundancy-free approach to active automata learning. In: Bonakdarpour, B., Smolka, S.A. (eds.) RV 2014. LNCS, vol. 8734, pp. 307–322. Springer, Cham (2014). https://doi.org/10.1007/978-3-319-11164-3_26
9. Peled, D., Vardi, M.Y., Yannakakis, M.: Black box checking. In: Wu, J., Chanson, S.T., Gao, Q. (eds.) Formal Methods for Protocol Engineering and Distributed Systems. IAICT, vol. 28, pp. 225–240. Springer, Boston (1999). https://doi.org/10.1007/978-0-387-35578-8_13
10. Pnueli, A.: The temporal logic of programs. In: FOCS Foundations of Computer Science, pp. 46–57 (1977)
11. Pnueli, A., Rosner, R.: On the synthesis of a reactive module. In: Conference Record of the Sixteenth Annual ACM Symposium on Principles of Programming Languages, Austin, Texas, USA, pp. 179–190, 11–13 January 1989
12. Rivest, R.L., Schapire, R.E.: Inference of finite automata using homing sequences. Inf. Comput. **103**(2), 299–347 (1993)
13. Sistla, A.P., Clarke, E.M.: The complexity of propositional linear temporal logics. In: STOC, pp. 159–168 (1982)
14. Vardi, M.Y., Wolper, P.: An automata-theoretic approach to automatic program verification (preliminary report). In: LICS Logic in Computer Science, pp. 332–344 (1986)
15. Vasilevskii, M.P.: Failure diagnosis of automata. Kibertetika **4**, 98–108 (1973)
16. Weiss, G., Goldberg, Y., Yahav, E.: Extracting automata from recurrent neural networks using queries and counterexamples. In: ICML International Conference on Machine Learning, pp. 5244–5253 (2018)

Author Index

A. Smolka, Scott   147
Ahishakiye, Faustin   108

Bjørner, Dines   35
Broy, Manfred   10

Chen, Xiaohong   3
Cleaveland, Matthew   137
Colombo, Christian   89
Cousot, Patrick   61

D. Stoller, Scott   147

Frohme, Markus   159

Grosu, Radu   147

Holzmann, Gerard J.   127

Jarabo, José Ignacio Requeno   108

Lee, Insup   137

Mehmood, Usama   147

Pace, Gordon J.   89
Peled, Doron   182
Pun, Violet Ka I   108

Roşu, Grigore   3
Ruchkin, Ivan   137

Schneider, Gerardo   89
Sokolsky, Oleg   137
Steffen, Bernhard   159
Stolz, Volker   108

Printed in the United States
by Baker & Taylor Publisher Services